# The Beer Option

# THE BEER

*Option*

## Brewing
*a*
## *Catholic Culture*
### YESTERDAY & TODAY

R. JARED STAUDT

Angelico Press

First published in the USA
by Angelico Press 2018
Copyright © R. Jared Staudt 2018

For information, address:
Angelico Press, Ltd.
169 Monitor St.
Brooklyn, NY 11222
www.angelicopress.com

978-1-62138-414-4 pb
978-1-62138-415-1 cloth
978-1-62138-416-8 ebook

Book and cover design
by Michael Schrauzer
Frontispiece:
Jan Steen, *The Dancing Couple* (1663) (detail).
Source: Wikimedia Commons

# CONTENTS

To my Dad, Joseph A. Staudt,
for the twentieth anniversary of our first trip
through our ancestral homeland, Germany.

*Semper Fidelis!*

# ACKNOWLEDGEMENTS

I want to thank Mark Giszczak and Michael Foley for their encouragement to write the book. Thanks also to Christopher Blum for encouraging me to attend sufficiently to the limits and problems of alcohol. I am very grateful to my friends and drinking buddies through the years, especially John O'Brien, Michael DiMarco, Joe Burns, Adam and Andrew Beach, John Ryan, Marco DiDomenico, Mike Towle, Nathan Aamot, Leo McNamara, John Carraux, and Bob Steuck. Special mention to Richard Meloche for trying some great monastic beers with me while discussing monastic spirituality. Special thanks to James Brown for completing a special beer mission with extraordinary perseverance. I'm also grateful to those who helped organize and promote the Saints, Monks & Beer pilgrimage while I was writing the book: Karna Lozoya, John Magee, Fr. John Riley, Aaron Lambert, Mike and Ken of Blind Faith Brewing, and everyone at *Those Catholic Men*, especially Jason Craig and James Baxter. Thanks to John LaBarbara, Richard Meloche, Joshua Hren, and Michael DiMarco (who deserves special thanks) for reading drafts and offering helpful suggestions. The library staff of the Cardinal Stafford Library, especially Tamara Conley and Stephen Sweeney, provided wonderful assistance tracking down books for my research. I am grateful also to Jennifer Woods and John Riess for their editorial work. And above all, I thank my wife, Anne, for putting up with so many beer conversations and years of "research."

# *The Beer Option*

Rod Dreher's 2017 bestseller, *The Benedict Option*, occasioned a wide debate about the nature of Christian culture, reaching even into the mainstream media. Dreher obviously touched a nerve, by asking the simple question of how Christians should live in an increasingly hostile, secular culture. Dreher was accused of advocating separation from society, while in reality his argument proposes the necessity to form intentional Christian communities to rebuild Western culture. *The Benedict Option* spurred a number of spin-offs — for example, the Francis Option, the Dominic Option, the Augustine Option, the Escrivá Option, and the Marian Option (which has its own book).

Rather than proposing another option, I offer the Beer Option as an extension of the Benedictine Option. Dreher looks to the Benedictine tradition for inspiration in forming pockets of stability — rooted in a spirituality of work, prayer, and community — to inspire new forms of Christian life. He contends that "the way of Saint Benedict is not an escape from the real world but a way to see that world and dwell in it as it truly is. Benedictine spirituality teaches us to bear with the world in love and to transform it as the Holy Spirit transforms us. The Benedict Option draws on the virtues in the Rule to change the way Christians approach politics, church, family, community, education, our jobs, sexuality, and technology. And it does so with urgency."[1] To that list we could add beer, which has a strong connection to the Benedictine tradition and when rooted in Catholic community provides opportunities for fellowship and evangelization.

So how can we speak of a Beer Option? Without entering into a debate on the relative merits of Dreher's views, I contend that beer presents one facet of a much larger project of cultural renewal. Dreher draws inspiration from the American monks who refounded monasticism in St. Benedict's hometown of Norcia, Italy. These same monks also brew

---

[1] Rod Dreher, *The Benedict Option: A Strategy for Christians in a Post-Christian Nation* (New York: Sentinel, 2017), 77.

John Rogers Herbert, *Laborare Est Orare* (1862). (Wikimedia Commons)

an acclaimed beer, witnessing to the enduring Benedictine tradition of brewing. They will factor centrally in this account, along with many other communities who brew regularly—Benedictines, Franciscans, Augustinians, and Norbertines (Premonstratensians). Benedictines have been the largest religious brewers, and thus will be featured prominently, but almost every major religious order has contributed as well (including the Jesuits and Dominicans).

For over twenty years I've been fascinated by beer's role in Western culture. Beer opens a door to many elements of Catholic culture: its history, social and economic influences, and even its spirituality. Catholicism has a rich sacramental culture, which recognizes how physical things mediate spiritual realities. This includes beer, referred to as a "creature" in the *Roman Ritual*'s official blessing for beer:

> Bless, O Lord, this creature beer, which thou hast deigned to produce from the fat of grain: that it may be a salutary remedy to the human race, and grant, through the invocation of thy holy name, that whoever shall drink it may gain health in body and peace in soul. Through Christ our Lord. Amen.[2]

---

[2]   Here is the Latin original: "Benedic, Domine, creaturam istam cerevisae, quam ex adipe frumenti producere dignatus es: ut sit remedium salutare humano generi: et praesta per invocationem nominis tui sancti, ut, quicumque ex ea biberint, sanitatem corporis, et animae tutelam percipiant. Per Christum Dominum nostrum. Amen."

Why does the Catholic Church bless beer? The answer to this question could be described as the purpose of this book. We situate beer as a creature of our world, a creation of man, which can be used for good and uplifting purposes, but can also be misused and can become an occasion for sin. The Church wants to show us how to use all things well, to order all things to our good and the glory of God. The Church's blessing is meant to teach us the purpose of beer and how it can serve the good. We could call this prayer a mini-catechesis on beer, as it shows us its key elements: its production as a healthful drink, its use for thanksgiving, and its goal to provide health in body and soul.

Looking at the prayer more deeply, we see that first, even though beer is a product of human culture, it originates in the kindness and power of God. God has created water, barley, yeast, and hops — the ingredients of beer — though, of course, humans are needed to combine them in the right way. Pope John Paul II, in his encyclical *Laborem Exercens*, refers to humanity as a co-creator with God in the work of culture. Nonetheless, the prayer recognizes that God is the ultimate source of beer, which he has deigned to provide, in the ingredients and the skill needed to make it, for the benefit of humanity.

Second, the prayer asks that beer serve as a healthful drink. This petition recognizes the scandal that alcohol presents an occasion of sin for so many people throughout the world. On the other hand, many studies have shown that moderate consumption of alcohol, even when daily, can benefit health, especially the circulatory system. Beer throughout history was a normal part of society's diet, providing a sanitary drink that was high in nutrients. Beer promotes health as a moderate and integrated part of a balanced diet.

Third, the prayer speaks of drinking with thanksgiving and praise. Beer provided in the past a sign of a successful harvest, which drew people together to celebrate with festivity and joy. Enjoying good food and drink (in moderation) fosters a cheerful and thankful heart for the many blessings that God has bestowed. Wine, however, gives us the ultimate example of a drink drawing us into thanksgiving, as it is used directly by the Church as the matter of the Eucharist (which means thanksgiving).

Fourth, the prayer asks for help in mind and soul when the beer is consumed in honor of God's holy name. St. Thomas Aquinas describes the virtue of religion as the most important moral virtue because by it we direct all that we do to the honor of God.[3] Literally, everything we do should honor God and that certainly includes even the mundane acts of eating and drinking. By giving these things to God they become more than mundane acts. Rather, they become invitations for God to enter our lives to transform us and to supernaturalize the fabric of our lives.

Ordering to God all that we do directs us to our final end and promotes true health in body and soul for an integrated life of holiness. When it comes to drink, the Bible describes how wine gladdens the heart of man (Ps. 104:15). The same could be said of beer, referred to as "strong drink" in translations of the Bible. Proverbs 31 speaks of avoiding the pitfalls of alcohol for rulers, lest they forget their decrees (or we could say their duty), but also speaks of the healing benefits of alcohol: "Give strong drink to him who is perishing, and wine to those in bitter distress; let them drink and forget their poverty, and remember their misery no more" (Prov. 31:6–7). Beer should serve as a soothing remedy, but we also know the pitfalls of abusing it. The promise and danger of alcohol have to be examined in tandem, as blessing when consumed rightly, but a curse when abused.

Peter Maurin, co-founder of the Catholic Worker Movement, offers an important principle of integration that helps lay a foundation for understanding alcohol's role in Catholic culture. Maurin spoke often of the need to unite the principles of cult, culture, and cultivation. For Maurin, cult means worship of God, the very heart of human culture. Culture means education, especially when experienced in open discussion and conversation with others. Cultivation demonstrates the necessity of working with one's hands, shaping and forming the earth and other artifacts.[4] This book will look at beer through the lenses of these three points: beer's relation to Catholic cult or worship, its place in Catholic thought and history, and the way in which it enables us to be in touch with nature and the craft of production.

---

[3] See Thomas Aquinas's *Summa Theologiae*, II-II, question 81. For an in-depth study of the virtue of religion see my dissertation, "Religion as a Virtue: Worship through Justice, Law, and Charity," PhD diss., Ave Maria University, 2009.

[4] See Dorothy Day and Francis Sicius, *Peter Maurin: Apostle to the World* (Maryknoll, NY: Orbis, 2004), 124–25.

Beer represents one particular outflow of Catholic culture. It may be a small one, but it serves as an image of the larger task of shaping the earth and ordering our goods to the highest spiritual reality. It is significant, however, that beer is used often for opposite purposes, leading us away from our spiritual good. The abuse of alcohol provides a serious objection to this book that should be met head on. Catholic theology recognizes that no thing is evil, but is good in so far as it has being and exists. According to St. Augustine, evil is a privation of good that arises from a perversion of the human will. Created realities like beer are not evil in themselves; rather, our own abuse of natural goods can twist a proper use toward evil. Think of the example of sex and the human body, both very good things created by God for the good of the human race and even for rightly ordered pleasure. The perversion of our bodiliness by no means makes sex bad. Rather, we need to recover its goodness and help people to order their desires rightly, as we see in John Paul II's Theology of the Body. This book proposes such a recovery of a Catholic culture of drinking through the lens of beer.

The book can also be seen as an attempt to show how the sacramentality of Catholic thought extends to the everyday goods of human life. In the Bible's sacramental vision, earthly realities symbolize hidden, spiritual realities. Drinking is one such symbol, which God uses to express the deeper meaning latent within our hearts and His design to fulfill the longings he elicits. According to the Psalms, wine is a sign of God's blessing: "wine to gladden the hearts of men" and "my cup overflows" (Ps. 104:15; 23:5). It is also a sign of thanksgiving and praise: "I will raise the cup of salvation and call on the name of the Lord" (Ps. 116:13). The abundance of wine is an image of the bounty of the earth and God's blessing within it. We can extend this same imagery to beer.

The Beer Option calls for a renewal of culture by finding God in the ordinary things of life and ordering them to Him, including beer. It does not offer a technical look at brewing, even if such elements are touched upon occasionally. Rather, it situates beer within a narrative of Catholic history and culture, examining beer as a microcosm of culture more broadly. Beer contains key elements of cultural production, communal use, and order toward the higher things. Beer also provides a concrete way for people to experience Catholic traditions, refine their sense of taste, and even begin crafting something themselves. The Beer

Option then discusses why today is a key moment in a beer renaissance, represented by the rise of microbrewing and homebrewing, and also a renewal of monastic brewing. This is an important return to tradition and also a move away from the international consolidation of breweries. Part One looks at a Catholic history of brewing, from its roots in the ancient world and the Bible, to the role of monks in the creation of modern brewing methods, through the destruction of most monastery brewers, finishing with their surprising resurgence. The second part looks at the key elements of culture and how beer relates to them, including cultivation and production, community and festive celebrations, local traditions, and even the spiritual life. The third part takes the reader through ways to experience beer and its cultural impact, beginning with how to appreciate and taste beer, how to use beer to evangelize, and how to produce beer within the home, and ending with examples of important monastic beers to try. The final part explores current cultural problems and how beer feeds into them, but can also help us to overcome them — namely alcoholism, the use of drugs (especially marijuana), and consumerism. The book concludes by situating beer within the broader task of restoring Christian culture.

I believe that we are living in a crucial moment when we must reassert our Catholic identity, rediscover lost traditions, and begin rebuilding a more Christian way of life. This will require a better understanding of the significance of culture and human flourishing and how to live differently in a secular world. Surprisingly or not, beer may provide one small opportunity for cultural renewal. This book will unpack this vision for renewal, offering a lighthearted yet earnest appeal to discover the Beer Option as one ingredient for fermenting Christian culture.

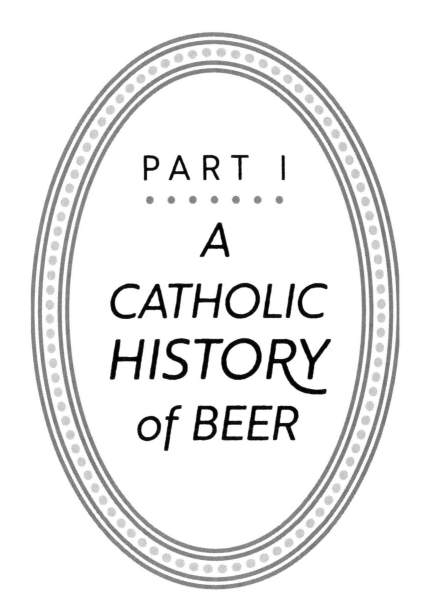

PART I

A
CATHOLIC
HISTORY
of BEER

CHAPTER 1

# *Beer in the Ancient World and the Bible*

The history of beer arose immediately with the origin of civilization itself. Indeed, there appears to be an even more cosmic backdrop to the origin of the drink. Patrick McGovern's *Uncorking the Past* traces the elemental role of alcohol in human history much further back in time to the very beginning of creation, in which ether (alcohol) first emerged.

> Astronomers probing our galaxy with powerful radio waves have discovered that alcohol does not only exist on the Earth. Massive clouds of methanol, ethanol, and vinyl ethanol — measuring billions of kilometers across — have been located in interstellar space and surrounding new star systems.... [A]s we peer into the night sky, we might ask why there is an alcoholic haze at the center of our galaxy, and what role alcohol played in jump-starting and sustaining life on our planet. If alcohol permeates our galaxy and universe, it should come as no surprise that sugar fermentation (or glycolysis) is thought to be the earliest form of energy production used by life on Earth.[1]

The creation of the first alcoholic beverages drew out the latent potential of creation, using another force inexplicably present in the universe: human intelligence. Since the dawn of time, agriculture, religious ritual, and beer have been intrinsically connected. They remain so throughout our story.

---

[1] Patrick McGovern, *Uncorking the Past: The Quest for Wine, Beer, and Other Alcoholic Beverages* (Berkeley: University of California Press, 2009), 1–2.

## WHAT IS BEER?

Beer is a drink composed largely of water, acquiring its quality and taste from malted grain, typically barley.[2] It contains a moderate level of alcohol, normally ranging from 4 to 6 percent. Yeast metabolizes the sugar content of this malt into alcohol during fermentation. It is usually flavored, containing hops for bitterness and preservation, but many other spices and flavors have been used through the millennia. We distinguish it from the other major forms of alcohol: wine made from grapes, cider from apples, mead from honey, and hard liquor, which uses a process of distillation. Some things have remained the same for five thousand years: namely, beer's main ingredient of malted barley. Other things are newer, such as the introduction of hops as the main flavoring in the Middle Ages. It was not until Louis Pasteur that the secret role of yeast in making alcohol was discovered.

Beer has been an important part of human culture from the beginning of recorded history. The story begins with barley, "the marrow of men," as Homer opined.[3] Barley is a hardy grass, which grew wildly and abundantly in the Fertile Crescent stretching from the Holy Land into modern day Iran, as well as in some areas of North Africa and further east in Asia. It was domesticated about ten thousand years ago and has been a staple cereal grain since (the fourth most consumed today). Although barley was used to make bread, it is coarser than wheat, more flavorful, and its seeds have a hull. Although the lighter wheat eventually won out as the key ingredient for bread, barley is the chief brewing grain for one reason: it malts easily and completely, creating the sugars necessary for fermentation.[4]

---

[2] There is no consensus on the origin of the word beer. The name may come from the Latin word *bibere*, to drink. To call beer simply "drink" reflects its central role in culture. In northern Europe in the Middle Ages it was *the* drink. Even though *bibere* is a Latin word, the Romans preferred the word *cervisia*, which they borrowed from the Celts, probably referring to the word soup. St. Isidore of Seville (560–636), in his *Etymologies*, had his own idea of the origin of *cervisia*, attributing it to Ceres, the goddess of agriculture. Others have suggested a Proto-Germanic origin from the word barley, *beuwo*, leading to the Old English word *beor*.

[3] Homer, *Odyssey*, XX, trans. Samuel Butler (London: A.C. Fifield, 1900).

[4] Rod Phillips notes that "the malting process raised the caloric value of the base cereal, giving beer more calories than bread made with an equivalent amount of grain. In addition, beer was rich in carbohydrates, vitamins, and proteins. It also gave

How did our ancestors discover brewing? No one knows for sure, but either hunters and gatherers or early famers must have stumbled across malted barley that had spontaneously fermented. As beer is so ancient, some wonder which came first—domestication of barley or the discovery of beer? If the discovery of beer came first, some wonder further if beer stimulated human civilization by pushing our ancestors toward the domestication of grain. Regardless of its exact origins, it is clear that beer emerged alongside human civilization.

Civilization began with the rise of agriculture, as nomadic groups learned to grow barley in the Ancient Near East. Eventually they put down roots and began to form villages. Usually we would think of the invention of bread as tying these groups to the fields, but we have now found very ancient archeological evidence of beer production from residue inside clay jars. Chemical tests confirm the existence of a rice beer dating to 7000 BC in Jiahu, China and barley beer from about 3,500 BC at the Godin Tepe archeological site in the Zagros Mountains of modern day Iran.[5] The latter site shows cultural links to the Uruk culture of Mesopotamia, possibly linking early beer production to the cities further West in the Fertile Crescent.

A view of the Zagros Mountains. (Wikimedia Commons)

---

its drinker a pleasant feeling." *Alcohol: A History* (Chapel Hill, NC: The University of North Carolina Press, 2014), 18. Barley's hull also helps in the filtering process.

   5  See McGovern, *Uncorking the Past*, chapters two and three.

## MESOPOTAMIA AND EGYPT

The earliest brews are prehistoric, but with the rise of civilization in Mesopotamia we have evidence of beer through the world's oldest writing, cuneiform. We actually have a Sumerian recipe, which was made by putting barley loaves into pots of water and allowing them to ferment. It was then consumed in a large, open vat with straws. The oldest description of brewing can be found in the Hymn to Ninkasi, the Sumerian goddess of brewing, dating from 1800 BC. It describes the use of bappir, the twice-baked barley bread used for brewing:

> You are the one who handles the dough [and] with a big shovel,
>> Mixing in a pit, the bappir with sweet aromatics (dates
>> and honey),
> You are the one who bakes the bappir in the big oven,
>> Puts in order the piles of hulled grains,
> You are the one who waters the malt set on the ground,
>> The noble dogs keep away even the potentates,
> You are the one who soaks the malt in a jar,
>> The waves rise, the waves fall.
> You are the one who spreads the cooked mash on large reed mats,
>> Coolness overcomes,
> You are the one who holds with both hands the great sweet wort,
>> Brewing [it] with honey [and] wine
> The filtering vat, which makes a pleasant sound,
>> You place appropriately on a large collector vat.
> When you pour out the filtered beer of the collector vat,
>> It is [like] the onrush of Tigris and Euphrates.[6]

Adding honey and grapes were important to stimulate fermentation as they naturally contain yeast, unlike barley. Sumer also gives us the world's oldest surviving epic, *Gilgamesh* (approximately 2000 BC), which makes a reference to beer in its passage on the civilizing of the wild man, Enkidu:

---

[6] Quoted in Joshua Mark, "The Hymn to Ninkasi, Goddess of Beer," *Ancient History Encyclopedia*, March 1, 2011, https://www.ancient.eu/article/222/the-hymn-to-ninkasi-goddess-of-beer/. I edited the text to remove some repetition.

Sumerian tablet detailing an allocation of beer from 3000 BC. (Wikimedia Commons)

Enkidu knew nothing about eating bread for food,
And of drinking beer he had not been taught.
The harlot spoke to Enkidu, saying:
"Eat the food, Enkidu, it is the way one lives.
Drink the beer, as is the custom of the land."
Enkidu ate the food until he was sated,
He drank the beer—seven jugs! and became
  expansive and sang with joy!

The world's oldest work of literature seems to testify to the role of beer in forming civilization, in taming the wild man to eat and drink like a civilized man. Beer also shows up in early law codes, including Hammurabi's, which stipulated death to shopkeepers who overcharged for it. It has also been hypothesized that cuneiform tablets inventorying beer contributed to the development of counting methods.

Beer also played a prominent role in Egyptian culture. It factored prominently into both Mesopotamian and Egyptian mythology and even ritual, indicating its significance. The Egyptians claimed that Osiris himself introduced the art of brewing. We also have Egyptian recipes, some of which have been recreated from hieroglyphic descriptions. Like Mesopotamian beer, it was thick like porridge (necessitating the use of straws) and was often flavored with honey, fruit, and other spices. Beer was a central part of the Egyptian diet, but was valued as medicinal, and is now thought to have included antibiotic qualities. Beer also served in Egypt as compensation for workers. Five liters of beer were given as daily wages for workers constructing the Great Pyramid. We have a good idea of the brewing process due to a miniature discovered at the tomb of Meketre, who was vizier to Pharaoh Mentuhotep II (2050–2000 BC). The Metropolitan Museum of Art in New York, which holds the piece, describes the scene: "The overseer with a baton sits inside the door. In the brewery two women grind flour, which another man works into dough. After a second man treads the dough into mash in a tall vat, it is put into tall crocks to ferment. After fermentation, it is poured off into round jugs with black clay stoppers."[7] The importance of beer in Egypt can be summarized through a hieroglyph inscription from about 2200 BC, which states: "The mouth of a perfectly contented man is filled with beer."

Closeup of model of Egyptian brewery from tomb of Meketre. (Wikimedia Commons)

---

[7] Quoted in Joshua Mark, "Beer in the Ancient World," *Ancient History Encyclopedia*, March 2, 2011, https://www.ancient.eu/article/223/beer-in-the-ancient-world/.

## BEER IN THE BIBLE?

Beer's role in the Bible all comes down to the meaning of the Hebrew word *shekar* (שֵׁכָר). Scholars generally translate it "strong drink," leaving no word for beer in the Bible, a decision dating back to St. Jerome.[8] Beer would be a surprising omission from the Bible considering that the Israelites lived between two beer-drinking cultures, Mesopotamia and Egypt, and lived in exile in both places. In fact, we have archeological evidence for the production of beer in ancient Israel.[9] Furthermore, God describes the Holy Land to the Israelites, just before they enter it, as being abundant in barley: "For the Lord your God is bringing you into a good land, a land of brooks of water, of fountains and springs, flowing forth in valleys and hills, a land of wheat and barley, of vines and fig trees and pomegranates, a land of olive trees and honey, a land in which you will eat bread without scarcity" (Deut. 8:7–9). Barley was a central part of Israel's agricultural life and diet.

Alcohol also related to the religious life of Israel. We see the word *shekar* used in the Nazarite vow (Num. 6:3), which renounces both wine and strong drink.[10] As there was no distilled alcohol prevalent at the time, it would make sense for the Scriptures to refer to the two main drinks of the time (often listed together). One scholar, Michael Homan, has made a strong case that *shekar* must be translated beer, noting that it certainly finds its origin in the Akkadian word for beer, *sikaru*.[11] *Shekar* would not

---

[8] Max Nelson, *The Barbarian's Beverage: A History of Beer in Ancient Europe* (New York: Routledge, 2005), 99. St. Jerome began the tradition of leaving *shekar* open ended, as he proposed the meaning of any alcoholic drink other than wine. Following Jerome's transliterated use of *sicera* in the Vulgate, the word would also be employed generically to indicate his meaning in the Latin West — any non-grape based alcoholic beverage, primarily beer, cider, mead, or perry. Charlemagne hired *siceratores* on his estate to make that range of beverages. Etymologically, *sicera* has given rise to the word cider. The abbeys of Normandy became leading producers of cider (*sidre* in French).

[9] See Ian Spencer Hornsey, *A History of Beer and Brewing* (London: Royal Society of Chemistry, 2003), 119. Hornsey notes that evidence points back even to the fourth millennium BC and extending into the first millennium BC (123).

[10] Jesus was criticized for "eating and drinking," implying that Jesus drank alcohol, unlike the Nazarite John the Baptist.

[11] Michael Homan, "Beer, Barley, and שֵׁכָר in the Hebrew Bible," in *Le-David Maskil: A Birthday Tribute for David Noel Freedman*, eds. Richard Elliot Friedman and William H. C. Propp (Winona Lake, IN: Eisenbrauns, 2004): 25–38; Michael Homan, "Did the Ancient Israelites Drink Beer?" *Biblical Archaeology Review* 36, no. 5 (2010): 49–56.

The Phillip Medhurst Collection, "The Tabernacle Set Up." (Wikimedia Commons)

refer to beer as we know it today, but a barley-based drink that may also
have included honey, grapes, dates, and other fruits. Translating *shekar*
with a link to barley-based beverages, which makes a lot of sense, would
mean that beer factored into the ceremonial rites of the Old Covenant.
Numbers 28:7–8 stipulates a drink offering of *shekar* as part of both the
daily and Sabbath sacrifice: "Its drink offering shall be a fourth of a hin
for each lamb; in the holy place you shall pour out a drink offering of
strong drink to the Lord. The other lamb you shall offer in the evening;
like the cereal offering of the morning, and like its drink offering, you
shall offer it as an offering by fire, a pleasing odor to the Lord."[12] The
drink offering, which also took the form of wine, occurred on Israelite
holy days as well as during monthly offerings.

   Homan points out one more significant, though overlooked, reference to beer in the Old Testament, without using the word *shekar*.[13]
Ecclesiastes 11:1–2 reads:

---

[12]   A hin is just over a gallon and a half. The first drink offering in the Bible was
performed by Jacob at Bethel in Genesis 35:14.
[13]   Michael Homan, "Beer Production by Throwing Bread into Water: A New
Interpretation of Qoh. XI 1–2," *Vetus Testamentum* 52 (2002): 275–79.

> Throw your bread upon the face of the water,
> because in many days you will acquire it.
> Give a serving to seven and also to eight,
> because you do not know what evil will be upon the land.

The verb "to throw" in the passage is the same verb for "to brew." This verb explains why it takes many days to acquire the results and why it should be served to many people, who should enjoy the fruit of the land. It also indicates that Israel brewed by placing loaves in water, with possibly seven or eight people with straws consuming at once. Wine clearly had precedence in Israel, though, which would be continued into the New Testament, as the Passover was drawn into the Paschal Mystery.

Although beer was also present in Greco-Roman society, the Greeks and Romans strongly preferred wine. Barley itself was disdained as a lower-class food source. Xenophon speaks of the beer he encountered in Armenia, more dispassionately, as an "acquired taste."[14] For the Romans, beer was the drink of the barbarians, whether the Celts or Germans. Pliny the Elder, speaking of Spain and Gaul, related: "The nations of the West also have their own intoxicant, made from grain soaked in water. . . . Alas, what wonderful ingenuity vice possesses! A method has actually been discovered for making even water intoxicated."[15] Tacitus described it in his *Germania* as a "liquor made from barley or wheat, fermented so as somewhat to resemble wine."[16] The northern barbarians, however, were soon to overrun the Roman Empire. With them, beer would rise to prominence once more and find a place within the new Christian culture coming into formation.

---

[14] Xenophon, *Anabasis*, V. The entire passage reads: "There were stores within of wheat and barley and vegetables, and wine made from barley in great big bowls; the grains of barley malt lay floating in the beverage up to the lip of the vessel, and reeds lay in them, some longer, some shorter, without joints; when you were thirsty you must take one of these into your mouth, and suck. The beverage without admixture of water was very strong, and of a delicious flavour to certain palates, but the taste must be acquired."

[15] Pliny, *Natural History*, XIV, 29.

[16] Tacitus, *Germania*, XXIII.

CHAPTER 2

# The Rise of
# Monastic Brewing

Although some early Christian writers maintained the Greco-Roman prejudice against beer, large-scale brewing arose and spread in Christendom alongside monasteries.[1] As little lights of civilization sprang up in the dark ages around communities of monks, so did breweries. Southern Europe continued to prefer wine, but the new culture of Christendom arose chiefly in the north in Charlemagne's court and the other newly civilized German tribes. Although we would not recognize ancient beer, the brew we know today developed through the care of the monks, as "over time, brewing knowledge accumulated among the learned and literate cloistered [monks], and brewing techniques and beer improved."[2] The monks perfected brewing, bringing new techniques (such as decoction), equipment (the coolship, lauter tun, and copper kettles), and greater sanitation — thereby providing sustenance and probably some holy mirth to European brewing.[3]

## BENEDICTINE FOUNDATIONS

St. Benedict lived in the early sixth century (480–547). He fled decadent Rome as a young student, gathering monks about him at Subiaco and later at Monte Cassino farther south. From central Italy, the moderate form of monasticism inspired by Benedict's *Rule* would spread throughout

---

[1] Max Nelson lists Sextus Julius Africanus, Eusebius, Cyril, and Theodoret as examples of Church Fathers who spoke negatively of beer and notes they were influenced by the Septuagint version of Isaiah 19:10, which condemns Egypt and says that those who labor for wages will be grieved. The Septuagint translates the Hebrew for those who labor as "those making beer" in Greek. See Nelson, *Barbarian's Beverage*, 75.

[2] Garrett Oliver, ed., *The Oxford Companion to Beer* (Oxford: Oxford University Press, 2011), 104.

[3] See Oliver, *Oxford Companion*, 343; 389.

Europe in the following centuries. Prayer constitutes the key work of the monastery, which Benedict calls the *opus Dei*, the work of God. Benedict also affirms the necessity of manual labor: "When they live by the labor of their hands, as our fathers and the apostles did, then they are really monks" (*Rule*, ch. 48).[4] Benedict also states that "the monastery should, if possible, be so constructed that within it all necessities, such as water, mill and garden are contained, and the various crafts are practiced" (ch. 66). The work of God and the work of the hands together form the *ora et labora* (prayer and work) that shape Benedictine life.

Although the self-sufficiency of the monastery insulates the monks from the world, the crafts St. Benedict mentions are important to provide an opportunity for the monks to witness to the world. He foresees the contributions of the monk to society: "Whenever products of these artisans are sold, those responsible for the sale must not dare to practice any fraud. . . . The evil of avarice must have no part in establishing prices, which should, therefore, always be a little lower than people outside the monastery are able to set, *so that in all things God may be glorified*" (ch. 57, quoting 1 Pt 4:11). Though speaking of prices, Benedict wants the monks to glorify God when they enter into contact with the outside world through their products.

Wine and beer are examples of two products the monks produced in their self-sufficient monasteries: wine in the south and beer north of the grape line. Benedict preferred that monks abstain from alcohol, but recognized that it formed a common (and sometimes even necessary) part of daily life at that time:

> Each one has his own gift from God, the one in this way, the other in that. Therefore it is with some hesitation that the amount of daily sustenance for others is fixed by us. Nevertheless, in view of the weakness of the infirm we believe that a *hemina* of wine a day is enough for each one. Those moreover to whom God gives the ability of bearing abstinence shall know that they will have their own reward. But the prior shall judge if either the needs of the place, or labor or the heat of summer, requires more; considering in all things lest satiety or drunkenness creep in. Indeed, we read that

---

[4] St. Benedict, *The Rule*, trans. Leonard Doyle, http://osb.org/rb/text/toc.html.

wine is not suitable for monks at all. But because, in our day, it is
not possible to persuade the monks of this, let us agree at least as
to the fact that we should not drink till we are sated, but sparingly.

Given his preference for abstinence, the daily allotment is quite generous. A *hemina* was an ancient measurement equaling a bit more than
half a pint. Little did Benedict know that his monks would become the
master brewers of Christendom.[5]

Wilhelm Ludwig Friedrich Riefstahl, *Mönche im Refektorium* (1888). (Wikimedia Commons)

## THE BREWING PRACTICES OF THE MONKS

Beer, as we know it, comes from the monks. They undertook "the first
large-scale production of beer in medieval Europe," in which "the first
signs of a new level of beer making included using more and better
equipment and the best of techniques. . . . Monks introduced a new form

[5] In fact, the first synod of Aachen in 816 decreed that monks could have twice as
much beer if they drank it instead of wine — a full pint or *sextarius* (Nelson, *Barbarian's
Beverage*, 101). Also, when the *Rule* was adapted for women in the seventh century in
the *Regula cuiusdam Patris ad Virgines*, it indicated that an elder nun should be placed
over the groups working in the brewery and that the nuns should receive "a draught of
strong drink, that is, the usual measure of beer." Quoted in and translated by Joseph
Strickland, "Beer, Barbarism, and the Church from Late Antiquity to the Early Middle
Ages" (master's thesis, University of Tennessee, 2007), 40.

of organization to brewing and the new form served as a model for later developments and for the long-term evolution of the industry."[6] The monks may even have invented the name, if one explanation of the etymology of the word is correct: a contraction of the Latin word for drink, *bibere.*

Regardless of the name, they perfected the brewing process, particularly on a large scale. A large part of this brewing success derives from the fact that monasteries became, according to the historian Christopher Dawson, "the most typical cultural institution" of the early Middle Ages, and centers from which Western culture would be reborn after the Fall of Rome and the onset of the Dark Ages of barbarian invasions.[7] In the midst of these Dark Ages, monasteries became lights of education, health care, and economics, which included brewing. Rod Phillips explains that

> the first large-scale brewing operations were set up in monasteries from the eighth century. Not only were monasteries wealthy enough to buy the equipment for commercial production, but they also owned the land that would provide the necessary supplies of grain. Beyond that, larger religious houses needed to produce more than a family household because they had to meet the dietary requirements of more people: the scores of monks in residence and the various travelers who might stay at a monastery.[8]

The monks developed a number of key innovations in their early monastic brewing. First, they began boiling the wort, created from soaking the malted barley before fermentation. This proved to be immensely important, particularly for purifying the water, making beer a sanitary beverage as well as a nourishing one. Throughout the Middle Ages, beer provided an important, safe alternative to contaminated water. It became a staple drink for men, women, and children, consumed throughout the day, especially by workers.[9] Nonetheless, historical sources point

---

[6] Richard W. Unger, *Beer in the Middle Ages and the Renaissance* (Philadelphia: University of Pennsylvania Press, 2004), 16.

[7] Christopher Dawson, *Religion and the Rise of Western Culture* (New York: Image, 1991), 44; 45.

[8] Phillips, *Alcohol*, 55–56.

[9] Rod Phillips estimates that "in the eighth and ninth centuries, monks drank 1.55 liters of ale, while nuns drank 1.38 liters. Among lay consumers, the volume of ale

to a hierarchy, with "wine as the drink of the rich, ale for the poor, and water for the poorest."[10]

The second major development came with a new flavor. As in the ancient world, there were many beer flavorings in the early Middle Ages: honey, heather, fruit, and herbs. The Germans used the word "ale" for their barley brew, but the monks' new drink (*biber*) would come from the boiled wort, flavored with hops. The first historical reference to hopped beer comes from the Benedictine Abbey of Corbie, France in 822, though records point to a hop garden given by Pepin the Short to the Abbey of St. Denis just outside of Paris in 768.[11] The Benedictines of northern France seem to be the first brewers to use hops regularly during the Carolingian period, and from there it spread to other monasteries, such as those in England in the tenth century and Germany in the eleventh.[12]

It was not until the period between the 1300s and the 1500s that hops became the universal additive, replacing gruit (a mixture of bog myrtle and other herbs), which varied by region.[13] An early example of its uniform adoption comes from France, where King St. Louis proclaimed in 1268 that "nothing shall enter into the composition of beer but good malt and hops."[14] Elsewhere, the traditional ale and the new "beer" were in competition (the latter even being banned in England and other localities

---

was calculated as varying between 0.6 and 2.3 liters of beer" (*Alcohol*, 55; see pages 90 ff. for the role of alcohol for laborers). Ken Follett captured accurately the familial nature of beer drinking as a daily staple, including its consumption by children in the Middle Ages, in his novel *Pillars of the Earth*: "A few minutes later Aliena came out with a pot of beer and a loaf of wheat bread. She broke the bread into hunks and handed out, then she passed the pot around" (New York: Penguin, 1990, 195).

[10]  Nelson, *Barbarian's Beverage*, 87.

[11]  Unger, *Beer in the Middle Ages*, 53–54; Nelson, *Barbarian's Beverage*, 107. The first mention of a hop garden (*humularia*) comes from the German Benedictine monastery of Hochstift, dating from about 859 (Hornsey, *History of Beer*, 307), though the plant itself was referenced at the Abbey of Weihenstephan in 768 (Oliver, *Oxford Companion*, 104) .

[12]  Unger, *Beer in the Middle Ages*, 54.

[13]  Richard Unger describes gruit as "a combination of dried herbs, including wild rosemary, with the most prominent ingredient being bog myrtle . . . most closely related to the willow" (*Beer in the Middle Ages*, 31). It has a "sharp taste" and was "bitter and astringent" (ibid.). The exact composition of gruit varied by region, with possible ingredients such as ginger, anise, cumin, laurel, marjoram, mint, sage, acorns, juniper, yarrow, ivy, thistle, heather, alecost, wormwood, and spruce.

[14]  Quoted in Hornsey, *History of Beer*, 294.

for a period of time). It was resisted by civil authorities because the Holy Roman Empire (through its nobility, bishops, and towns) controlled the production of gruit and used it as the means of taxing ale. The ability to sell the right to make gruit was called the *gruitrecht*, a coveted and valuable privilege. Hopped beer eventually won out for one main reason: hops turned out to be a great preservative, adding significant shelf life to the drink and enabling it to travel further distances for trade. It also provided a citrusy, acidic balance to the maltiness of beer, and was thought to be medicinal.

The medicinal qualities of beer attracted the attention of one particular Benedictine, though not a monk: the abbess, musician, artist, preacher, mystic, and now Doctor of the Church, St. Hildegard of Bingen (1098–1179). In addition to her artistic and ecclesial roles, Hildegard acted as a renowned healer and naturalist. In her book, *Causes and Cures*, she notes that "beer puts flesh on the bones and gives a lovely color to the face, on account of the strength and good juices of the grain. Water has a weakening effect. . . . Whether people are healthy or sick . . . they should drink wine or beer, not water."[15] In another work, *Physica*, which focuses on the natural qualities of plants and how they can be used for remedies, she provides a few tidbits on the making of beer. She speaks of the qualities of hops, for instance: "It is warm and dry, and has a moderate moisture, and is not very useful in benefiting man, because it makes melancholy grow in man and makes the soul of man sad, and weighs down his inner organs. But yet as a result of its own bitterness it keeps some putrefactions from drinks, to which it may be added, so that they may last so much longer."[16] While speaking of ash trees, she advises: "If you also wish to make beer from oats without hops, but just with grusz [i.e., gruit], you should boil it after adding a very large number of ash leaves. That type of beer purges the stomach of the drinker, and renders his heart light and joyous."[17] For the swelling of man's virile parts, she recommends the mixing of fennel, fenugreek,

[15] Hildegard of Bingen, "Causes and Cures," in *Hildegard of Bingen: Essential Writings and Chants of a Christian Mystic — Annotated & Explained*, trans. Sheryl Kujawa-Holbrook (Woodstock, VT: Sky Light Paths, 2016), 129, 2.256.

[16] Hildegard of Bingen, *Physica*, trans. Priscilla Throop (Rochester, VT: Healing Arts Press, 1998), 36, 1.61. She also cautioned that hops could have negative effects, such as making one insane! See Nelson, *Barbarian's Beverage*, 110.

[17] Hildegard of Bingen, *Physica*, 124.

and butter, after which one should "take the little cakes from which beer is made, heat them moderately in warm water, and place them over the tumor."[18] Women are not left out—she points to beer as a remedy for excessive menstrual blood.[19]

St. Hildegard von Bingen, *The Celestial Influences on Animals and Plants.* (Wikimedia Commons)

Hildegard provides a striking image of one of the Benedictines' central tasks: hospitality. "Let all guests who arrive be received as Christ" (*Rule,* ch. 53). It is no coincidence that the word "hospital" comes from the word "hospitality." *Hospes* means "stranger" in Latin and the monks embraced a mission to care for strangers as Christ Himself, which entailed providing the only clear medical treatment of the early Middle Ages. Hospitals grew

[18]  Ibid., 41.
[19]  Ibid., 100.

out of monastic hospitality and the sick houses run by monasteries. [20] Beer, naturally, factored into hospitality, with special brews specifically for guests, including the infirm. The monks brewed a variety of beers for their own consumption, to sell to the surrounding villages, and to provide for pilgrims and guests. There were at least two distinct strengths: strong and small. Small beer would be given to the sick, pregnant women, and even children, as it contained only about 2 percent alcohol.

## THE GROWTH OF MONASTIC BEER

From Benedict's first foundations in Italy, monasticism quickly spread throughout Europe, though a distinct Egyptian-inspired monasticism predominated in France for some time and from there spread to Ireland. Eventually, monastic breweries numbered in the thousands throughout northern Europe. The Irish monasteries brewed as well, and their missionary monks laid the foundation for many of the German monasteries that would later take up the mantle of monastic brewing. We know from the life of St. Columban (543–615), an Irish monk who took a lifelong vow of pilgrimage as a missionary from his homeland, that beer was important in the life of the Irish monks. His biography, written by Jonas of Bobbio in the seventh century, describes no less than three beer miracles.[21]

In the first beer miracle, Columban saved the monastery's beer from spilling throughout the cellar. The cellarer was pouring from the barrel into a jar, but left it in haste to be obedient: "After he had done what the man of God wished, he returned quickly to the cellar, thinking that nothing would be left in the vat from which the beer was running. But he saw the beer had run into the jar and not the least drop had fallen outside, so that you would have believed that the jar had doubled in size." Interestingly, it also offers a definition of beer, describing how the cellarer "was ready to serve out the beer (*cervisia*), which is boiled down from the juice of corn or barley, and which is used in preference to other beverages by all the nations in the world." The second is reminiscent of the miracle of the Lord's multiplication of the loaves, but this time with bread and beer! Working

---

[20] See Guenter Risse's *Mending Bodies, Saving Souls: A History of Hospitals* (Oxford: Oxford University Press, 1999).

[21] See "The Life of St. Columban by the Monk Jonas," Fordham University, accessed June 2, 2018, https://sourcebooks.fordham.edu/basis/columban.asp.

in the fields and hungry, his monks tell Columban: "Father, believe me, we have only two loaves and a very little beer." Columban answered, "Go and bring those." After praying, "all were satisfied and each one drank as much as he wished. The servant carried back twice as much in fragments and twice the amount of drink." Finally, while travelling through Germanic lands, Columban encountered some Swabians who were on their way to offer beer to the god Oden. "They had a large cask that they called a *cupa*, and that held about twenty-six measures, filled with beer and set in their midst.... When he heard of this abomination, he breathed on the cask, and lo! it broke with a crash and fell in pieces so that all the beer ran out." We see from these short passages that the monks made and consumed beer regularly, and that barbarians used beer in their religious rituals.

Other Celtic monks followed the example of St. Columban as they established monastic breweries on continental Europe, contributing to the evangelization of the Germans. One of Columban's disciples, St. Gallus, established one of the most important foundations near Lake Constance, Switzerland, in 613. In the following century, his simple hermitage grew into an abbey that was named after him, and which received the patronage of Charlemagne's grandfather. Interestingly, a blueprint of the abbey, called "the Plan of St. Gall," still exists today.

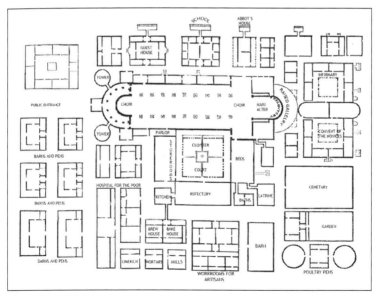

Plan of St. Gall. (Wikimedia Commons)

Although the plan may not have been fully executed, it is the oldest existing overview of the structure of a monastery and shows us how the brewery was integrated into a much larger economic unit, which supported the monks as well as guests and the local community.

We can see how the abbey was a small town in its own right, with a school, library, workshops, and livestock, and indeed, like many monasteries, it did give birth to an adjacent town. Significantly, it contained not only an infirmary for monks, but also a hostel and a hospital for the poor—one of the oldest in Europe. The brewery was central to the monks' practice of hospitality and care for those in need, producing 350–400 liters a day.[22] In addition to beer, the monks offered food, clothing, herbal remedies, and Europe's first individualized care (and quarters) to the sick.

The monks of St. Gall developed what is thought to be the first large-scale brewery in Europe. It consisted of a kiln for roasting malt and three distinct brewing operations, producing three different kinds of beer and developing practices that stimulated fermentation. The *Oxford Companion of Beer* describes their brewery in detail:

> Each of the monastery's three breweries was dedicated to making a different type of beer. One brew was a strong beer called *celia*, made from barley, sometimes from wheat, or frequently from both. It was reserved only for the abbot and his inner circle and his high-ranking visitors. The second brew, called *cervisa*, was a beer of milky-sour taste, usually made from oats, and flavored with herbs and sometimes with honey; the latter version was called *cervisa mellita*. This was the monks' and pilgrims' everyday beer and was consumed like water throughout the day. The third brew, called *conventus*, was a thin "small beer" made from the final runnings of the stronger beers and mixed with fresh extract from malted oats. It was brewed specifically for the abbey's lay workers and for beggars.[23]

Eventually, almost all the monasteries of Europe, including the ones founded by Celtic monks, embraced the *Rule* of St. Benedict.

---

[22] Unger, *Beer in the Middle Ages*, 29.
[23] Oliver, *Oxford Companion*, 767.

Charlemagne, and his son Louis the Pious, played a pivotal role, standardizing monastic practice as well as beer-making, thereby creating Europe's first rules governing the quality of beer. Key centers of monasticism could be found in Burgundy (the home of Cluny and Cîteaux, where they perfected viticulture) and central Europe, especially Bavaria and Austria. Munich serves as a great example of the expansion of monastic culture into central Europe. Even the name Munich (München) comes from the German *Mönch*—monk—as the city sprouted from a monastic foundation. In Bavaria, monks began selling beer commercially for the first time.[24] We see remnants of this today, as the two oldest breweries in the world, Weihenstephaner (1040) and Weltenburger (1050), were Benedictine breweries. Although Weihenstephaner was secularized in the early 1800s, Weltenburger is still connected to the Weltenburg Abbey.

Because the *Rule* of St. Benedict allows only one meal a day in Lent (after Vespers), the Bavarian monks are known for brewing a particular Lenten beer that sustained them during the fast.[25] Pretzels may have the same origin, as it has been suggested that they were developed for Lent when no animal products could be eaten. Their shape also suggests hands folded in prayer, as well as three loops for the Trinity. Pretzels, therefore, reinforce the monks approach to brewing—linked to fasting and ordered toward prayer.

The monks helped to make beer the staple drink of northern Europe and a central element in the growth of Christian culture. Their prayer and work provided advancements in health and nutrition, as well as centers of culture where local peasants, the sick, and pilgrims gathered in fellowship with the monks. Beer played an important role in their overall work of building up culture during the Dark Ages and laying the foundations for a new flowering of Christian culture. Eventually, breweries became commercial enterprises in the High Middle Ages; the monks still brewed, but monastic beer lost its unique, cultural role. A few hundred years later, it would lose much more with the onset of the modern world and the near extinction of monastic brew.

[24] Unger, *Beer in the Middle Ages*, 34.
[25] The Lenten beer we know today, Paulaner's *Salvator*, actually comes from the Franciscan tradition of St. Francis Paola's Friars Minim. A strong double-bock style, known as liquid bread, it supplied nourishing sustenance during the fast.

Detail from medieval illumination. (Wikimedia Commons)

Nonetheless, the monks tendered a last major contribution on the eve of the Reformation. Bavarian monks created a new method of brewing and a new style of beer: the lager. Lager means "storeroom" and derived from storing beer in caves and cellars. Brewing used to be a seasonal endeavor, as the summer months were too warm to brew. Beer would be stored in caves and cellars, with chestnut trees planted in the surrounding area for further shade (making a convenient location for the beer garden). The cold temperature and the settling of the yeast to the bottom of the storage containers brought about a new strain of yeast, which ferments at lower temperatures and at the bottom of the brew tanks.[26] The monks unintentionally fostered this new beer, but it

---

[26] The bottom fermenting lager yeast is named *Saccharomyces pastorianus*, versus the top fermenting ale yeast, *Saccharomyces cerevisiae*. Laws regulated brewing throughout Europe, stipulating when beer could be brewed and with what ingredients. The most famous example of a brewing law is the long-lasting Reinheitsgebot of 1516, by which the Bavarian ruling family, the Wittelsbachs, decreed that only beer, hops, and water

was taken up and developed more intentionally by Bavarian breweries such as Spaten, known for their dunkel or dark lager. The bright and crisp lager style dominant today developed further east in the town of Pilzen, Bohemia (modern day Czech Republic), from where we get the name Pilsner. Despite all of the monks' contributions to brewing, the modern period has been nearly fatal to monasticism and its culture.

could be used in brewing (as yeast had not yet been identified). The Wittelsbachs kept the right to brew wheat beer themselves, occasionally leasing out this right to others. The Reinheitsgebot continues today throughout Germany.

CHAPTER 3

# *The Decline and Fall of Catholic Brewing*

The modern world is riddled with the remains of monasteries. The last five hundred years has seen the steady dismantling of the Catholic culture of medieval Christendom. Although the Middle Ages had its problems, its key characteristic could be found in the central role of the Catholic faith in society. The Catholic core arose not simply from the fact that everyone was Catholic, but because the faith shaped politics, economics, education, and the arts. Monastic life offers one palpable expression of this culture, a Christendom in miniature, and thus it stood out as a target for the modern forces bent on creating a more secular world. How did the attack on monasticism affect beer production? Brewing would follow the direction of modern culture, decisively turning away from the Church and toward the secular realm.

## THE REFORMATION

Ironically, the orgy of destruction monasticism faced in the sixteenth century began with an Augustinian monk (or friar), Martin Luther. Although he abandoned his vows and married a nun (who had a brewing license) and wrote a work on the nullity of monastic vows, he maintained the practice of hospitality and conversation over beer in his table talks. The talks occurred in his new home, his old confiscated monastery, over beer brewed by his wife. Accordingly, he described his work (or lack thereof as he tells it) in light of his drinking habits: "I simply taught, preached, and wrote God's Word; otherwise I did nothing. And then, while I slept, or drank Wittenberg beer with my friends . . . the Word so greatly weakened the papacy that never a prince or emperor did such damage to it. I did nothing. The Word did it all."[1]

---

[1]  Martin Luther, "Eight Sermons at Wittenberg: The Second Sermon, March 10,

Luther's house, the former Augustinian Friary. (Wikimedia Commons)

Drinking beer indeed! Luther certainly did not do nothing. Not only did he add words to his German translation of the Bible, but he defended his choices in quite colorful language. Speaking of the all-too-crucial passage, Romans 3:28, Luther responded to Catholic criticism that he had added the word "alone" — absent from the original text — with a response that surely must have become a popular drinking song:

> If your Papist annoys you with the word "alone," tell him straightaway, Dr. Martin Luther will have it so: Papist and ass are one and the same thing. Whoever will not have my translation, let him give it the go-by: the devil's thanks to him who censures it without my

---

1522," in *Martin Luther's Basic Theological Writings*, 3rd ed., eds. W. R. Russell & T. F. Lull (Minneapolis, MN: Fortress Press, 2012), 292.

will and knowledge. Luther will have it so, and he is a doctor above all the doctors in Popedom.[2]

During one table talk, the former friar contrasted his own drinking practices, which were known to be generous, to the "Friar's Fast in Popedom," which entailed "three days of feasting for every fast day," including "two quarts of beer, a quart of wine, spice cakes, or bread prepared with spice and salt, to better relish their drink."[3] Another leading "reformer," John Calvin, also accused the monks of "license in drinking" and their "abstinence in eating alone . . . a mere mockery of God."[4] King Henry VIII, who destroyed the English monasteries, allegedly also rejected one of the monks' major contributions to brewing, calling hops "a wicked and pernicious weed," destined to ruin England's ales.[5]

The Reformation began the process of secularization in the modern world, by insisting on the essential interiority of faith. For the reformers, the Church became essentially invisible and the Christian life consisted of faith apart from reason, and grace divorced from nature. For instance, Luther taught that "reason is the devil's greatest whore."[6] While Luther denigrated reason in favor of faith, the Enlightenment accepted this dichotomy between the natural and supernatural, though it turned the tables on faith. This matters for our discussion of beer because of a fundamental shift in Catholic culture: isolating faith from the ordinary affairs of the world. The Reformation struck at the central role of monasteries in society, affecting much more than beer, of course, by removing an institution central to caring for and educating the poor.[7]

---

[2] Martin Luther, "Open Letter on Translating," 1530. http://bible-researcher.com/luther01.html.

[3] Martin Luther, *Luther's Table Talk* (London: Longman, Rees, Orme, Brown, and Green, 1832), 85–86.

[4] *Calvin's Commentaries*, trans. John King, vol. 3, *Harmony of the Law*, Part 1, accessed May 19, 2018, http://www.sacred-texts.com/chr/calvin/cc03/cc03065.htm.

[5] Rod Phillips actually claims that Henry was motivated against hops due to the fact that they came from Protestant Northern Europe. See Phillips, *Alcohol*, 100. Henry continued to persecute Protestants even after his schism with Rome.

[6] Martin Luther, "Sermon for the Second Sunday in Epiphany," January 17, 1546, his last sermon in Wittenberg. See *Luther's Works*, vol. 51, ed. John Doberstein and Helmut Lehmann (Philadelphia: Fortress Press, 1959), 374.

[7] Arthur J. Penty notes that "after the suppression [of the monasteries], the poor were deprived at one fell swoop of alms, shelter and schooling. The consequence was

## THE ENLIGHTENMENT AND FRENCH REVOLUTION

The Enlightenment called for the final destruction of Catholic culture (and monasticism in particular) which was begun by the Reformation. As Voltaire put it, "Quoi que vous fassiez, écrasez l'infâme," translated as, "Whatever you do, crush the infamous thing" — the infamous thing being the Church. The French Revolution accomplished this dastardly goal in France and the tyrant Napoleon spread the destruction across the rest of Europe. The revolution abolished all monastic vows on February 13, 1790, assuming responsibility for education and charitable works formerly handled by the Church. Monks who complied were given a stipend; those who did not were martyred or exiled.

Napoleon saw monks as useless, and closed over a thousand monasteries throughout Europe. French monasteries were not the center of European brewing, but the effects of the French Revolution rippled throughout Europe. After seizing territory of the Holy Roman Empire in Alsace-Lorraine and the lowlands, France forced a review of the entire constitution of the Empire. In 1803, with French supervision, all ecclesiastical lands, prince-bishoprics and monasteries were dissolved and confiscated.[8] A decree of July 28, 1811, from Napoleon himself, also shuttered all Trappist monasteries in his Empire, directly impacting the Belgian Trappist breweries. When it came to the great, and highly lucrative, monastic breweries of Bavaria, however, many of them were secularized, taken over by the state or private bidders. Only thirty out of fifteen hundred Benedictine monasteries survived the Napoleonic Wars.

Take the example of Weihenstephan Abbey, founded by St. Corbinian in 720 in honor of St. Stephen. Records point to a hop garden next to the Abbey from the year 768, with a license to brew from the city of Freising in 1040, which is the date on their label, establishing them as the oldest continually operating brewery in the world. Like the other Bavarian monasteries, it was secularized in 1803 and taken over by the

---

that great numbers, left entirely destitute of the means of existence, took to begging and thieving." After the suppression, new landlords "speedily raised the rents and enclosed the commons. In other cases the peasantry were simply turned out of their holdings." *A Guildman's Interpretation of History* (New York: Sunrise Turn, 1919), 165; 167.

[8] For an overview of the dissolution of monasteries in this time period, see Derek Beales, *Prosperity and Plunder: European Catholic Monasteries in the Age of Revolution, 1650–1815* (Cambridge: University of Cambridge Press, 2003).

Baron Lejeune, *Assault on San Engracia Monastery* (1827). (Wikimedia Commons)

State of Bavaria, which controls it to this day. The second oldest brewery, founded at Weltenburg Abbey, suffered the same fate, but under the patronage of King Ludwig I the abbey was refounded in 1842 along with its brewery. The Benedictines were not the only victims. The Franciscan Minim Friar's Paulaner brewery, named after St. Francis Paola, was purchased by its lay workers, and Augustiner-Bräu, Munich's oldest brewery, was taken from the Augustinians and eventually passed to the Wagner family.

## BEER IN AMERICA

Even if the Enlightenment opposed Catholic brewing culture, it did not oppose beer itself. In fact, the United States, itself a product of Enlightenment thought, created its own drinking culture. As the traditional beer culture was under attack in Europe, a new culture formed in America. We can see this even in the Founding Fathers. George Washington brewed at Mount Vernon, where he grew hops, and he even gave out beer to voters. Sam Adams, as we all now know, has a connection to beer, but primarily in his father's malt house, not as a brewer. Thomas Jefferson waited until 1812 to begin brewing at Monticello. The phrase "Beer is proof that God loves us and wants us to be happy" has been attributed to Benjamin Franklin. We cannot find evidence of this quotation, but Franklin did write a letter to André Morellet, in which he said: "Behold the rain which descends from heaven upon our vineyards, there it enters the roots of the vines, to be changed into wine, a constant proof that God loves us, and loves to see us happy."

The brewing culture of America stretches back even further to the Pilgrims and the earliest colonies of Virginia in the 1500s. The first brewery in the Americas was founded by the Spanish in 1544 in Mexico City, but in the North, it was the Dutch in New Amsterdam (later New York) in 1613. A little later, around 1634, a Jesuit, Br. Ambroise, became the first recorded brewer in Canada.[9] Brewing grew slowly but steadily in North America. As most beer was brewed in the home and in local taverns, by 1810 there were only 132 commercial breweries. By 1850 that number would grow to 431, peaking in the 1870s at over 4,000. Why the exponential growth in breweries in the middle of the nineteenth century? Immigration from Germany soared in the 1840s and these new Americans would found large and successful breweries. The oldest operating brewery in the United States was started by David Yuengling in 1829 in Pottsville, Pennsylvania. The Pabst brewery followed in 1844; Anheuser-Busch in 1852; Miller in 1855; Schell in 1860; Leinenkugel's in 1867; Coors in 1873; and Shiner in 1909. All were founded by German immigrants and still operate today, though many as subsidiaries of international conglomerates.

It was not just lay Catholics who fled the political upheavals of Europe. As many European Catholics sought refuge and new opportunities in America, monks followed them, seeing themselves in the missionary tradition of St. Augustine of Canterbury and St. Boniface. Archabbot Boniface Wimmer, for instance, came to America and in 1846 founded the Archabbey of St. Vincent in Latrobe, Pennsylvania, America's first

---

9  Allen Winn Smith, *Brewed in Canada: The Untold Story of Canada's 350-Year-Old Brewing Industry* (Toronto: Dundurn, 2001), 21.

St. Vincent Archabbey. (Wikimedia Commons)

Benedictine monastery. Wimmer's abbey raised their own crops, mined coal, and established a brewery. Monastic brewing had arrived in America! Fr. Omer Kline, in a history of the Archabbey buildings, describes the role of the brewery:

> The beginnings of a brewery operation at Saint Vincent were very modest in comparison with the major public issues that were made in 1849–1852 and in the 1890s concerning Saint Vincent being in the "beer business." To build this little brewery and to brew beer for consumption by the monks was not viewed as out of place by these early Saint Vincent Benedictines. In fact these hard working monks, most of whom had emigrated from the territory around Munich, Bavaria, craved for the beer for which that area of southern Germany had long been famous. It was a time-honored practice for Bavarian monasteries to make and sell beer.[10]

---

[10] Omer U. Kline, OSB, *The Saint Vincent Archabbey Gristmill and Brewery: 1854–2000* (Latrobe, PA: St. Vincent Archabbey, 2000), 40–41.

The monks ran into trouble quickly, though, as the Bishop of Pittsburg, Michael O'Connor, the Irish-born Jesuit, belonged to the temperance movement. Abbot Wimmer, however, had the support of King Ludwig I of Bavaria, who, with support from Pope Pius IX, provided funds to build the monastery's brewery. Trouble would arise again, however, due to the sale of the monks' beer to the general public, which turned more clergy against the Archabbey. Some critics even changed the Benedictine abbreviation of OSB to the "Order of Sacred Brewers" and one newspaper wrote of "Saint Vincent's 'Holy Beer' Brewed by Papal Authority."[11] The brewery was not to last, as the monks cut production: "The fate of the Saint Vincent Brewery was finally sealed on January 29, 1919, with the ratification of the Eighteenth Amendment to the United States Constitution."[12] The shuttered brewery burnt to the ground in the following decade.

Not too long after monks began brewing in Latrobe, other monks established a brewery at St. Meinrad's Archabbey in 1860 (after being derailed five years earlier by prohibitionists). They quickly leased it out to laymen, after their own failed attempt to brew. Some of Meinrad's monks are currently trying it again, hopefully with more success. The Capuchins of Munjor, Kansas, also began brewing in 1902, though their efforts were short-lived as Prohibition shuttered their brewery as well.

## INDUSTRIALIZATION

Some monastic breweries, having weathered the storm of political revolution, reopened in Germany and Belgium, and a few more sprang up in America. At the same time a new revolutionary force, industrialization, would upend traditional brewing practices. In 1777, just a year after the Declaration of Independence, the first steam engine appeared in a brewery in Stratford-le-Bow, England, which was used for milling grain (taking the place of horses). Engines soon began to pump water, wort, and beer around the brewery. These machines drastically increased production. Concrete, transportation, refrigeration, and stronger iron all followed, making beer production more efficient and the product more mobile.

[11] Ibid., 51.
[12] Ibid., 52.

The scientific revolution also greatly increased precision in brewing. The hydrometer measured the density of sugars. The thermometer allowed for more precision in maintaining the right level of sugars to enhance fermentation through temperature control—between 145°F and 160°F during the mash. The microscope enabled more advanced knowledge of yeast, observable for the first time as an organism. Yeast was once known as *godesgood* because the spontaneous fermentation it caused was attributed to God's providence. Louis Pasteur was not the first to see yeast through the microscope, but he decisively advanced the understanding of yeast as a microorganism and thus advanced sanitation in brewing, especially through the pasteurization process he invented.

The industrial revolution also enabled greater distribution of beer. This ended up being of enormous consequence, moving beer more from a cottage industry to an industry. Breweries grew larger as they could export their goods. Anheuser-Busch, in particular, made use of refrigerated train cars to extend the life and quality of their beer as they built a brewing empire across the United States. Anheuser-Busch also pioneered bottling in 1873. Bottling had been around for a while, but industrialization enabled large-scale bottling on the assembly line, which, combined with rail transportation and refrigeration, only increased the growth of large breweries.

Industrialization marked a turning point in Western society, creating many social problems, which alcohol only exacerbated. Mass migration to cities decimated rural populations, brought higher crime and social problems to overcrowded cities, and contributed to the secularization of cultural life. With the decline of home life, public houses proliferated in London to serve as new cultural centers, eventually growing to one for every sixteen houses.[13] Brewers responded to the new working-class population of London and other English cities with a new beer style called porter, named for a large segment of their customers, as well as stronger and highly-hopped Indian pale ales to ship across the globe to England's growing colonies. In addition, gin became a craze in industrialized London. As alcoholism became a growing problem in the industrialized West, temperance movements stepped in to limit and even prohibit the use of alcohol.

---

13   Phillips, *Alcohol*, 106.

## PROHIBITION

The American drinking culture that grew out of the colonies experienced this same tension. Before the formation of the large German breweries in the mid-nineteenth century, it was whiskey, not beer, that dominated the American drinking scene. Monks popularized spirits in the late Middle Ages, originally for medicinal purposes, and Protestant Scotch-Irish immigrants brought the tradition to colonial America. Through distillation, whiskey enabled farmers to preserve extra grain indefinitely. It became a staple commodity and even currency for the pioneers pushing into modern day Kentucky (location of Bourbon County, named in honor the French King Louis XVI, who crucially supported American independence). The dominance of whiskey, which is much higher in alcohol than beer and more prone to abuse, led to the creation of a powerful temperance movement to combat the effects of alcohol.

Temperance movements grew slowly but steadily throughout the 1800s. The American Temperance Society formed in 1826 and within ten years had a million and a half members. The next stage of the movement was taken up by women, who formed the Women's Christian Temperance Union in 1873, linking prohibition to women's suffrage. Some Christian denominations, such as Methodists and Baptists, also strongly supported prohibition. Starting in 1881, states began to ban the production and sale of alcohol, paving the way for the Eighteenth Amendment to the Constitution, passed in 1919 and taking effect the following year. Interestingly, national prohibition was part of a worldwide movement in the early 1900s, with at least seven other countries banning alcohol. Prohibition had many unintended consequences, such as bootlegging (a profession that included my great-great grandfather), speakeasies, organized crime, and doctor's notes for medicinal whiskey. Brewers survived by making other malt products, near beer, and even ice cream. President Franklin Roosevelt campaigned to repeal prohibition and delivered with the passage of the Twenty-First Amendment in 1933. The president celebrated at the White House with a special brew from Yuengling, begun before brewing was technically legal.

Catholics, in general, strongly resented prohibition, as would be expected. William Henry Cardinal O'Connell (1859–1944), Archbishop of Boston, summed up the Catholic view well: "Compulsory prohibition, in general, is flatly opposed to Holy Scripture and Catholic Tradition." A Bavarian Capuchin friar, Fr. Hyacinth Epp, residing in the dry state of Kansas, also expressed in 1902 that "without beer, things do not seem to go as well." The friars started their own brewery on the condition they would not sell it, but when prohibition became federal law the friars noted: "A day to remember: we had our last beer. . . . How shall we stand it without beer next summer?"[14] Germans across the country were devastated, as a central component of their diet and tradition had been made illegal. Further, Germans saw it as a "threat to cultural activities such as Sunday beer-gardens."[15] Anti-German sentiment stemming from World War I did not help their cause. Due to the Irish proclivity for whiskey, though, some Irish Catholics supported prohibition, as seen in the Catholic Total Abstinence Union of America.

When the alcohol ban ended in 1933, only a fraction of the old breweries reopened. Restrictive laws remained on the books, prohibiting microbreweries, brew pubs, and homebrewing. After weathering the storm of Prohibition, yet another challenge to traditional brewing emerged: commercialization. Even fewer breweries survived the rise of large, industrial breweries, consolidated through aggressive advertising in the mid-twentieth century. The twentieth century saw a steady decline in the number of breweries until by 1983 the top six breweries—Anheuser-Busch, Miller, Heileman, Stroh's, Coors, and Pabst—controlled 92 percent of beer production in the United States. By the 1980s, however, a new brewing revolution took hold.

[14]  Earl Meyer, O.F.M. Cap., *St. Francis Parish, Munjor, Kansas, 1876–1976* (Munjor, KS: St. Francis Church, 1976), 38.
[15]  Phillips, *Alcohol*, 159.

# CHAPTER 4

# *The Renaissance of Benedictine Brewing*

The Psalmist asks, "If foundations are destroyed, what can the just one do?" (Ps. 11:3). The Benedictine order has survived for fifteen hundred years because of the enduring validity of its charism—the need for stability, silence, work, and contemplative prayer. The Benedictines not only survived, but flourished in the Dark Ages. They survived the competition of new forms of religious life, with the rise of the mendicant orders in the 1200s. They survived the great revolutions of the modern world. Monasteries may have been sacked and abandoned through the centuries, but the foundations laid by St. Benedict, rooted in the foundations of the Gospel, have endured. Even when things are lost, they can be found again.

## TWO RESILIENT MONASTERIES

As an example of Benedictine resilience, witness St. Benedict's own monastery, Monte Cassino, founded in 529 on the mountain site of a Temple of Apollo. St. Benedict later had a dream that Germanic tribes would destroy the monastery after his death, and in prayer he obtained the grace that none of his monks would be harmed. The Lombards destroyed the abbey in 581 and it lay vacant for more than a century, until refounded in 718 with Charlemagne's great-uncle among their number. It was then sacked again by the Saracens in 884, with the abbot, Bertharius, martyred. Refounded once again, it became a center for the study of medicine and was the first school of St. Thomas Aquinas, who became an oblate there in 1230. It suffered an earthquake in 1349 and was sacked by Napoleon in 1799. Most recently, the Americans and British bombed it needlessly during the battle of Monte Cassino in

1944, wrongly suspecting its defensive occupation by the Germans.[1] The abbey typifies the ups and downs of Christian life and culture through the centuries. Pope Benedict XVI spoke of the resiliency of the abbey:

> I am particularly glad to pause in this sacred place, in this Abbey, four times destroyed and rebuilt for the last time after the bombing of the Second World War 65 years ago. "Succisa virescit" ("Pruned, it grows"): the words of the new coat of arms clearly convey its history. Monte Cassino, like the age-old oak planted by St. Benedict, "stripped of its leaves" by the violence of the war, sprang up even more vigorously than before. More than once I have been able to enjoy the hospitality of the monks and have spent unforgettable moments of stillness and prayer in this Abbey.[2]

More recently, the basilica and monastery sitting above St. Benedict's childhood home collapsed during a series of earthquakes in 2016. The Monastery of St. Benedict in Norcia, Italy, was refounded by a group of international monks, mainly Americans, in the year 2000. They have focused on returning to the Benedictine charism with strict faithfulness to the *Rule* and the monastic *horarium* guiding the daily schedule of prayer and work. Through their perseverance, the monks symbolize the larger work of rebuilding Christian culture.

The monks of Norcia featured prominently in *The Benedict Option*, as Rod Dreher notes that their monastery is an unusual place in the modern world, a sign of contradiction. One of the monks, however, spoke of how the rebuilding project can extend beyond the monastery's walls:

> Father Martin flashed a broad grin from beneath his black beard and said that all Christians can have this if they are willing to do what

---

[1] For details on the German defenses and their refusal to enter the monastery, see Fr. Gereon Goldmann, *The Shadow of His Wings* (San Francisco: Ignatius Press, 2000). The Germans did use the ruins for defensive positions, however, after it was bombed by the Allies. Fr. Goldmann's narrative is one of the most riveting I have ever read. He survived the S.S., the smuggling of Bibles into France, the invasion of Sicily and Italy, and internment camps in North Africa.

[2] Benedict XVI, "Address at Monte Cassino" (May 24, 2009), http://w2.vatican.va/content/benedict-xvi/en/homilies/2009/documents/hf_ben-xvi_hom_20090524_vespri-montecassino.html.

Church of St. Benedict, Norcia. (Wikimedia Commons)

After the earthquake. Photograph courtesy of the monks of Norcia.

it takes to mount the recovery, "to pick up what we have lost and to make it real again." "There's something here that's very ancient, but it's also new," Father Martin said. "People say, 'Oh, you're just trying to turn back the clock.' That makes no sense. If you're doing something right now, it means you're doing it right now. It's new and it's alive! And that's a very powerful thing."[3]

Sifting through the rubble on October 30, 2016, it became clear that only one room in the monastery remained without serious damage: the brewery. Though the monks relocated to the mountains outside of town, the reestablished brewery there will be at the center of their rebuilding efforts. Beer is helping the monks to rebuild, in a sign of beer's potential for cultural rebuilding more broadly. The monks, finding even some humor in the rubble, released a "Quake beer," with the beer that survived the quake in the brewery. The Norbertine canons behind the Belgian Abbey beer, Leffe, jumped in to support as well, releasing a beer called "Leffe per Norcia," with proceeds funding a new chapel.[4]

## THE REBIRTH OF BREWING CULTURE IN AMERICA

If 1920 marks a pivotal year in American brewing with Prohibition, then 1978 deserves equal prominence. Prohibition not only dried up Americans' enjoyment of alcohol, it also precipitated the demise of a local brewing culture, especially for German Catholics. When Prohibition ended, many blue laws made brewing and distribution of beer difficult. For instance, laws restricted brewers from selling directly to retailers, limited the hours one could purchase alcohol, and made homebrewing illegal. Then in 1978, Congress lifted the six-decade ban on homebrewing, and the next year the beer market was deregulated. Together, these changes enabled the rebirth of microbrewing. There were only forty-four microbreweries nationwide in 1979, but today there are more than four thousand, the highest number since 1870. America truly has experienced a brewing rebirth in the last four decades. Growing from a few dozen to a few thousand breweries is an amazing thing, but an entire beer culture

---

[3]  Dreher, *Benedict Option*, 76.
[4]  See "Leffe per Norcia," accessed Aug. 4, 2018, http://leffepernorcia.it/.

has arisen along with it. The enormous growth of homebrewing and craft breweries has been spurred by a new generation of American drinkers, who want locally produced, more sophisticated, and flavorful beer.

The craft brewing movement began earlier though. It was pioneered by Fritz Maytag (a descendant of the founder of the Maytag washer company) who purchased the Anchor Steam brewery in San Francisco in 1965. Though he took over an established, historic brewery (dating to the Gold Rush), it pointed the way to the coming resurgence of American brewing by pioneering craft styles at a time when the pilsner was standard. In one innovative project, the brewery attempted to reconstruct the Ninkasi recipe of ancient Sumer described in chapter one. The growth of homebrewing also laid an important foundation for Charlie Papazian, who formed brewing clubs and taught classes beginning in the late 1970s (eventually founding the American Homebrewers Association). Homebrewing formed a group of Americans who were passionate about good beer and were ready to change a dismal market with few options and style varieties. With the change in the law in the late seventies, new breweries began to emerge, some from those who had already begun homebrewing.

Some of them became large breweries in their own right. Jim Koch founded the Boston Beer Company in 1984, the early days of the craft beer revolution. He began brewing an old family recipe in his kitchen, which became Samuel Adams and has grown to be the second largest craft beer in the United States after Yuengling (a survivor of the old German family breweries). Third in line is Sierra Nevada, which began operations in 1980 as a pioneering homebrew store, sourcing its own hops and then building its own microbrew equipment since none was available. It specializes in highly hopped beers, helping to set a trend in American craft beers. They are also known, like many other new breweries, for sustainability, investing in a beer laboratory, and promoting cultural events such as concerts and a beer camp. The fourth, New Belgium, specializes in Belgian-style beers, including monastic styles. It is employee-owned and based in Fort Collins, contributing to northern Colorado's status as "the Napa Valley of beer."

In addition, there are so many smaller breweries, coming in many varieties. Brew pubs sell primarily what they brew in-house, though technically must sell on-site at least 25 percent of what they brew. Microbreweries produce less than fifteen thousand barrels a year. Craft breweries can be larger, but not too large. The Brewers Association gives the following definition:

> An American craft brewer is small, independent and traditional. Small: Annual production of 6 million barrels of beer or less (approximately 3 percent of U.S. annual sales). Beer production is attributed to the rules of alternating proprietorships. Independent: Less than 25 percent of the craft brewery is owned or controlled (or equivalent economic interest) by an alcoholic beverage industry member that is not itself a craft brewer. Traditional: A brewer that has a majority of its total beverage alcohol volume in beers whose flavor derives from traditional or innovative brewing ingredients and their fermentation. Flavored malt beverages (FMBs) are not considered beers.[5]

Brew pubs, microbreweries, and craft breweries have become common across the United States, creating local beer culture and innovative beer styles.

## REVIVAL OF MONASTIC BREWING

Following the Napoleonic-led destruction of monastic brewing, the Trappists of Belgium became the first to bounce back, along with some stalwart survivors in Bavaria. Napoleon fell at Waterloo in Belgium in 1815. The Belgian Trappist monks at Westmalle reestablished brewing in 1836, followed by Westvleteren in 1839, and Chimay in 1850. Apart from these isolated instances, monastic brewing clearly looked like a relic of the past. Prohibition shut down monastic brewing in the United States, but, just as craft and microbrewing eventually experienced a rebirth, so did Benedictine brewing. What is it about monks and beer? Even after centuries of disruption, the two just can't be kept apart! And as craft beer continues to rise in popularity in the United States, the holy craftsmen responsible for creating European brewing practices are reclaiming their own.

Three factors came together for the rebirth of monastic brewing in the US. First, Belgian Trappist beers have been growing in popularity; they

---

[5] "Craft Brew Defined," Brewers Association, accessed May 20, 2018, https://www.brewersassociation.org/statistics/craft-brewer-defined/.

are consistently rated among the best in the world and the US market continues to pay higher-than-average prices for them. Second, as the growing beer culture in the US has generated interest in monastic styles, the monks have realized they can tap into this market. Third, the monks have had to deal with a huge identity crisis, which began plaguing the monasteries in the 1960s. They need to rediscover lost elements of their tradition and find new ways of generating income and interest in their mission. Abbeys abandoned the Benedictine schedule of prayer and work (the *horarium*), and many abandoned longstanding practices of manual labor. I know of a monastery that prays in common only three times a day, versus the *Rule*'s eight specified times. When Assumption Abbey stopped ranching in 2011, it made the front page of the *New York Times*: "With No More Cowboys Taking Vows, Monastery Quits the Cattle Business."[6] I asked the now-deceased abbot why this made the front page and he had no idea, but it clearly indicated a decrease in vocations and vitality. Even the *Times* could recognize the loss of a "rich connection to the earth as the monks go about their days of prayer and humble work." In an odd case, South Carolina's Mepkin Abbey stopped selling eggs, its major source of income, after attacks from PETA in 2007.[7] Prayer and manual labor have declined together at Benedictine monasteries throughout the world.

In the midst of declining faithfulness to the *Rule* and consequently in vocations to the monastic life, we have seen a conscious return by some monasteries to a more traditional monastic life. Monasteries such as Clear Creek Abbey in Oklahoma, the Monastery of St. Benedict in Norcia, Italy, Mariawald Trappist Abbey in Germany, Pluscarden Abbey in Scotland, Silverstream Priory in Ireland, Stift Heiligenkreuz in Austria, Fontgombault Abbey and its dependent monasteries in France, as well as others in France such as Saint-Joseph de Clairval, have all preserved or returned to the *Rule*'s directives for prayer, the daily schedule of monastic life, and more traditional Gregorian chant and liturgy. These abbeys have experience a dramatic rise in vocations and have become

6  Erik Ekholm, "With No More Cowboys Taking Vows, Monastery Quits the Cattle Business," *New York Times*, August 13, 2011, https://www.nytimes.com/2011/08/14/us/14monks.html.

7  Doug Pardue, "Mepkin Abbey to Stop Selling Eggs under Pressure from PETA," *Post and Courier*, December 19, 2007, https://www.postandcourier.com/mepkin-abbey -to-stop-selling-eggs-under-pressure-from-peta/article_118dcd8b-07b3-5198-b34d-76c49ae1d763.html

magnets for the renewal of Catholic spirituality and culture.

Likewise, monastic beer has seen a revival around the world. The prestigious Trappist brand has expanded from just seven breweries in two countries (Belgium and Holland), to twelve in six countries. In just the last few years new Trappist beers have emerged in Holland (Zundert), Austria (Engelszell), France (Monts de Cats), Italy (Tre Fontane), the United States (Spencer), and England (Mount St. Bernard Abbey). Plans are also being laid in Spain (San Pedro de Cardeña).[8] As the average age of the monks increases and financial pressures mount, Trappist monasteries are finding that the "Trappist brand" points to a viable financial future.

Northern France, once a center of monastic brewing, has seen its first monastic beer revival in decades. Before the French Revolution, France was home to nine Trappist breweries and a few of them revived in the post-Napoleonic era, though they did not survive the World Wars.[9] Recently, Mont des Cats (named for the Germanic tribe of the Chatti, not for cats) revived its brewing with the help of the Chimay Trappist brewery in Belgium. Mont des Cats brewed from 1848 until 1905, when restrictions on monasticism imposed by the Third French Republic exiled many monks. The First World War destroyed their brewery and it was not rebuilt, as the monks turned instead to cheese production. In 2011 the monks reached out to the Chimay Brewery of the Abbey of Scourmont in Belgium and created a new recipe, which Chimay brews on behalf of Mont des Cats.

The second Benedictine abbey to take up brewing again in France is St. Wandrille Abbey. It is actually listed as one of the first places to make hopped beer, which Brother Matthew, one of the monks, described as "Cervisia humulone."[10] The monks of Wandrille make their beer within the monastery and use the proceeds to finance a number of restoration projects, including ruins of the ancient abbey and the library, as well

---

[8] The Monasterio de San Pedro de Cardeña in Spain already contracts with a secular brewer to make a Trappist style beer, though it cannot be considered an official Trappist product until it is brewed within the monastery.

[9] See Nancy Hoalst-Pullen and Mark Patterson, *Atlas of Beer: A Globe Trotting Journey through the World of Beer* (Washington, DC: National Geographic, 2017), 89–90.

[10] Claire Lesegretain, "French Benedictines Launch New Brewery: Beer Project Takes Monks Back to the Future," *La Croix International* (Dec. 8, 2016). Unger describes how "Abbot Ansegis of Wandrille (c. 830) talked about beer made with hops" (*Beer in the Middle Ages*, 54).

Abbey of St. Wandrille. (Wikimedia Commons)

as providing for new housing for pilgrims. Wandrille provides another example of how beer is helping to restore monastic life.

In 2012, Ampleforth Abbey in Yorkshire, England, introduced a beer to complement their cider and liqueur production. One surviving member of Westminster Abbey took a group of newly professed English monks with him in exile to France in 1605, where they continued brewing their *bière anglaise*, bringing their own hops with them.[11] Later, the monks had to return to their original homeland for refuge, leaving France under the Revolution in 1792. Father Terrence, the current Prior, describes the monastery's historic brewing: "In the 18th century we were granted a license by Louis XIV to brew and sell beer throughout France. The recipe for our new beer is based on that historic one. We have worked with an expert Dutch brewer who set up the Little Valley Brewery at Hebden Bridge, here in Yorkshire. He visited several Trappist breweries in Belgium and Holland to study their brewing techniques and we think he has helped us produce a first-rate beer. One of St. Benedict's rules is that monks should be self-sufficient. Our orchards and cider production have been a success, so making our own beer seemed a natural progression

---

[11] Brett Tremble and Jayne Lutwyche, "Ampleforth Abbey: How monks mix God, booze and business," BBC, January 15, 2013, http://www.bbc.co.uk/religion/0/18786736. In the article, Fr. Petersburs commented that "these are small beers, they come in small bottles — to be clear that our position is not to encourage excessive drinking." The *Downside Review* traced the beer's enormous popularity in France, even with the local Duke, brewed at the English monk's foundation in exile, St. Lawrence at Dielouard. See *The Downside Review* 4 (1885).

for us."[12] The monks have restored both their monastery and their beer to Protestant England.

In Prague, the ancient Norbertine monastery, Strahov, opened a brewery and restaurant as part of its own restoration. The canons were expelled under Communism, but the building was returned to them recently. Within walking distance from the Prague Castle and near St. Vitus's Cathedral, the historic buildings, including a beautiful basilica and library, needed repair. The on-site brewery dates back to the thirteenth century.[13] The canons are truly rediscovering their roots and using the proceeds to rebuild in a central tourist destination, ideal for hospitality, with seating in the brewery, restaurant, and the outdoor courtyard. One of their main beers is named after St. Norbert himself, which they pair well with the restaurant's traditional Czech cuisine.

## MONASTIC BEER COOPERATIVES IN THE UNITED STATES

Somewhat surprisingly, the revival of monastic brewing has reached the United States as well. We can trace three main stages of this development. First, new craft breweries began brewing in the monastic style, including New Belgium, Ommegang, and Lost Abbey, among others. Second, some of these breweries decided to form cooperatives with monasteries to brew abbey-style beers. Finally, some monasteries decided to begin brewing, an encouraging sign for the renewal of Catholic culture in the United States. New monastic breweries hopefully will spark interest in monastic history and its brewing culture.

The first example of an abbey cooperative beer in the United States, brewed by arrangement between an independent brewer and a monastery, is Abita's Abbey Ale. While not brewed by an abbey directly, Abita donates twenty-five cents to St. Joseph Abbey in St. Benedict, Louisiana, for each bottle of Abbey Ale that it sells. I think that the novelist Walker Percy, an oblate who is buried on the monastery grounds, would

[12] "Trappist Beer," TESCO Real Food, accessed March 7, 2018, https://realfood.tesco.com/our-food/yorkshire-monks-brew-up-a-classic-british-beer.html#HlfJBIRYYHbr1jop.99.

[13] "About Us," Klášterní Pivovar Strahov (Monastic Brewery Strahov), accessed March 25, 2018, http://www.klasterni-pivovar.cz/index.php?process=00000000-0105-2b58-11b1-9bf77b8e3731&languageID=00000000-0105-2b58-11e9-475211a79c15.

be quite pleased by this arrangement. Not only are devotees rumored to place his favorite drink upon his grave, but his own theory of drinking reveals its "sacramental" character, as we will see in chapter seven.

Another abbey cooperative, Ovila, takes its name from a medieval Spanish monastery, Santa María de Óvila, founded in 1181 in Trillo, Guadalajara. The stones from the monastery's chapter house were imported to San Francisco by the media tycoon, William Randolph Hearst, for incorporation into one of his fantasy houses. After sitting unused for decades in a public park in San Francisco, the Abbey of New Clairvaux acquired the stones to restore its chapel. In order to fund the project, they partnered with the brewery Sierra Nevada to brew a series of high quality abbey-style beers. This is a clear example of the revival of abbey beers and the renewal of Catholic culture, which is literally rebuilding its fallen structures.

Chapter house, New Clairvaux Abbey. (Wikimedia Commons)

Benedictine sisters are brewing too. In 2015, a new brewery opened on the grounds of the Sisters of St. Benedict in Ferdinand, Indiana. St. Benedict's Brew Works is owned by two laymen, Vince Luecke and Andy Hedinger, but operates at the monastery. Hedinger said: "I can't think of a better place to be than on the grounds of this monastery. It's peaceful, it's just absolutely beautiful."[14] The brewery's menu, dubbed "The Daily

---

[14] "About," St. Benedict Brew Works, accessed June 2, 2018, http://www.saintbenedictsbrewworks.com/index.php/about/.

Missal," plays up its Benedictine location. They have brewed beers such as The Abbess, a hefeweizen with banana and clove; Sanctimonious Stout, brewed with lactose sugar and hints of chocolate and roasted coffee; Walburga's Wheat IPA; and Sister Mary Kölsch. The brewery has a fitting slogan: "Pray-Work-Brew."

## AMERICAN BREWING MONKS

The revival of monastic brewing in the United States is just beginning, but it appears the initial beers have already spurred more interest, with additional monasteries considering brewing. Some monasteries, such as Clear Creek Abbey and St. Gregory's Abbey (which brews mead), both in Oklahoma, brew solely for their own consumption. (My students continue to tease me for being a little overeager in the refectory to pour myself a glass of Clear Creek's Belgian style ale before prayers had been completed when we were on retreat there.) Some other monasteries have brewed small batches of homebrew, or rather "monastery brew," such as St. Meinrad Abbey in Indiana, St. Mary's Monastery of Petersham, Massachusetts, and the Capuchins in Denver, who brewed for the city's Oktoberfest.

The first example of the revival of monastic brewing began at the Abbey of Christ in the Desert in New Mexico in 2005, when the monks formed the Abbey Beverage Company (initially in conjunction with another monastery in Pecos). The monks host a small brewery on their property and grow their own local subspecies of hops, *neomexicanus*. In addition, larger scale production occurs through an alternating proprietorship with Sierra Blanca Brewing, which enables wider distribution. They have five regular beer styles: Monks' Ale Single, Dubbel, Tripel, Wit, and Dark, with labels featuring profiles of the monks of the abbey. The beer's motto, "Brewed with Care and Prayer," is a fitting image of Catholic culture in general. Initially, the monks directly controlled the brewing project, though the Abbey Beverage Company now rests primarily in lay hands.

There is also a promising new beer coming out of Mount Angel Abbey in Oregon and their Benedictine Brewery. Hops had already been grown on abbey-owned land for decades. The abbey began experimenting with small batches and then contract brewed (with some help from Oregon State's fermentation program), before planning to brew on-site under the direction of Fr. Martin Grassel and director of enterprises, Chris

Jones. Fr. Martin remarked: "This started as a revenue project, but it has become an evangelization project. . . . [It] has been inspired by God."[15] They named their first beer Black Habit Ale, after the Benedictine habit with a dark beer style to match. The back of the label reads:

> We, the monks at Mount Angel Abbey, in the spirit of a centuries-old monastic tradition, are dedicated to our craft for a higher purpose. We use pristine Oregon water, and hops grown in our own backyard and brewed in facilities located right on Abbey grounds. It's a place where monastic life cultivates work and prayer, with every bottle brewed to the glory of God. We welcome all to enjoy our beer in food and fellowship, nourishing both the body and the spirit.

A good summary of a Catholic brewing philosophy! The abbey held a "brewery raising" gathering in November of 2017, with over one hundred people participating, including monks and seminarians. Built with wood harvested on the monastery's land, the monks opened the Benedictine

Brewery raising at Mount Angel. Photograph courtesy of Benedictine Brewery.

[15] Don Williams, "Father Martin Grassel Beerchaser-of-the-Quarter," *The Beer Chaser,* accessed May 5, 2018, https://thebeerchaser.com/2017/07/26/father-martin-grassel -beerchaser-of-the-quarter/.

Brewery and the St. Michael taproom in the summer of 2018 and now oversee the brewing themselves.[16]

In a historic move, St. Joseph's Abbey in Spencer, Massachusetts launched the first American Trappist beer, Spencer Trappist, in 2014. They began by training with local craft brewers and "recognized that brewing was a very traditional monastic enterprise," leading them to consult with their Belgian brethren.[17] They constructed a large brewery on the monastic grounds, where eight monks work, with the aim to brew four thousand barrels a year, eventually increasing to ten thousand. Their flagship beer is a Pater beer, a style the monks usually reserve for their own consumption. The abbey website describes the beer as follows:

> Our recipe was inspired by the traditional refectory ales known as patersbier ("fathers' beer" in Flemish) in Belgium. These sessionable beers are brewed by the monks for their dinner table and are typically only available at the monastery. Spencer is a full-bodied, golden-hued ale with fruity accents, a dry finish and light hop bitterness. The beer is unfiltered and unpasteurized, preserving live yeast that naturally carbonates the beer in the bottle and keg and contributes to the beer flavor and aroma.[18]

It has found a warm reception, living up to the Trappist reputation. In addition to two other Trappist styles, they have branched into American styles, such as an IPA, a pilsner called Feierabendbier, an imperial stout, a festive lager, and even fruit beer. In this sense, they are behaving in a more American fashion than the traditional Belgian Trappist Abbeys, who generally focus on a few classic styles.

The Benedictine life has survived many challenges through the centuries. Monastic brewing, though almost extinct the last two hundred years, has undergone a remarkable rebirth. As we will see in future chapters, this rebirth may also help rebuild Christian faith and culture more broadly.

---

[16] See Benedictine Brewery, https://www.mountangelabbey.org/benedictine -brewery/.

[17] "Our Story," Spencer Brewery, accessed May 5, 2018, "https://spencerbrewery. com/index.php/our-story.

[18] "Spencer Trappist Ale," Spencer Brewery, accessed May 5, 2018, https://spencer-brewery.com/index.php/our-beers/spencer-trappist-ale. See also *The Oxford Companion to Beer*'s entry for "Singel."

PART II

BEER
&
CULTURE

CHAPTER 5

# *Beer as an Expression of Culture*

So far, we have seen the story of beer and how it fits into the narrative of Catholic history. We will now explore its place in human culture. The story of human culture begins, well . . . in the beginning. The first commands God gave to humanity were cultural commands: "Be fruitful, multiply, fill the earth and subdue it" (Gen. 1:28). "The Lord God took the man and put him in the garden of Eden to till it and keep it" (Gen. 2:15).[1] God entrusted the world to humanity to care for it, to bring it under cultivation for the good of humanity, and to give glory to God its Creator. Man is a cultural animal, fashioning the earth as part of his likeness to God. Beer is an important image for our broader cultural vocation of shaping the earth for the sustenance and joyful flourishing of the human community.

## THE ORIGINS OF CULTURE

The world in its natural state contains a myriad of latent possibilities, and it belongs to human intelligence to draw them out. Bread does not grow out of the earth, but wheat does. Wine does not drip forth from the vine. Culture comes from the Latin word for "cultivation," *colere* (interestingly also the Latin word for "worship"). Cult, culture, and agriculture all derive from *colere*'s participle, *cultus*, meaning to tend to or care for something.

---

[1] In fact, the words used by the Bible reinforce cultural practice and possibly even the cultivation of wine: "The language used to describe the royal status of the human pair is unambiguous. They are to have dominion (*rādâ*) over the earth and subdue (*kābâš*) it. These words are associated with power and authority. The word *rādâ* may have originally denoted the treading activity taking place in a wine press. . . . As for the word *kābâš*, it reinforces *rādâ*. Wherever it occurs in the Bible it always means an action in which man reduces something to his use through the application of force" (Stephen Dempster. *Dominion and Dynasty: A Theology of the Hebrew Bible* [Downers Grove, IL: IVP, 2003], 59–60).

61

Culture entails the shaping of things in the world, impressing a human stamp upon them. Producing works of culture clearly reminds us that the rest of creation is subordinate to us and is meant for us. When it comes to agriculture (the tending of fields), we see how planting seeds, tending plants, and harvesting crops give us a glimpse of humanity's role in cultivating God's creation in order to sustain and uphold us.

Culture as a social reality comes forth from the sum total of human work, as we fashion a complete way of life in society. Nature is given to us by God, but culture exists only as an artificial creation of humanity, working with and perfecting nature. Christopher Dawson, who devoted his life's work to tracing the role of religion in culture throughout history, notes that there are four major elements of culture: a group of people, working in a particular natural environment, forming social institutions and economic practices, and guided by common beliefs and moral convictions.[2] All of these elements are necessary, as we shape both nature and human life as a community, but Dawson argued that religion is the very heart of culture, giving an organizing vision and the highest perspective to all its other elements. Pope John Paul II argued that culture makes us more human, in that it enables us to express our identity and creativity in community with others. "Man lives a really human life thanks to culture," he argued, as we move beyond mere bodily needs to shape our life in a rational way toward higher goods.[3] Culture becomes an inheritance as we pass its customs from one generation to the next. A culture enters a crisis when this mode of transmission, through family, education, and religion, breaks down.

We tend to think of culture in terms of being cultured, as participating in the higher elements of life that impart sophistication, such as the fine arts. Art may be one of its particularly dramatic and significant expressions, but culture encompasses every aspect of our social life. In fact, we should become creators of culture at all levels — through work, family life, religious practice, education, sports and entertainment, and all other social practices. The need to participate in the formation of culture has been emphasized by Pope Francis, speaking of our response to God's primal command:

---

[2] See Christopher Dawson, *The Age of the Gods* (London: Sheed & Ward, 1933), xxiv.
[3] John Paul II, "Address to UNESCO" (Paris, June 2, 1980), http://inters.org/John-Paul-II-UNESCO-Culture, §6.

Pieter Bruegel the Elder, *The Corn Harvest* (1565). (Wikimedia Commons)

> Cultivating and caring for creation is an instruction of God which he
> gave not only at the beginning of history, but has also given to each
> one of us; it is part of his plan; it means making the world increase
> with responsibility, transforming it so that it may be a garden, an
> inhabitable place for us all.[4]

When God entrusted Adam with the care of the Garden, it was a trust
given to us all. We need to care for the world and exercise dominion
over it through our work. Every person has been given the command
by God to shape the world through culture. Work did not result simply
from the Fall, although it became toilsome, but rather reflects the call
to impress our personality upon the world. Everyone has his or her
own contribution to make through work, family life, and friendships.

Culture forms a fundamental reality of life, and yet it has become
threatened in many ways. Not only has work lost its direct contact with
nature, imparting an abstract character to modern culture, but the very
center of culture has been removed by secularism. Faith should be the

---

[4] Francis, "Catechesis," (June 5, 2013), https://w2.vatican.va/content/francesco/
en/audiences/2013/documents/papa-francesco_20130605_udienza-generale.html.

center of our way of life, but Christians live within a culture that seeks to keep God on the fringes, relegating religion to private belief and practice. John Paul II spoke of the renewal of culture as a priority of the New Evangelization because "a faith that does not become culture is not fully accepted, not entirely thought out, not faithfully lived."[5] Culture, therefore, has taken on an even greater prominence for Christians, who have the vital task of reconnecting its lost strands: community, nature, economics, education, and faith.

## MONASTICISM AND CULTURE

Monks have played a central role in the history of beer for a reason. They are the ones most attuned to the work of God, the *opus Dei*, both in the spiritual and natural sense. They have immersed themselves in the contemplation of God and His creation. Bl. John Henry Newman recognized this by ascribing the poetic spirit to the monks of Benedict, as opposed to the predominantly intellectual mission of the Dominicans and practical apostolate of the Jesuits. Newman describes how the contemplation of the poetic "demands, as its primary condition, that we should not put ourselves above the objects in which it resides, but at their feet. . . . It implies that we understand them to be vast, immeasurable, impenetrable, inscrutable, mysterious."[6] The monks have put themselves at the feet of the Lord and also at the feet of the created things in which they live and work. It is because of this humility that they have shown themselves the great innovators of beer and other crafts that have shaped our culture.

In a way, the monks point us back to the Garden, not simply to restore it, but to recreate the world in accord with God's plan. Pope Benedict XVI has given us a powerful expression of how the natural and supernatural mission of building culture are intertwined in the life of the monastery:

[5] John Paul II, "Address to the Italian National Congress of the Ecclesial Movement for Cultural Commitment" (January 16, 1982), https://w2.vatican.va/content/john-paul-ii/it/speeches/1982/january/documents/hf_jp-ii_spe_19820116_impegno-culturale.html. See R. Jared Staudt, "Culture in the Magisterium of Pope John Paul II: Evangelization through Dialogue and the Renewal of Society," *Claritas* 3, no. 1 (March 2014): 53–65, https://docs.lib.purdue.edu/cgi/viewcontent.cgi?article=1066&context=claritas.

[6] John Henry Newman, "The Mission of St. Benedict," in *Historical Sketches*, vol. 2 (London: Longmans, Green, & Co., 1906), 387.

In fact Bernard explicitly states that not even the monastery can restore Paradise, but he maintains that, as a place of practical and spiritual "tilling the soil," it must prepare the new Paradise. A wild plot of forest land is rendered fertile — and in the process, the trees of pride are felled, whatever weeds may be growing inside souls are pulled up, and the ground is thereby prepared so that bread for body and soul can flourish. Are we not perhaps seeing once again, in the light of current history, that no positive world order can prosper where souls are overgrown?[7]

Catholic culture should root out the weeds of the world and our souls. Work enacts the call to exercise dominion over the earth, a priestly toil ordered toward the Kingdom that will never end. The work of the monks gives us a glimpse of how all of our work and culture should be directed toward the Kingdom of God.

As we have seen, St. Benedict tells the monks to strive for self-sufficiency, having all the goods and crafts needed to support themselves within the monastery walls. The monastery, therefore, becomes a culture in miniature, a culture saturated with prayer. Pope Benedict once again illumines this reality, speaking to the Cistercian monks at Heiligenkreuz Abbey in Austria:

Cistercian monks at work (13th century). (Wikimedia Commons)

7  Pope Benedict XVI, *Spe Salvi*, encyclical letter, Vatican website, November 30, 2007, http://w2.vatican.va/content/benedict-xvi/en/encyclicals/documents/hf_ben-xvi_enc_20071130_spe-salvi.html, §15.

The core of monasticism is worship—living like the angels. But since monks are people of flesh and blood on this earth, Saint Benedict and Saint Bernard added to the central command: "pray," a second command: "work." In the mind of Saint Benedict, part of monastic life, along with prayer, is work: the cultivation of the land in accordance with the Creator's will. Thus in every age monks, setting out from their gaze upon God, have made the earth life-giving and lovely. Their protection and renewal of creation derived precisely from their looking to God. In the rhythm of the *ora et labora*, the community of consecrated persons bears witness to the God who, in Christ, looks upon us, while human beings and the world, as God looks upon them, become good.[8]

Prayer and work, *ora et labora*, both reach toward the Kingdom, one by fulfilling the primal command of God to bring the natural world to perfection, continuing His act of creation; the other by straining directly for the world to come, participating in the Heavenly City even in the midst of the earthly one. Prayer leads us into the presence of God, giving us the supernatural strength to direct our work rightly—for our good, the good of others, and the glory of God.

## BEER AS AN EXPRESSION OF CULTURE

Beer is a work of culture, an act of perfecting God's creation by drawing out its hidden possibilities. Its foundation is water: the source of life, needed continually to refresh us. To this we add barley, providing beer its nourishing power. Finally, yeast makes this barley water turn into something distinct, beer, with alcohol to lighten the heart and foster joy. Man brings these three ingredients together through his work. Let's look back to the prayer of blessing for beer, which describes beer as a "creature," something that is created.

> Bless, O Lord, this creature beer, which thou hast deigned to produce from the fat of grain: that it may be a salutary remedy to the

---

[8] Benedict XVI, "Address at Heiligenkreuz Abbey" (Sep. 9, 2007), http://w2.vatican.va/content/benedict-xvi/en/speeches/2007/september/documents/hf_ben-xvi_spe_20070909_heiligenkreuz.html.

human race, and grant, through the invocation of thy holy name,
that whoever shall drink it may gain health in body and peace in
soul. Through Christ our Lord. Amen.

Beer is a creature of both God and man. God has established in His
providence everything humans needs to create it. He has provided
the ingredients and the natural processes, and has created the human
intelligence that understands and harnesses them. Beer does not simply spring forth from the earth; we take the fat of the earth that God
has given us, and we shape it and bring about a higher development.
Drinking beer is much more enjoyable and even healthier than simply
eating barley!

This brings us to the very heart of culture: the cultivation of the earth
to make it suitable for human life. Ultimately it entails, as for the monks,
shaping our own lives, creating a way of life through our work and by
ordering our lives rightly. Beer springs forth from the nature of culture
itself and for most of human history it has been a crucial element of
society, providing nourishment and comfort for humanity. This points us
to the very purpose of beer as a creature, a work of human culture. The
prayer points us to a startling reality: that it may be a salutary remedy
to the human race. The word "salutary" may sound a bit extreme as
it sounds like salvation. The words used for toasting in the Romance
languages, however, reveal its meaning in the prayer: *salute* asks for
good health. Salutary does not mean that beer leads us to salvation, but
should bring us health, as part of our overall flourishing of body, mind,
and soul. Yes, this salutary benefit extends to the soul as well. The Bible
itself points to this when it says that God has given us wine "to gladden
the heart of man" (Ps. 104:15). This does not mean that drinking beer
will automatically make us holy or healthy; actually we know that too
much beer will do just the opposite! Beer provides nourishment and
good cheer, leading to both bodily and interior refreshment. Health
in body and peace in soul at the end of the prayer point us to the goal
of our drinking. We want beer to contribute not just to any physical
flourishing but to our whole lives.

Édouard Manet, *A Good Glass of Beer* (*Le bon bock*) (1873). (Wikimedia Commons)

## BEER AND LEISURE

Leisure is the basis of culture, as Josef Pieper tells us. We work for leisure, for the time needed to pursue the highest things in life. Work is "activity," "toil," and "function," while leisure is a "mental and spiritual attitude" of "non-activity" and "inward calm," ordered toward the capacity to receive the reality of the world.[9] Humans are cultural creators, but they are also called to the contemplation and peace that raise us above the distractions

---

[9] See Josef Pieper, *Leisure the Basis of Culture* (San Francisco: Ignatius Press, 1992), 26.

and pressing demands of life. Making beer constitutes work, but we enjoy it in leisure. Beer should be consumed in the context of our meals with others, celebrations of feast days and holidays, and conversations with friends. The concept of leisure provides a central underpinning for the remaining chapters of this section on beer's relation to culture.

Beer has played a crucial role in Western culture, especially in northern Europe (above the grape line), as it helped shape the rhythm of life: food, work, and celebration. Reflecting on the nature of beer brings us in touch with the basic realities of nature: plants, soil, cultivation, the movement of the seasons. Robert Burns, the famous and festive poet of Scotland, situates beer in the midst of the seasons and human culture, even giving us a little tutorial on brewing. His ballad, drawing on a traditional theme and the fictitious figure representing beer, John Barleycorn, stands as a testimony to the beer made and enjoyed by the workers who enjoyed singing its praises.

### JOHN BARLEYCORN
Robert Burns (1759–96)

There was three kings into the east,
Three kings both great and high,
And they hae sworn a solemn oath
John Barleycorn should die.

They took a plough and plough'd him down,
Put clods upon his head,
And they hae sworn a solemn oath
John Barleycorn was dead.

But the cheerful Spring came kindly on,
And show'rs began to fall;
John Barleycorn got up again,
And sore surpris'd them all.

The sultry suns of Summer came,
And he grew thick and strong;

His head weel arm'd wi' pointed spears,
That no one should him wrong.

The sober Autumn enter'd mild,
When he grew wan and pale;
His bending joints and drooping head
Show'd he began to fail.

His colour sicken'd more and more,
He faded into age;
And then his enemies began
To show their deadly rage.

They've taen a weapon, long and sharp,
And cut him by the knee;
Then tied him fast upon a cart,
Like a rogue for forgerie.

They laid him down upon his back,
And cudgell'd him full sore;
They hung him up before the storm,
And turned him o'er and o'er.

They filled up a darksome pit
With water to the brim;
They heaved in John Barleycorn,
There let him sink or swim.

They laid him out upon the floor,
To work him farther woe;
And still, as signs of life appear'd,
They toss'd him to and fro.

They wasted, o'er a scorching flame,
The marrow of his bones;
But a miller us'd him worst of all,
For he crush'd him between two stones.

And they hae taen his very heart's blood,
And drank it round and round;
And still the more and more they drank,
Their joy did more abound.

John Barleycorn was a hero bold,
Of noble enterprise;
For if you do but taste his blood,
'Twill make your courage rise.

'Twill make a man forget his woe;
'Twill heighten all his joy;
'Twill make the widow's heart to sing,
Tho' the tear were in her eye.

Then let us toast John Barleycorn,
Each man a glass in hand;
And may his great posterity
Ne'er fail in old Scotland!

We see many of the elements of beer and culture coming out in Burns's poem: nature and seasons, work, festivity, and devotion to one's place (a theme we'll pick up in chapter seven). The highest element of culture, however, cult, is missing from the ballad (and we will come back to that theme in chapter eight). In the meantime, we will maintain the festive theme of raising a glass in our continuing exploration of beer and culture in the next chapter.

# CHAPTER 6

# *Feasting, Fasting, and Friendship*

Although beer provides refreshment and nutrition, we do not primarily drink it for those reasons, of course. We like to drink with others, and even should, as the old phrase goes: "never drink alone." Alcoholics are not social, but retreat into themselves in their addiction. Chesterton also said, "The sign of decay is not in the public-house, but in the private bar."[1] Drinking should be communal and requires an occasion: a meal, a meeting of friends, an important event to celebrate. We will look at how drinking forms an integral part of festivity and friendship, but also how it is moderated by the Christian tradition of fasting.

## RAISING A FESTIVE CUP

We call the celebration of a saint's day a feast day. We need an occasion to celebrate, to express our joy and thanks for God's blessings. Pope Francis has added that we need a good drink to facilitate our feasting: "Water is necessary for life, but wine expresses the abundance of a banquet and the joy of a feast. . . . [J]ust imagine ending a wedding feast drinking tea; it would be a shame."[2] In the early Church and Middle Ages, feast days were days of rest and worship and eventually days of public celebration, giving rise to town fairs.

Eating and drinking have always been a part of any feast. Psalm 116 indicates drinking's role in ritual worship throughout history: "What shall I render to the Lord for all his bounty to me? I will lift up the cup of salvation and call on the name of the Lord, I will pay my vows to the Lord in the presence of all his people." We see the foundation for

---

[1]  G. K. Chesterton, *George Bernard Shaw* (New York: J. Lane Co., 1909).
[2]  Francis, "Catechesis" (June 8, 2016), https://w2.vatican.va/content/francesco/en/audiences/2016/documents/papa-francesco_20160608_udienza-generale.html.

Christian festivity in Acts 2:46–47: "And day by day, attending the temple together and breaking bread in their homes, they partook of food with glad and generous hearts, praising God and having favor with all the people." This feasting was no selfish indulgence, for as we read in the previous verse, "they sold their possessions and goods and distributed them to all, as any had need." Christian festivity expresses itself in joy and generosity to those in need.

Feast days were also kept in classical culture. Typified by the Jewish libations, wine was poured out of a cup as a sacrifice to recognize and honor the source of blessing in the divine. *The Odyssey*, in particular, gives us a glimpse of this tradition through Pisistratus's command to Telemachus: "'Offer a prayer, sir,' said he, 'to King Neptune, for it is his feast that you are joining; when you have duly prayed and made your drink-offering, pass the cup to your friend that he may do so also. I doubt not that he too lifts his hands in prayer, for man cannot live without God in the world.'"[3] Even the pagans recognized the necessity of honoring the divine with a thanksgiving sacrifice for the good things of life.

In his biography of St. Augustine, the historian Peter Brown described what a feast day looked like in the early Church:

> A festival of a martyr was a time of torchlight vigils in the war summer nights. It was a time of glory, marked by a suspension of the ordinary — by the chanting of songs, by the elevation of good wine, even by rhythmic dance.... To go to a feast of the martyrs was to draw sustenance through deep, almost non-verbal participation — through excited throngs, through liquor, music and swaying movement — in triumph of the martyr's victory. The high cheer of such occasion, associated with the earthy ingredients of any ancient festival, celebrated a blinding flash of supernatural power that brought a little luster to the dull, constrained existence of the average Christian.[4]

Though this is the origin of a feast, Brown notes that Augustine wanted to spiritualize the celebration, focusing more on prayer and moderation.

---

[3]   Homer, *The Odyssey*, III.

[4]   Peter Brown, *Augustine of Hippo: A Biography* (Berkeley: University of California Press, 2000), 453.

Nonetheless, the feasts demonstrate the celebratory and joyful nature of the commemoration of the saints and liturgical life of the Church.

We associate one feast in particular, St. John the Evangelist on December 27, with the raising of a festive glass to celebrate Christmas, with a special blessing at the end of Mass for wine. This tradition may have arisen because John's Gospel teaches us how God uses the image of drinking to symbolize the blessings he wants to bestow on us. The fourth chapter of his Gospel gives us one of the clearest symbols: Jesus is thirsty; a disgraced Samaritan woman comes to Jacob's well; Jesus, breaking taboos, asks her for a drink; she is scandalized. Jesus responds: "If you knew the gift of God, and who it is that is saying to you, 'Give me a drink,' you would have asked him, and he would have given you living water." What is beautiful is that Jesus asks her for a drink: "I thirst," that line from the Cross that proved foundational for Mother Teresa's spirituality. Drinking should not focus on oneself, but the needs of the other. Rather than even noticing Jesus's thirst, we usually focus on satiating ourselves. We drown away our sorrows, or even try to obliterate them in excess.

John's Gospel also shows us how the Lord transforms our festivities into a sign of the eternal wedding feast. O happy fault that caused the wedding feast to run dry of wine! The simple line "they have no wine" reveals our true emptiness before the Lord. He fills the cup for the feast, as a sign of his hour to come. It is of course during "His hour" that He shows us just how profoundly He will satiate us. Now Christ does not turn water into wine, but wine into his Blood. First, He provided wine for the feast, but now He provides the new wine that draws us into the eternal wedding feast. And there will be a mystical wine in this feast: "I tell you I shall not drink again of this fruit of the vine until that day when I drink it new with you in my Father's kingdom" (Matt. 26:29). The Book of Revelation shows us that God reveals the joy of heaven precisely as a feast: "And the angel said to me, 'Write this: Blessed are those who are invited to the marriage supper of the Lamb'" (Rev. 19:9). God does not suppress the natural joy we have on earth, but fulfills it in a much higher way. Our own feasting is a small sacramental sign of our eternal happiness in heaven.

In the Gospels, Jesus asks us to "do this in memory of me," which we do at every Mass. In an elusive phrase, Paul relates the words of institution as "Do this, as often as you drink it, in remembrance of me" (1 Cor.

11:25). No earthly drinking can surpass the Eucharistic feast in which our earthly wine becomes a new, heavenly fruit of the vine. Nonetheless, Paul seems to exhort us to remember the Lord whenever we drink (cf. 1 Cor 10:13). In this way, we see how our earthly celebrations, like the wedding feast at Cana, can point beyond the present moment, in sacramental fashion, to the new vine of heaven.

Josef Pieper, in his great work on festivity, *In Tune with the World*, contrasts true Christian festivity with our modern inability to celebrate truly. He points to the artificiality of our secular celebrations: "The artificial holiday is not only a sham festival; it borders so dangerously on counterfestivity that it can abruptly be reversed into 'antifestival.'"[5] He also challenges our "true existential poverty... in having lost the power to celebrate a festival festively," which includes food, wine, song, dancing, art, and the praise of God.[6] Our own celebrating has become flat, lacking not only the religious heart of festivity, but also the true joy and merriment that marked ancient feasts. As Odysseus said, speaking simply of the human reality of feasting: "It is a good thing to hear a bard with such a divine voice as this man has. There is nothing better or more delightful than when a whole people make merry together, with the guests sitting orderly to listen, while the table is loaded with bread and meats, and the cup-bearer draws wine and fills his cup for every man. This is indeed as fair a sight as a man can see."[7] In addition to this human joy, we must recognize the true occasion of a feast, a day meant to praise God and thank Him for His blessings.

A key cause of our existential poverty comes from the breaking of the temporal from the eternal. Our feasting should be a sign of heaven, that angelic "festal gathering" (Heb. 12:22). The link to the eternal enlivens our ability to raise a festive glass, truly rejoicing in the Lord, the goodness of His creation, and His arrival in this world to sanctify it. Pieper affirms that "to celebrate a festival means: to live out, for some special occasion and in an uncommon manner, the universal assent to the world as a whole."[8] This assent to the world, as a moment of leisure,

---

[5] Josef Pieper, *In Tune with the World* (South Bend, IN: St. Augustine's Press, 1999), 79.

[6] Ibid., 52.

[7] Homer, *Odyssey*, IX.

[8] Pieper, *In Tune with the World*, 30.

Pieter Brueghel the Elder, *Peasant Wedding* (1567). (Wikimedia Commons)

entails a breaking out of the mundane ritual that confines us. It opens us to the transcendent so that "in celebrating festivals festively, man passes beyond the barriers of this present life on earth."[9] The joy of the festival, drawing together the memory of both earthly and divine blessings, points to the eternal joy of heaven, by giving us a small, imperfect glimpse of the eternal feast.

In *Drinking with the Saints*, Michael Foley suggests special drinks to pair with saints' feast days. For instance, he recommends a Trappist beer for February 6, the feast day of the patron saint of brewers and inn-keepers, St. Amand, who was also an apostle to the great brewing nation of Belgium.[10] There are also many Christmas beers, usually seasoned with festive flavors, to accompany our wine for St. John's feast day on December 27. I don't think anyone with Irish heritage (or perhaps *any* heritage) needs to be encouraged to have a beer on St. Patrick's Day. Foley recommends some stouts to sample beyond the staple Guinness, such as Murphy's, Beamish, or O'Hara's, or for a different style, Kilkenny

[9] Ibid., 43.
[10] Michael Foley, *Drinking with the Saints: The Sinner's Guide to a Happy Holy Hour* (Washington, DC: Regnery, 2015), 29.

Irish Cream or Murphy's Red.[11] Germans can take up celebrating their apostle, St. Boniface, on June 5 with some good German beer. Personally, I would recommend a German Benedictine beer, such as Weltenburger or Andechs, to honor the Benedictine bishop and martyr. In addition to listing a variety of Benedictine beers for St. Benedict's feast on July 11, Foley also recommends some great liqueurs, such as Bénédictine, used to make B&B.[12]

## FASTING

Fasting is a natural complement to feasting. The Church asks us to fast and do penance for forty days in preparation for Easter, and Advent began in the same way for Christmas. Eating and drinking are part of our feasting, a sign of the heavenly feast, and so fasting represents the battle in preparation for this heavenly feast. Originally, Christian fasting included abstaining from alcohol, though this has relaxed through the centuries (like so many other things). It relaxed even to the point that some Bavarian monks and friars were known for drinking a strong doppelbock to sustain them during the Lenten fast, banking on the maxim, *liquida non frangunt ieiunium* (liquids do not break the fast). According to legend, when the pope (possibly Urban VIII, d. 1644), heard of this Lenten brew, he asked to taste some of it. The Franciscan Minim Friars, who originated the Salvator doppelbock, allegedly sent him a barrel that spoiled during the long journey over the Alps. After tasting it, the pope told them to keep drinking as much as they wanted for their penance!

We saw earlier that the word for beer (*shekar*) appears in the Bible as part of the vow of the Nazarites to renounce wine and strong drink. Although beer aids our celebration of religious festivals, and through libations even constituted a part of Israel's formal sacrifices, our devotion also drives us to sacrifice it. Likewise, St. Benedict told his spiritual children: "We read that monks should not drink wine at all, but since the monks of our day cannot be convinced of this, let us at least agree to drink moderately, and not to the point of excess" (*Rule*, ch. 40). Perhaps paradoxically, we find the highest use of drink by abstaining from it, but

---

[11]   Ibid., 56.
[12]   Ibid., 59.

those who cannot accept this counsel must embrace moderation and its right ordering to holiness. One way to build moderation is through fasting, periods of time without drinking alcohol. This keeps one from getting too attached and puts drink in its right perspective.

St. Thomas tells us that the virtue of religion not only gives God worship, but also orders everything that we do toward God. This would include beer, of course. One of the main expressions of this virtue is sacrifice, which surrenders the good things of life from time to time so as to possess and use them with less attachment. Aquinas describes sacrifice as a "tendering of submission" to God using material things, "by offering them to God in sign of the subjection and honor due to Him, like those who make certain offerings to their lord in recognition of his authority."[13] Fasting presents one particular kind of sacrifice, subordinating our eating and drinking habits to God. St. Thomas tells us there are three reasons to fast. "First, in order to bridle the lusts of the flesh . . . since fasting is the guardian of chastity. For, according to Jerome [*Contra Jov.* ii.], 'Venus is cold when Ceres and Bacchus are not there,' that is to say, lust is cooled by abstinence in meat and drink. Secondly, we have recourse to fasting in order that the mind may arise more freely to the contemplation of heavenly things. . . . Thirdly, in order to satisfy for sins."[14] Therefore, fasting provides us with a necessary way of ordering our lives to God by purifying our desires and making penance for our overattachment to earthly things in sin.

Originally the Lenten fast included alcohol (and still does for some Eastern Churches, whose members may abstain from alcohol every Wednesday and Friday). Ven. Dom Guéranger explains in *The Liturgical Year* that "in the early ages of Christianity, fasting included also abstinence from wine, as we learn from St. Cyril of Jerusalem, St. Basil, St. John Chrysostom, Theophilus of Alexandria, and others."[15] For instance, St. Cyril says in his fourth catechetical lecture: "For we fast by abstaining

---

[13] Thomas Aquinas, *Summa Theologiae* (*ST*), II-II, q. 85, a.1. Translation by English Dominican Province (New York: Benzinger Bros., 1947), accessible at www.newadvent. org/summa. I will use the standard citation format for Aquinas's *Summa*, abbreviating the title as *ST*, then indicating the part (part I, parts I-II and II-II, and part III), followed by the question and article numbers.

[14] *ST* II-II, q. 147, a. 1.

[15] Dom Prosper Guéranger, OSB, *The Liturgical Year*, vol. 5, *Lent*, http://www. liturgialatina.org/lityear/.

from wine and flesh, not because we abhor them as abominations, but because we look for our reward; that having scorned things sensible, we may enjoy a spiritual and intellectual feast."[16] Early Christians did not frown on alcohol, but abstained from it because they recognized its goodness and desired an ever better drink! By the Middle Ages, Catholics were still not permitted to eat "flesh meat, eggs, and milk foods," but were "not forbidden to drink wine."[17]

Jesus pointed us to the goal of fasting when He said, "The days will come, when the bridegroom is taken away from them, and then they will fast in those days" (Luke 5:35). When we fast from beer and other alcohol, we are looking toward the goal of reuniting with the Bridegroom. In fasting, we can already anticipate drinking the greater cup of the feast of heaven. As Pope Francis reflected, linking the wedding of Cana to the Cross: "Yes, the Lord continues to reserve the best wine for our salvation, just as it continues to flow from the pierced side of the Lord. . . . We are all invited to the wedding feast, because the new wine will never run short!"[18] We are waiting for a better draught to come, which means we cannot become too attached to any earthly drink.

It has been claimed that Bavarian monks fasted by drinking only beer during Lent. Rather, they drank beer to sustain them until their one small meal after Vespers. We know the monks sought other ways to make their fast easier, such as moving Vespers from the evening into the afternoon and moving None (usually recited at three o'clock in the afternoon, the "ninth" hour) to twelve o'clock, which is how we get the word "noon"! Author and homebrewer J. Wilson took the Lenten beer fast quite literally and lived only on beer during Lent. He lost 25 pounds over 46 days, but said he "felt more focus and self-discipline," and felt he had proved that the monks' fast was not only possible but probable.[19] Even if this type of fasting was not a regular monastic practice, one Belgian Cistercian nun, St. Lutgardis of Aywières (1182–1246), fasted only on bread and beer for seven years. More normally, though, the Bavarian

[16] Cyril of Jerusalem, "Catechetical Lectures," in *Nicene and Post-Nicene Fathers, Second Series*, vol. 7, ed. Philip Schaff and Henry Wace, trans. Edwin Hamilton (Buffalo, NY: Christian Literature, 1894).

[17] *ST* II-II, q. 147, a. 8.

[18] Francis, "Catechesis" (June 8, 2016).

[19] J. Wilson, *Diary of a Part-Time Monk* (Hampstead, MD: Old Line, 2011).

monks and friars did brew special strong beers for Lent. Martin Zuber of the Paulaner Brewery explains that "they needed something other than water to sustain them, so the monks turned to a common staple of the time of their region — beer. They concocted an 'unusually strong' brew, full of carbohydrates and nutrients, because 'liquid bread wouldn't break the fast.'"[20] Beer in moderation might help one to fast, but conversely it would strengthen spiritual discipline to give it up altogether.

## PASSING THE CUP IN FRIENDSHIP

As we advance to the heavenly banquet, we need friends to help us along the path of our pilgrimage. Beer draws men together for friendship and conversation; too much fasting can put a strain on fellowship. When in graduate school, I felt moved to give up beer for a year and it was the loneliest year of my life! Beer draws people together by creating a setting for fellowship and lively conversation.

Pope Francis describes how drinking promotes one of his favorite themes, "a culture of encounter." During his visit to Columbia, he said: "For you, young people, it is so easy to encounter one another. All you need is a good coffee, a good drink or any other excuse to meet."[21] When sitting down without a drink, it can feel awkward, like something is missing — the fuel of fellowship! Shortly after I started my first teaching job, my graduate students were not much younger than I was and a few were older. We formed a strong men's group, enjoying mountain hikes, visiting microbreweries, and enjoying a behind-the-scenes tour of a large brewery, and many long evening discussions.

There's a long tradition of profound conversation over drinks. Think of Plato's *Symposium*, where Socrates gathered with friends in the house of Agathon to give praise to love. "Socrates took his place on the couch, and supped with the rest; and then libations were offered, and after a hymn had been sung to the god, and there had been the usual ceremonies,

[20] Quoted in Matt Hadro, "The 17th Century Monks Did a Beer Fast for Lent," *Catholic News Agency*, March 1, 2017, https://www.catholicnewsagency.com/news/these-17th-century-monks-did-a-beer-fast-for-lent-90886.

[21] Francis, "Apostolic Visit to Columbia" (Bogota, Columbia, September 7, 2017), https://w2.vatican.va/content/francesco/en/speeches/2017/september/documents/papa-francesco_20170907_viaggioapostolico-colombia-fedeli.html.

they were about to commence drinking."[22] The guests agreed to drink moderately so as to be able to enter into a deeper conversation, taking turns speaking the praise of love. We know that drinking with friends does not always promote the love of wisdom (to say the least), but friends gathering to pursue this end will be aided by moderate drinking. Roger Scruton argues that wine includes an "opening out of the self to the other" and, unlike drugs, "paints the truth of the world as the true one."[23]

It seems to be a key part of masculinity to gather around a drink and talk shop. How many times has my wife asked me about a male friend's personal life after we got together for a drink. I always reply, "I don't know. We didn't talk about that." Chesterton provides a piercing analysis of male camaraderie: "Women speak to each other; men speak to the subject they are speaking about."[24] Men spend much more time talking about work, politics, sports, and ideas, and come to personal matters through these more objective discussions. When guys get together, all that matters is that they are guys who share time together and work out problems. And men are more physical, as Chesterton reminds us, with "the insistence upon the body and its indispensable satisfaction. No one has even begun to understand comradeship who does not accept with it a certain hearty eagerness in eating, drinking, or smoking, an uproarious materialism. . . . It is at root a resistance to the superciliousness of the individual."[25] The material element of eating, drinking, and smoking helps to form a bond between the men, drawing them into the encounter before them.

Just as we find masculinity itself under attack, so camaraderie needs commitment and protection. Men need to stand together. Chesterton once again champions this important cause: "And, perhaps, you will agree with me that the thread of comradeship and conversation must be protected because it is so frivolous. It must be held sacred, it must not be snapped, because it is not worth tying together again. It is exactly because argument is idle that men (I mean males) must take it seriously; for when (we feel),

[22]   Plato, *Symposium*, trans. Benjamin Jowett.
[23]   Roger Scruton, *I Drink, Therefore I Am: A Philosopher's Guide to Wine* (New York: Continuum, 2009), 132.
[24]   Chesterton, *What's Wrong with the World* (New York: Cassell and Co., 1910), 92.
[25]   Ibid., 90.

Édouard Manet, *The Beer Drinkers* (1878). (Wikimedia Commons)

until the crack of doom, shall we have so delightful a difference again?"[26] Camaraderie is more important than ever today, as we need to overcome the growing isolation brought on by technology and social media. True camaraderie opposes the juvenility of men acting like boys; rather, it encourages men to support one another as men, talking about problems and ideas and encouraging each other to stand against the crises facing the family and our culture.

[26]  Ibid., dedication.

The revival of genuine masculinity and camaraderie will only happen when men open their homes and make room for others there. For men with families, this entails sacrifice of time and space to include others. Hospitality was at the heart of the monks' breweries, and as they drew people to settle around the monasteries culture was rebuilt. Even in the midst of an epic argument (literally), Achilles still hosted Odysseus, sent on embassy by Agamemnon: "With this he led them forward, and bade them sit on seats covered with purple rugs; then he said to Patroclus who was close by him, 'Son of Menoetius, set a larger bowl upon the table, mix less water with the wine, and give every man his cup, for these are very dear friends, who are now under my roof.'"[27] Even in a feud, having a drink in the context of hospitality proved a powerful opening. Men need to work out problems together and not be afraid of controlled argument. In a time of "safe spaces," there must be more confrontation and a working out of problems, not less. Engaging in true hospitality will help us in welcoming others, receiving and sharing opposing viewpoints, and creating the conditions for fellowship.

I have seen that beer brings people together and provides an opportunity for fellowship to form. We enjoy the time spent drinking together: the taste of the drink and its effect, the time with friends, the movement through the conversation. Sitting down over a beer lightens the heart and eases conversation, enabling mutual self-disclosure and receptiveness. Talking over a drink is not the same as "dry" talk. We gather to mark important moments, to discuss business, or just to have a time to be together as men. Marking these occasions with a beer provides a moment of unity and friendship. As Plutarch says, "the goal of drinking is friendship," though excess, he makes clear, surely undermines it. He speaks of "firm and lasting friendship" forming "over a glass of wine, which like fire softened and melted [the] tempers and disposed them for a happy union."[28] Or more simply, as Homer put it: "Mix a cup . . . and hand it round."[29]

---

[27] Homer, *Iliad*, IX, trans. Samuel Butler.
[28] Plutarch, *De Moralia*, II, trans. William Watson Goodwin.
[29] Homer, *Odyssey*, VII.

# CHAPTER 7

# The Importance of
# Place and Tradition

We have become dislocated in so many ways — forgetful of our cultural heritage, distant from the land, and not committed to preserving traditions that have been handed down through the centuries. Surely beer alone cannot overcome this problem, but it can point us to how local traditions can be sustained and developed in new ways. Beer has pointed me back to my own heritage and opened up a path for learning about local traditions throughout the world. Local beer culture also provides us with an opportunity to strengthen our own communities.

## REDISCOVERING HOME

At age sixteen, I left home for a year to study abroad in Poland. One of the highlights of that amazing year was a trip with my Dad around Germany. My Dad is just about 100 percent German, and while I am mostly German, I also have what I like to call an Irish flare. As we sought out the oldest and best pubs in Berlin, Cologne, and Munich, we found ourselves tracking many of Napoleon's old haunts (little did I know at that time his role in destroying monastic beer). I will never forget sitting in Munich, drinking the oldest beer in the world! We stayed an extra day in Bavaria, being taken by the culture and scenery: the beer, the churches, the mountains, the castles, and the beer (did I say that already?)! We immediately connected with our *Vaterland* and had the sense of reconnecting to a lost home.

Staudt is a small town located between the cities of Cologne and Frankfurt, evenly divided between Catholics and Protestants. My own family was Lutheran (though my branch later became Catholic through marriage to the Snyder family). The town had a unique form of ecumenism through the inn, described as part of the culture of the surrounding

Staudt, Germany. (Wikimedia Commons)

region of the Bann of Wirges: "The inhabitants . . . show themselves to
be sensible, are hardworking (that is to say enterprising), and yet docile,
love foreigners, are at home thrifty to the point of miserliness and at
the inn wasteful to the point of showing off; can be called more cleanly
than uncleanly."[1] Staudt clearly had a drinking culture surrounding its
local virtues, which followed its emigrants to the new world.

During World War I, many German Americans anglicized their names
to distance themselves from their homeland, now turned enemy. Even for
some of my family, Staudt became Stoudt or even morphed to the English
name Stout. (Knowing my love for beer, friends can't resist punning my
name with stout beer!) I'm from Harrisburg, Pennsylvania, only a short
drive from the Stoudt Brewery, which was established by some of our
distant relatives. My brother and I enjoyed stopping in and sampling
our kin's brew. Further afield, other distant relatives run the Gourmet
Haus Staudt in Redwood City, California, featuring a beer garden and
over one hundred German beers. Why do I mention this family back-
ground? We suffer from cultural amnesia in our country, having become
disconnected from our past and family traditions. Brewing, on the other
hand, involves unbroken tradition stretching back to the beginning of
civilization. I am proud that my forebears played a role in continuing

---

[1] Court Council Linz, quoted in "Staudt," *Wikipedia*, accessed May 20, 2018,
https://en.wikipedia.org/wiki/Staudt. My wife says the description fits me to a "T."

this tradition. Beer provides an opportunity for reconnecting with old traditions and places, each with its own unique methods and styles.

Beer still shapes the culture of northern Europe and draws people together to celebrate. The largest gathering, Oktoberfest, runs each year from mid-September through the first Saturday in October. It is a large gathering — six million people just in Munich, with many other imitations throughout the world. The celebration began in honor of the wedding of Prince Ludwig and Princess Therese in 1810 (the same Ludwig I who helped reestablish monasteries after the downfall of Napoleon). The public gathering with horse races and a parade was so popular that it has continued for over two hundred years now. It is a great time of year when Germans through the world, including my family, celebrate our German heritage with friends, brats, and beer. Other gatherings reflect Pieper's definition of festivity more closely by holding a festival in honor of the town's patron saint. One example in Germany can be found in the Annafest of the town of Forchheim. They brew a special festbier for St. Anne's feast day on July 26. About fifty thousand people attend, with plenty of food, music, and games and rides for the kids.

But of course, I'm a long-displaced German. A more recent émigré, Pope Emeritus Benedict XVI, still maintains his drinking connections to his homeland. A delegation came from Bavaria to bring beer and pretzels for his ninetieth birthday on April 16, 2017. His favorite beer is Franziskaner Weissbier, a wheat beer brewed near a Franciscan friary, hence the friar on the label. Before becoming pope, he was a regular at the Cantina Tirolese, a Bavarian restaurant near the Vatican. There is a famous picture of Ratzinger raising a glass with Peter May, CEO of

Cardinal Ratzinger Visiting the Andechs Abbey in Bavaria. KNA. Used with permission.

the Stuttgarter Hofbräu brewery, inside the Vatican on September 22, 2003 (see the cover of *The Bad Catholic's Guide to Wine, Whiskey, and Song*). May's brewery later was reported to have delivered 185 US gallons of beer to Pope Benedict XVI and claimed the Pope's endorsement of their beer.[2] Word must have gotten out, because the Anglican Archbishop of York presented a gift of English beer to Benedict, including one named after the Holy Grail, when he visited the Vatican for the Week of Prayer for Christian Unity in 2008.[3]

There also have been beers brewed in his honor. The Bavarian brewery, Weideneder, brewed a Papst-Bier (Pope's Beer) for a number of years in honor of their local hero. They must have been expecting his election, as "only 19 hours after the election of Pope Benedict XVI, Fritz Weideneder present[ed] the first bottles of his Pope's Beer in Marktl," which is Benedict's hometown.[4] Though the beer was discontinued in 2017, other beers have been dedicated to the German Shepherd. For instance, a hefeweizen with a badly punned name, "Beer-nedict XVI: Pint-ifex Maximus," was served at the Society for Catholic Social Scientists in Steubenville, Ohio in the fall of 2017. The beer was produced at the request of the Benedict XVI Centre for Religion and Society at St. Mary's University in Twickenham, England, but brewed locally in Ohio by the Hightower Brewing Company.[5]

## REVIVING LOCAL BREWING TRADITIONS

Munich is a place that attracts beer drinkers from around the world every year. There are great places to imbibe the German beer traditions in the United States as well. I have visited many of the oldest breweries in the United States, which are commonly of German origin, such as Yuengling, Schell, Leinenkugel's, and Coors, dragging along my wife

---

[2] "Brewery Says New Pope Loves Its Beer, Stuttgarter Hofbräu." *First Coast News* (2005).

[3] "Anglican Archbishop Gives Pope 'Holy Grail' Beer," *CNA*, January 29, 2008, https://www.catholicnewsagency.com/news/anglican_archbishop_gives_pope_holy_grail_beer.

[4] "The Pope's Beer," Weideneder, accessed April 24, 2018, http://www.weideneder.com/papstbier/33-papst-bier-en.html.

[5] Dan Hitches, "New Pintifex Beer Honours Benedict XVI," *Catholic Herald*, November 1, 2017, http://www.catholicherald.co.uk/news/2017/11/01/new-pintifex-beer-honours-benedict-xvi/.

and kids (more or less unwillingly) and my Dad and friends (more readily). These visits presented an opportunity to encounter local history and tradition. The tours paid off in some small measure: as my family and I were touring a historic farm, my son Louis (only five at the time) successfully identified a hop vine, exclaiming that we could make beer!

The English philosopher Roger Scruton speaks powerfully of the importance of place in the appreciation of drink and its power to draw us into local traditions. He describes a pivotal moment in his life when he was captivated by his first truly great bottle of French wine:

> I was about to fall in love — not with a flavour or a plant or a drug but with a hallowed piece of France. That bottle from which I had unfurled the loving hands contained a glinting, mahogany-coloured liquid, an intoxicating aroma, a subtle and many-layered flavor, but also something more precious than all of these, summarized in the ancient and inscrutable names of Rotanoy, the château, and Pomerol, the place. I was overwhelmed by the sense of this drink as a distillation of a place, a time and a culture.[6]

Wine enthusiasts may quickly jump in and claim superiority and greater complexity for wine. They refer to the "terroir," the combination of soil, geography, climate, sun exposure, etc., that gives each wine its unique character. Although beer does not have quite the same rootedness in the soil, nonetheless, beer does evoke precise localities and traditions. Nancy Hoalst-Pullen and Mark Patterson, the authors of National Geographic's *Atlas of Beer*, do not hesitate to apply the term terroir to beer as well. They note that "in essence, terroir is about acknowledging that place is something you can taste.... [A] beer's character can be greatly shaped by its four main ingredients: grains, hops, water and yeast. The quality and character of these ingredients change from place to place, and the conditions under which they are grown and found creates unique and

---

[6] Scruton, *I Drink*, 12. He describes further: "Visitors to Burgundy... will sense all around them the history and religion.... They will know that this soil is hallowed soil: it has been blessed and cajoled and prayed over for centuries, many of the vineyards being worked by monks for whom wine was not just a drink but a sacrament.... Even in this skeptical age their vine is, for the Burgundians, something more spiritual than vegetal, and their soil more heaven than earth" (35–36).

discernable flavors that can make each beer unique."[7] Furthermore, they take the reader on a journey to six continents to discover the beer *cultures*, not just ingredients, that shape local styles and drinking habits. Randy Mosher adds that "climate, soil, moisture, geology, micro-nutrients" all make an impact.[8] Beer has a long history and carries many local traditions. Think of German lagers, English ales, Irish stouts, Czech pilsners, Scottish ambers, French farmhouse ales, Belgian Trappist beer, etc. It is hard to compare beer and wine, but beer has a greater range of taste and local diversity than wine.

When it comes to Italy, the heart of wine country, we can see how "brewers accentuate terroir by using local adjuncts and utilizing local equipment such as wine barrels. In the Piedmont region, brewers make their beer unique by incorporating the ingredients at hand: indigenous grains, local fruit such as peaches or blueberries, vegetables such as green peppers and spices such as basil."[9] Craft brewing became legal only a little more than twenty years ago, but Italian brewers translated their great culinary skills to produce innovative beers, emphasizing their pairing with food as well. The Italians give us one example of how a local culture shapes beer production, rooting it in broader traditions and ingredients.

Beer draws us into these rich traditions of style, place, and history, helping to build a sense of place and community. The public house provides the essential, local gathering place in the British Isles for conversation, watching sports, and music. Ales were generally local and England developed its own styles — bitter, old ale, mild, barley wine, brown ales, stouts, porters, and IPAs. One important tradition in the English pub concerns its particular way of serving cask ale: allowing it to ferment in the cask in-house as it builds up natural carbonation, then serving it without filtering or pasteurizing. This results in a beer fresher and warmer than normal for Americans. Cask ale came under threat and almost saw extinction in the 1970s with consolidation by larger brewers. In response, a grassroots effort formed to protect traditional cask or "real ale" (called the Campaign for Real Ale, CAMRA) and proved highly successful. Not only did it successfully preserve cask ale and a greater

7 Hoalst-Pullen and Patterson, *Atlas of Beer*, 16.
8 Randy Mosher, *Tasting Beer: An Insider's Guide to the World's Greatest Drink*, 2nd ed. (North Adams, MA: Storey, 2017), 89.
9 Ibid., 106.

Hopgarden in Hallertau.

variety of beer served in pubs, but now with over 180,000 members, it continues to advocate for the preservation of local pubs and to protect brewers from punishing taxes.

Germany, on the other hand, perfected the lager, served cold and crisp, with a lighter and clearer color (which has become the dominant beer throughout the world). Germans frequent pubs as well, but also enjoy both large beer halls and more intimate settings, such as beer gardens and tents. Bavaria is the center of Germany's beer culture, not only as the origin of Oktoberfest, but also as the center of international hop production. Its Hallertau region produces a third of the world's hops.[10] The Germans, Czechs, and Austrians consume more beer per capita than any other country. They form the heart of the beer belt, where beer is a normal part of the culture and might be consumed at any time of day. Germans even mix beer with soda and lemonade to form shandy, consumed in place of soft drinks.

My first beer was an experience drastically different from that of most American teenagers. It was not snuck from my parents' fridge or guzzled at an underage drinking party. It was in Wrocław, Poland, in the basement of the city hall, which sported a brewpub. It was not a Bud

[10]  Hoalst-Pullen and Patterson, *Atlas of Beer*, 60.

Max Liebermann, *Munich beer Garden* (1884). (Wikimedia Commons)

Light, but a dark, sweet beer made at that very spot, unlike anything I had tasted before. Was it the kind of falling in love that Scruton experienced? It was not just the beer; it was the friendship of two other Americans also living in a foreign country. It was the history of the town, with its mix of Polish and German heritage. It was the building, with its brightly colored tile roof, beautiful, intricate medieval clock, and Gothic spires.

It was an experience — a meeting of a particular time, people, history, and culture — made possible by the warm feeling and exuberant taste of a unique and beautiful beer. Would anything less have captured me so?

Monasteries may have built up brewing in Europe, but the medieval town eventually displaced them as the center of brewing culture, and of the culture more generally. People gathered in the towns for business, worship, and celebration. In the late Middle Ages, brewer guilds formed, through which brewers exercised political influence. Unlike other medieval guilds, which have disappeared, brewing guilds persist as groups of professionals who provide training and support for their craft. One such guild is in Belgium: "On the Grand Place in Brussels stand the ornate guild houses of the city's ancient trades. The bakers' and butchers' houses are now restaurants. Another has become a bank. Yet the brewers' house is still home to the Brewers' Federation."[11]

Belgium, where beer is not simply a drink but a culture, has preserved its distinctive brewing traditions such as using wild yeast and bacteria for fermentation and adding herbs and fruit for flavorings. Some of these distinctive styles are lambic, oude gueuze, oude kriek, Flemish red ale, saison, and other sours. Belgium has preserved the Catholic tradition of brewing more than any other place. We see this especially in the famous strong Trappist beers. When the new monastic breweries arose around the world recently, they all looked to the Belgian Trappists for inspiration, and some even for training. Belgian brewing is at once the most traditional and the most modern of any nation's, preserving old techniques while venturing into bold experimentation.

Belgium represents the opposite end of the spectrum from Germany — with its purity law that allows only water, barley, hops, and yeast — as brewers boldly experiment with added ingredients and innovative styles. Randy Mosher describes this exciting beer culture well:

> There's a huge variety of strengths, colors, textures, and brewing methods; hundreds of distinctive yeasts and other microorganisms; fermentation in barrels; blended beers; sugar, honey, and caramel syrup in addition to malt; unmalted grains, like oats, wheat, spelt,

[11] "Brewed Force: How a Small, Unremarkable Country Came to Dominate the World of Beermaking," *The Economist*, December. 17, 2011, https://www.economist.com/node/21541708.

Brewers Guild (center), Brussels, Belgium. (Wikimedia Commons)

and occasionally buckwheat; a whole basket of fruit; every conceivable kind of spice, including grains of paradise, chamomile, cumin, star anise, and a "medical lichen." The list is long, deep, wide, and exhilarating.[12]

Belgium is also home to the largest brewer in the world, AB InBev, and yet preserves many small, family-owned breweries.

In 2016, UNESCO added Belgian beer culture to its Representative List of the Intangible Cultural Heritage of Humanity. Belgium has not only unique and unusual beer styles, but also some unique practices. Bruges may be the only city in the world to have a two-mile-long beer pipeline, running under the city streets. Beer flows from the Brouwerij De Halve Maan, dating from 1564, to an out-of-town bottling plant, keeping the beautiful city free from delivery trucks. Belgians have also recently served "small beer" at an elementary school as a pilot program to promote a drink healthier that soda. The school succeeded in promoting better health, but for some reason parents still did not feel comfortable

---

[12] Mosher, *Tasting Beer*, 289.

serving beer to kids in school.[13] Only Belgians would try! One brewer, Randy Thiel of Ommegang, became the first American to be inducted into the *Chevalerie de Forquet* (Knights of the Mashing Fork) by Belgian brewers in Brussels. He commented: "It almost brings a tear to my eye seeing how the Belgian community takes so much pride in this organization."[14] Brewers there still hang on to the old traditions, even with the arrival of more scientific methods.

The purpose of local traditions is not to keep us stuck in the past, but to guide us as we move forward. We preserve and continue the legacy we have received from our ancestors, but we make our own contributions to the tradition, keeping it alive and growing organically. The old and new traditions are coming together through the Cistercian monks in California, as we saw in chapter four. One of the most modern and successful brewers in America, Sierra Nevada, has been brewing to support the reconstruction of a building lost to time. The old-world traditions continue in the new world — and sometimes are given new life — just as the medieval Spanish chapter house rises at New Clairvaux's monastery in California.

In the face of modern technology, so many places, traditions, and cultures are under attack. Pope Francis used his encyclical on the environment, *Laudato Si'*, to speak of the need to defend our homes and heritage. He reminds us:

> The history of our friendship with God is always linked to particular places which take on an intensely personal meaning; we all remember places, and revisiting those memories does us much good. Anyone who has grown up in the hills or used to sit by the spring to drink, or played outdoors in the neighborhood square; going back to these places is a chance to recover something of their true selves. (§84)

Although the environment gets the most attention in the encyclical, Francis also tells us that we need to defend our cultural heritage: "Together with the patrimony of nature, there is also an historic, artistic and

---

[13] Julia Davis, "The Belgian Plan to Give Beer to Schoolchildren," *Mental Floss*, August 14, 2012, http://mentalfloss.com/article/12248/belgian-plan-give-beer-schoolchildren.

[14] Quoted in Stan Hieronymus, *Brew like a Monk: Culture and Craftsmanship in the Belgian Tradition* (Boulder, CO: Brewers Publications, 2005), 135–36.

cultural patrimony which is likewise under threat. This patrimony is a part of the shared identity of each place and a foundation upon which to build a habitable city" (§143). Continuing and developing local brewing traditions represents one small element of the overall task of preserving our cultural and social identity. Beer can shape and help us to retain our sense of place and culture.

In general, we have become culturally and socially disoriented. Walker Percy calls this "the lost self," in *Lost in the Cosmos*, his psychoanalysis of our culture.[15] Going deeper with Percy's existential probing on this dislocation, Michael Barruzini reflects on how he helps us to perceive

> the question of *how to be* in a particular time and place. Percy slyly suggests that bourbon is the answer. No, not in the sense of drowning sorrows in alcoholic stupor, but in recognizing that it is in concrete things and acts that we are able *to be* in the world.... It is distinctively personal acts, like having an evening glass of bourbon, that construct a life. It is this aesthetic, this incarnation, simply this way to be, which gives a glass of bourbon its real value. But this incarnation of being extends beyond evening drinks, and informs every action we make in our lives.[16]

Like bourbon, beer helps us to incarnate our community and traditions, accompanying our family meals and celebrations, fostering our time with friends, and providing moments to be with others in our place and time.

Beer itself cannot build a local community, but its production does help us to reflect on this process. In the United States, we have developed a very local and innovative beer culture, as brewpubs, microbreweries, and craft breweries have popped up all over our neighborhoods, providing a place to meet. These brewers often use local ingredients, stimulating us with unique flavors. I live in the center of this movement in northern Colorado, the Napa Valley of beer. I have been able to visit many of the breweries in the area—Great Divide, Odell, New Belgium, Breckenridge,

---

[15] Walker Percy, *Lost in the Cosmos: The Last Self-Help Book* (New York: Picador, 2000), 12.

[16] Michael Barruzini, "Walker Percy, Bourbon, and the Holy Ghost," *First Things*, September 22, 2011, https://www.firstthings.com/web-exclusives/2011/09/walker-percy-bourbon-and-the-holy-ghost.

Left Hand — to name some of the major ones. Denver is also home to the Great American Beer Festival, the largest beer gathering in the US, attracting sixty thousand people and over eight hundred brewers with thirty-five hundred beers. Breweries have created a culture of craft and innovation in Colorado, giving us local gathering places that serve local brews using local ingredients.[17] We are continuing the great brewing traditions of Europe, shaping them through our own new local traditions, stemming from the great mountain water and sense of place at the base of the Rockies.

## FROM THE SHIRE TO THE PRAIRIES

J. R. R. Tolkien understood the importance of place and the need to fight to preserve it. Within the mythical world he created, Middle Earth, the Shire represents the ordinary life of the country, which Tolkien knew was passing away. *The Lord of the Rings* movies leave out the climax of the story, when the hobbits return home to see the Shire industrialized, and worse, regulations placed on beer! Insufferable! After their epic quest to destroy the ring, the key battle for the hobbits was yet to take place. The Scouring of the Shire is a call to action. Not only were their homes and families under attack, but so were other things the hobbits loved: their beer and tobacco.

As the hobbits returned home, "there was no beer and very little food." After hearing the dreadful news, Sam breaks in: "All right, all right! . . . That's quite enough. I don't want to hear no more. No welcome, no beer, no smoke, and a lot of rules and orc-talk instead." What they found was prohibition. Farmer Cotton explained to them:

> So things went from bad to worse. There wasn't no smoke left, save
> for the Men; and the Chief didn't hold with beer, save for his Men,
> and closed all the inns; and everything except Rules got shorter and

[17] The United States has become the world's leader in hops production as of 2016, and even with this growth it has remained difficult to keep up with demand. Coors brews a Colorado native beer with only local ingredients, though Colorado only has about 200 acres out of more than 50,000 nationwide. See Elizabeth Hernandez, "Colorado Farmers Help Lift U.S. Hop Production to the Top of the Heap Worldwide," *Denver Post* (September 11, 2016). There is a boom in hop production in the Western slope of Colorado and a family from our Catholic school is moving to the other side of the state to take part.

Hobbiton set. (Wikimedia Commons)

> shorter, unless one could hide a bit of one's own when the ruffians
> went round gathering stuff up "for fair distribution": which meant
> they got it and we didn't, except for the leavings which you could
> have at the Shirriff-houses, if you could stomach them. All very bad.
> But since Sharkey came it's been plain ruination.

The hobbits organized the resistance to defend their land, their freedom, and their traditions. The hobbits' restoration was well rewarded:

> In the Southfarthing the vines were laden, and the yield of "leaf"
> was astonishing; and everywhere there was so much corn that at
> Harvest every barn was stuffed. The Northfarthing barley was so
> fine that the beer of 1420 malt was long remembered and became a
> byword. Indeed a generation later one might hear an old gaffer in
> an inn, after a good pint of well-earned ale, put down his mug with
> a sigh: "Ah! that was proper fourteen-twenty, that was!"

Seeing their community in shambles, the hobbits did not just sit back and give in to helplessness. The Scouring of the Shire provides a clarion call to act before it is too late.

Throughout *The Lord of the Rings*, Tolkien uses pubs such as the Green Dragon and the Inn of the Prancing Pony to represent community — the latter being the subject of Frodo's memorable song:

> There is an inn, a merry old inn
> beneath an old grey hill,
> And there they brew a beer so brown
> That the Man in the Moon himself came down
> one night to drink his fill.[18]

Beer provided some comfort to the travelling hobbits throughout their journeys, even amidst the rubble of Isengard, though they had to fight for it in the end.

The Shire has inspired some local culture and community amidst the Dakota prairies. I had the privilege of teaching in the Catholic Studies program at the University of Mary in Bismarck, North Dakota for two years. The University took a cue from Tolkien in creating a pub with an atmosphere conducive to conversation and fellowship for faculty and students (of age):

> Chesterton's is proudly named for G. K. Chesterton (1874–1936), the English writer, literary critic, poet, and Catholic apologist. The design of Chesterton's was inspired by The Eagle and the Child pub in Oxford, where J. R. R. Tolkien, C. S. Lewis, and the rest of The Inklings used to gather for good cheer and conversation. Three nights a week, Chesterton's operates as our "campus pub," offering concessions and beverages. ... The Tolkien-themed beer on tap, "Southfarthing Stout" and "Green Dragon Ale," are locally brewed for Chesterton's at Buffalo Commons in Mandan, ND.[19]

Overlooking the beautiful Missouri River valley, it is quite the place. The inside is decorated with quotes from Chesterton and the images of saints when they were college-aged. It serves food, hosts games and

[18] And what's an inn without an innkeeper? We cannot resist liking Barliman Butterbur even though he is "a fat innkeeper who only remembers his own name because people shout it at him all day," according to Strider. Barliman cannot fathom that his former customer has become king: "What's The Pony to him, or mugs o' beer? Not but what my beer's good, Gandalf. It's been uncommon good, since you came in the autumn of last year and put a good word on it. And that's been a comfort in trouble, I will say."

[19] "Chesterton's," The University of Mary, accessed May 5, 2018, https://www.umary.edu/student-life/campus-activities/chestertons.php.

events, and has a cozy place by the fire to keep warm during the North Dakota winters. We had many wonderful evenings of live music, poetry, philosophical discussions, and conversations by the fire. Having enjoyed many conversations there and being on the shorter side myself, I take comfort in Tolkien's insight that "at the table small men may do the greater deeds."[20] Chesterton's has truly formed a culture and community on campus and provides a model for us to emulate in our own communities.

---

[20] As Beregond tells Pippin in *The Return of the King*.

# CHAPTER 8
# *A Spirituality of Beer*

Can we really speak of a spirituality of beer? Yes, but with important caveats. We would be deluded, or maybe tipsy, if we thought that drinking beer in and of itself brought us closer to God. We can begin by saying what a spirituality of beer is not. I was actually consulted for my theological opinion about a man who had brewed beer with holy water. My response was that holy water should be reserved for prayerful purposes, not mundane uses. So we can use holy water to bless beer, not make it. Just as holy water should not be used to make beer, beer should not be used in place of holy water. In the thirteenth century, the custom had arisen in Norway to baptize with beer when water was not available. Pope Gregory IX had to intervene: "Since according to the Gospel teaching, a man must be born again of water and the Holy Ghost, those are not to be considered validly baptized who have been baptized with beer."[1] A proper spirituality of beer focuses not upon drawing beer into sacraments and sacramentals, but rather on helping Christians to draw drinking into a life rightly ordered to God. Beer finds its place in Catholic culture in light of the Eucharist, the spirituality of the monks, and the life of the saints. Catholic culture is sacramental in a broad sense, finding meaning in every aspect of life and ordering it all to God's glory. Catholic culture includes eating and drinking as signs of joy, fellowship, and even of the spiritual life. This chapter will explore how we should understand beer within the context of the interior life, offering a basic sketch of a spirituality of beer.

---

[1] Quoted in William Fanning, "Baptism," in *The Catholic Encyclopedia*, vol. 2 (New York: Robert Appleton, Co., 1907), http://www.newadvent.org/cathen/02258b.htm.

## BEER AS A SIGN

"So, whether you eat or drink, or whatever you do, do all to the glory of
God" (1 Cor. 10:13). Drinking constitutes an essential part of the Catholic
faith, through the consumption of the Eucharist, Christ's Body and Blood
under the appearance of bread and wine. But, not beer drinking. Only
in the Old Testament do we see the practice of a beer (*shekar*) offering
(although Paul speaks of himself as a drink offering in Philippians 2:17).
In the New Covenant, however, without wine, we have no Eucharist,
and without the Eucharist, we lose the source and summit of our faith.
In the Eucharist we also find the source and summit of culture: nature,
work, and the divine meet as we receive the grace needed to order all
things rightly to God.

The Eucharist shows us the goal of work and culture. John Senior asks
the question, "what is Christian Culture?" and provides an answer: "It
is essentially the Mass." In *Restoration of Christian Culture*, he describes
how Christendom "is the Mass and all the paraphernalia which protect
and facilitate it. All architecture, art, political and social forms, economics, the way people live and feel and think, music, literature — all
these things when they are right, are ways of fostering and protecting
the Holy Sacrifice of the Mass."[2] The focus on the Mass even shows the
purpose of work as "not profit but prayer . . . that we live for Him and
not for ourselves."

If beer has a place in Christian culture, it must be understood in
light of the essential drinking of Christ's blood. The Eucharistic cup
draws upon the work of human culture. Culture, as we have seen, can
be understood simply as a way of life. A Christian culture, therefore, is a
way of life that draws its source and finds its fulfillment in the Christian
faith. Just as grace builds upon nature, the Eucharist builds upon human
culture. Bread and wine are two of the most important and fundamental
works of culture. They do not just grow out of the earth, but we use our
intelligence to form them from the fruits of the earth. The matter of the
Eucharist cannot be wheat and grapes, but the works of culture made
from them. The sacrament transforms our works of culture into acts of
cult (worship), making them supernatural and divine.

[2] John Senior, *The Restoration of Christian Culture* (Norfolk, VA: IHS, 2008), 17.

The Eucharist transforms not only our soul, but our entire life, as we incarnate its fruits in our family life, work, and leisure. Christian culture as a whole becomes sacramental, an expression of the divine bursting forth from God's entrance into the world. Pope Benedict taught that a "Eucharistic spirituality... embraces the whole of life," and "as a mystery to be 'lived,' meets each of us as we are, and makes our concrete existence the place where we experience daily the radical newness of the Christian life."[3] Therefore, the Eucharist should give life to all of our eating and drinking.

Lucas Cranach the Younger, *Last Supper* (1565). (Wikimedia Commons)

[3] Benedict XVI, *Sacramentum Caritatis*, apostolic exhortation, Vatican website, February 22, 2007, http://w2.vatican.va/content/benedict-xvi/en/apost_exhortations/documents/hf_ben-xvi_exh_20070222_sacramentum-caritatis.html, §77; 79.

How, then, does beer relate to the Eucharist? Despite what anyone said in the 1970s, beer and pretzel Masses are invalid and sacrilegious! The Protestant artist, Lucas Cranach, painted leading reformers into his *Last Supper*, but also placed a mug of beer centrally on the table, with an attendant holding another mug in the lower right corner (frankly, I'd take the beer over his other additions!). Germans can't resist putting beer close to the centrality of the Eucharist.

Eularia Clarke's *Last Supper* (1962) offers a more serious argument for extending the Eucharist into our everyday eating and drinking. Clarke places the Lord's Supper within a café, with coffee and other drinks,

Eularia Clarke, *Last Supper* (1962). Eularia Clarke Trust. Used with permission.

offering an image of that event that continues to permeate our everyday lives. Without altering how we see the original event, like Cranach, Clarke helps us to recognize how the reality of the Last Supper continues, as we eat and drink in memory of Our Lord—though we also continue to betray Him by listening to the temptations and distractions of the enemy, who uses food and drink to turn us away from the saving meal. We take for granted that Christ chose to communicate His life to use through food and drink, these basic realities of life, which He elevated to a divine reality. Clarke may have represented this reality by showing Christ distributing eggs, signs of growth into new life.

Our entire life should be Eucharistic, as we give thanks to God for His blessings and as we toast with our friends and family, which is a form of blessing. A blessing is to "speak well" to another (*bene dicere* in Latin, whence St. Benedict got his name) and when we toast we wish health, good will, and honor to others. In Latin, the traditional beer toast is *prosit*, literally "may it be beneficial," asking for good fortune. In German, it contracted to *prost*. An alternative Latin toast is *salutaria*, asking for health, which in the Romance languages became *santé* in French, *salute* in Italian, and *salud* in Spanish. Our drinking should be a moment of blessing and thanksgiving, drawing grace from the supernatural cup of blessing at Mass.

It is also a good idea to bless our beer, as we saw in the traditional blessing of the *Roman Ritual*. St. Benedict followed this practice and it saved his life, as the monks of his first monastery tried to poison him because of his strictness. St. Gregory the Great describes how "the glass wherein that wine was, according to the custom, offered to the Abbot to bless, he, putting forth his hand, made the sign of the cross, and straightway the glass, that was held far off, broke in pieces."[4] This is the origin of the prayer of exorcism on the reverse side of the Medal of St. Benedict, abbreviated with the first letter of each word in Latin, V RSNSM V–SMQLI V B: "Begone Satan! Never tempt me with your vanities! What you offer me is evil. Drink the poison yourself!"

Although beer is not a sacramental in the theological sense, it nonetheless can be sacramental in a lesser way, as a sign of both the bounty of the earth and the joys of the higher life. You have probably heard the polka song: "In heaven there ain't no beer, that's why we drink it here, and when we're gone from here, our friends will be drinking all the beer!" *Sed contra*, or on the other hand, as Aquinas would say, the Lord will provide a celestial drink from his own cup that perfects and surpasses the beer we know here. The Irish saint, Brigid of Kildare (451–525), famously prayed for beer in heaven (at least as described in a later medieval manuscript). She was known to perform her own beer miracles; she changed water into beer on three occasions and stretched a small amount of grain to brew enough beer to serve during Easter week for eighteen churches.[5] St. Brigid the brewer provides us with the ultimate toast:

---

4   Gregory the Great, *Dialogues*, Bk. II, http://www.osb.org/gen/greg/.
5   See Nelson, *Barbarian's Beverage*, 76. Her name can also be written as Brigit.

I'd like to give a lake of beer to God.
I'd love the heavenly
Host to be tippling there
For all eternity.

I'd love the men of Heaven to live with me,
To dance and sing.
If they wanted, I'd put at their disposal
Vats of suffering.

White cups of love I'd give them
With a heart and a half;
Sweet pitchers of mercy I'd offer
To every man.

I'd make Heaven a cheerful spot
Because the happy heart is true.
I'd make the men contented for their own sake.
I'd like Jesus to love me too.

I'd like the people of heaven to gather
From all the parishes around.
I'd give a special welcome to the women,
The three Marys of great renown.

I'd sit with the men, the women and God
There by the lake of beer.
We'd be drinking good health forever
And every drop would be a prayer.

There will be a new heaven and a new earth as earthly culture passes away. There may not be beer in heaven in the way we experience it now, but there will be a drink that far exceeds it. God will transform every good thing in a way we cannot even imagine. We do have earthly analogies of that happiness through the joy, satisfaction, and yes, even inebriation of earthly drinks. We get a sense of this through the idea of sober intoxication, the drunkenness we experience when the Holy

Spirit moves us beyond our normal senses and thoughts. The Apostles were accused of being drunk at Pentecost, but St. Paul tells us, "do not get drunk with wine, for that is debauchery; but be filled with the Spirit" (Eph. 5:11). We also pray in the Anima Christi, "Blood of Christ, inebriate me." The intoxication of the Spirit makes all the world spin as if nothing before the beauty of God, which makes us seem out of our minds in the eyes of others. This sober intoxication will continue forever. Jesus drank with his resurrected body, showing us that drinking will continue in some form even in our glorified state. He did not drink out of physical necessity, which shows that there must be a deeper meaning to drinking. Drinking will have a place in the wedding feast of the Lamb as an eternal sign of the life and joy that comes from our love and union with God. We will celebrate an unending feast!

## BREWING AND BENEDICTINE SPIRITUALITY

If we need proof of beer's place within Catholic spirituality we need look no further than the monastery. Why is it that those devoted to prayer develop the best beer? It is because the monks know how to rightly order it. And when beer is rightly ordered, it can promote a small foretaste of the joy and unity with others that we are meant to experience in heaven. Dom Erik, of Mount St. Bernard, the newest Trappist brewing abbey, even suggests that "the brewery provides us with a parable for our monastic life, with the Lord as virtuoso brewmaster. The Scriptures favour wine as an image of the Gospel—but that is culturally conditioned; beer, it seems to me, is a much neglected theological symbol."[6] The monks must have intuited this spiritual insight on brewing and communicated it to Western culture. As Patrick McGovern notes, "we owe a debt to the monastic communities of the Middle Ages for most of the European beverages we enjoy today. As well as patiently dedicating themselves to a spiritual life and preparation for the next world, the monks explored, selected, and nurtured the plant life of this world (including hops), concocted new alcoholic drinks, and made beer and wine on a large scale."[7] The monks' pursuit of heaven created more earthly mirth.

6 "Tynt Meadow Trappist Ale," Mount Saint Bernard Abbey, accessed Aug. 6, 2018, http://mountsaintbernard.org/tynt-meadow-ale.

7 McGovern, *Uncorking the Past*, 129.

St. Benedict was named a patron saint of Europe for his role in laying the foundation for Christian culture after the fall of the Roman Empire in the West. Pope Benedict, speaking to the monks of Monte Cassino, described how the spiritual life of Benedict's monks stimulated culture: "Embodying the Gospel in his life, he became the pioneer of a vast movement of spiritual and cultural rebirth in the West." In his Paris lecture given to UNESCO, Pope Benedict clarified that

> it was not their intention to create a culture nor even to preserve a culture from the past. Their motivation was much more basic. Their goal was: *quaerere Deum*. Amid the confusion of the times, in which nothing seemed permanent, they wanted to do the essential — to make an effort to find what was perennially valid and lasting, life itself. They were searching for God.[8]

The spirituality of the monks followed the Sermon on the Mount: "But seek first his kingdom and his righteousness, and all these things shall be yours as well" (Matt. 6:33). Seeking God led them to be secure and even excellent in their pursuit of earthly goods as well.

Bl. John Henry Newman called the element that connected the heavenly and earthly in the monastery the "poetic sense" of the Benedictines, which imbued their integration of work and prayer. Newman describes how the monks "were not dreamy sentimentalists, to fall in love with melancholy winds and purling rills, and waterfalls and nodding groves; but their poetry was the poetry of hard work and hard fare, unselfish hearts and charitable hands. They could plough and reap, they could hedge and ditch, they could drain; they could lop, they could carpenter; they could thatch, they could make hurdles for their huts; they could make a road, they could divert or secure the streamlet's bed, they could bridge a torrent."[9] They approached the created world and their cultural work with the attentiveness and contemplation that came from the depth of their prayer. Gisela Kreglinger describes the same attitude in relation to wine: "A well-crafted wine . . . can rekindle within us a sense

---

[8] Benedict XVI, "Address to UNESCO" (Sep. 12, 2008), http://w2.vatican.va/content/benedict-xvi/en/speeches/2008/september/documents/hf_ben-xvi_spe_20080914_lourdes-vescovi.html.

[9] Newman, "Mission of St. Benedict," 398.

of wonder and awe for God, a deep gratitude for creation and all its rich blessings, and can enhance our joy and festive play before God."[10]

The monks shaped culture by their spirituality of work, which led them to create a self-sustaining culture that united prayer, learning, work, hospitality, and evangelization. Pope Benedict's Paris lecture also draws this out: "Monasticism involves not only a culture of the word, but also a culture of work, without which the emergence of Europe, its ethos and its influence on the world would be unthinkable. Naturally, this ethos had to include the idea that human work and shaping of history is understood as sharing in the work of the Creator." The works of culture, even the monk's production of beer and wine, become part of their prayer, their spirituality of ordering all things to the glory of God. John Senior describes this holistic spirituality of the Benedictines, shaping all of life within the culture of the monastery:

> In the moral and spiritual order, we become what we wear as much as what we wear becomes us — and it is the same with how we eat and what we do. That is the secret of St. Benedict's Rule, which in the strict sense regulated monasteries and in the wider sense, through the influence and example of monasteries . . . civilized Europe. The habits of the monks, the bells, the ordered life, the "conversation," the music, gardens, prayer, hard work and walls — all these accidental and incidental forms conformed the moral and spiritual life of Christians to the love of Mary and her Son.[11]

Senior was attracted to the Benedictines, and recommended that young people consider the contemplative life because its "poetic" nature incarnates the faith in a way particularly lacking today. Just as we have separated body from soul, we have separated faith from culture.

This spirituality is what drew me to become a Benedictine oblate. I spent time at a Cistercian abbey in high school, praying with the monks in choir and working on the abbey grounds. Years later, as I was discerning a spiritual tradition to guide my family life and teaching classes on culture, I was drawn back to those days. The *Rule* has provided a

[10] Gisela Kreglinger, *The Spirituality of Wine* (Grand Rapids, MI: Eerdmans, 2016), 141.
[11] Senior, *Restoration of Christian Culture*, 130.

principle of integration for my life and a vision of Christian culture. Even beer could fit into this integration, as it provides a key example of the way Benedictines have shaped Western culture. They became master brewers as an extension of their dedication to prayer, redeeming both time (Eph 5:16) and earth through their efforts. Catholic culture exists so that we can live out our faith as a way of life, just as the monastery forms a culture dedicated to God. These words of John Paul II have become my motto: "Culture and holiness! We must not be afraid, when saying these two words, of pairing them unduly."[12]

The monks embody the Christian balance of being in the world but not of the world, a balance that models the relationship between beer and Catholic culture. Even as the monks retreat from the world and pursue heaven, they have become the best brewers in the world! How do these things go together? St. Josemaría Escrivá provides a fitting answer: "Have you not noticed that mortified souls, because of their simplicity, have a greater enjoyment of good things, even in this world? Without mortification there is no happiness on earth."[13] Saying no to earthly things allows us to make proper use of them. Putting God first offers the proper perspective on culture, because the wisdom of God allows us to see things as they are and how they entwine into the ordering of the whole. Cult is the highest aspect of culture and, when it enjoys the priority of place, it stimulates cultivation, providing the freedom and creativity to produce great works of art and culture.

The monks at Norcia are a perfect example of this blending of prayer and brewing. In an interview with *Crux*, Fr. Benedict Nivakoff, then director of the brewery, now prior, said, "People see that for us it's not just a job. . . . Our job is to do something which, by the standards of the secular world, is pretty useless: to pray. . . . There's a comparison with beer, because in a sense, [beer] is useless, it's not something that you have to have to survive. . . . But it's something you can enjoy and it makes life better, like God." Br. Francis Davoren, a self-proclaimed beer-geek, who first conceived the monastic brewery, added: "We're seeking God

[12] John Paul II, "Address to the Catholic University of the Sacred Heart" (Nov. 9, 2000), http://w2.vatican.va/content/john-paul-ii/en/speeches/2000/oct-dec/documents/hf_jp-ii_spe_20001109_gemelli.html.

[13] Josemaría Escrivá, "Penance," in *The Furrow*, ch. 32, 982–83, http://www.escriva-works.org/book/furrow-chapter-32.htm.

Photograph courtesy of the Monks of Norcia.

above all. . . . The focus of our day is God. We work to support ourselves, but also for the glory of God: The beer helps support the monastery, so that the monastery can support his work in the world."[14] Benedictine brewers provide witness precisely on how to place beer within a proper spirituality of prayer and work.

The embrace of beer in the Catholic tradition should not lead one to think that it exists for its own sake. Beer is one means by which the fruits of the earth are enjoyed to praise God, to bring cheer into man's heart, and to lead one into genuine fellowship. Chesterton famously and rightly proclaimed that "we should thank God for beer and burgundy by not drinking too much of them." The fact that Benedictines created modern brewing demonstrates that Catholic culture can be most fully appreciated with a view toward the eternal. Unexpectedly, focusing on the highest things enables us to better appreciate lesser things and order them properly toward what is highest.

[14] Ines San Martin, "Benedictine Brewer-monks Say Beer, Like God, Just Makes Life Better," *Crux*, April 5, 2016, https://cruxnow.com/church/2016/04/05/benedictine-brewer-monks-say-beer-like-god-just-makes-life-better/.

## PATRON SAINTS FOR BEER DRINKERS

### ST. GERMANUS OF AUXERRE (378–448)

Germanus was a Roman nobleman from Gaul (modern day France), who after a superb education became an unexpected bishop and a friend of St. Patrick's, held back the invading Saxons in England, and helped stamp out the Pelagian heresy there. Known as St. Germain in France, his name has been given to many beverages, including the famous St. Germain liqueur, a strong seasonal brew in the Trappist quadrupel style made by Birra Toccalmatto in Italy and the Brasserie St. Germain in France (which also brews a beer in honor of another key beer saint, St. Hildegard). Germanus may not have been named an official patron saint of beer, but we do have a good cause to remember him while we are drinking. Hilaire Belloc immortalized him in his "Pelagian Drinking Song," contained within his work, *The Four Men — A Farrago*:

> Pelagius lived in Kardanoel,
>    And taught a doctrine there,
> How whether you went to Heaven or Hell,
>    It was your own affair.
> How, whether you found eternal joy
>    Or sank forever to burn,
> It had nothing to do with the Church, my boy,
>    But was your own concern.
>
>    *Semi-chorus*
> Oh, he didn't believe
> In Adam and Eve,
>    He put no faith therein!
> His doubts began
> With the fall of man,
>    And he laughed at original sin!
>
>    *Chorus*
> With my row-ti-tow, ti-oodly-ow,
>    He laughed at original sin!
>
> Whereat the Bishop of old Auxerre
>    (Germanus was his name),

> He tore great handfuls out of his hair,
>   And he called Pelagius Shame:
> And then with his stout Episcopal staff
>   So thoroughly thwacked and banged
> The heretics all, both short and tall,
>   They rather had been hanged.
>
>   *Semi-chorus*
> Oh, he thwacked them hard, and he banged them long,
>   Upon each and all occasions,
> Till they bellowed in chorus, loud and strong,
>   Their orthodox persuasions!
>
>   *Chorus*
> With my row-ti-tow, ti-oodly-ow,
>   Their orthodox persua-a-a-sions!
>
> Now the Faith is old and the Devil is bold,
>   Exceedingly bold indeed;
> And the masses of doubt that are floating about
>   Would smother a mortal creed.
> But we that sit in a sturdy youth,
>   And still can drink strong ale,
> Oh—let us put it away to infallible truth,
>   Which always shall prevail!
>
>   *Semi-chorus*
> And thank the Lord
> For the temporal sword,
>   And howling heretics too;
> And whatever good things
> Our Christendom brings,
>   But especially barley brew!
>
>   *Chorus*
> With my row-ti-tow, ti-oodly-ow,
>   Especially barley brew![15]

Raise a glass and fight heresy!

15  Hilaire Belloc, *Complete Verse*, ed. W. N. Roughead (London: Gerald Duckworth, 1970), 90–92.

## ST. AUGUSTINE (354–430)

Drinking did not factor much into Augustine's conversion, but in *Confessions* he tells of how his mother had to overcome alcoholism in her youth. He himself apparently did not struggle with drink, but was held in bondage to the sins of the flesh, even while part of a Manichaean sect that disdained the body. After his conversion, he became a model of temperance and charity, but he drank wine to prove he was no longer a Manichaean, which forbade it as evil. His biographer, Possidius, described his eating and drinking habits: "But Augustine, as I have said, held a middle course, turning neither to the right hand nor to the left. His table was frugal and sparing, though indeed with the herbs and lentils he also had meats at times for the sake of his guests or for some of the weaker brethren; but he always had wine because he knew and taught, as the Apostle says, that 'every creature of God is good and nothing is to be rejected if it be received with thanksgiving, for it is sanctified through the Word of God and prayer.'"[16]

We associate him with brewing not because of his own life, spent in the wine-drinking terrain of the Mediterranean, but because of the brewing efforts of his friars. There are a number of beers dedicated to him, especially the Augustiner bräus brewed by the Augustinian friars in Munich, Germany (1328), Salzburg, Austria (1621, now operated by the Benedictines), and Ghent, Belgium (1295, though relaunched in 1982 with the help of Brewery Van Steenberge). The brewery in Salzburg has the largest restaurant in Austria, called the Bräustübl, seating fifteen hundred people and serving beer from wood barrels stored in a traditional stone cellar, described as "a place of encounter, of tradition — a piece of living history in the center of the Salzburg World Cultural Heritage."[17] Likewise, the Munich brewery, now secularized, operates a beer garden and cellar, which are popular gathering places.

[16] Possidius, *Life of St. Augustine*, trans. Herbert Theberath Weiskotten, ch. 22.
[17] "Austria's Biggest Beer Stop," Augustiner Bräu, accessed June 3, 2018, https://www.augustinerbier.at/das-braeustuebl/geschichte-tradition/.

## ST. BRIGID OF KILDARE (451–525) AND ST. COLUMBAN (543–615)

Along with St. Patrick, who traveled through Ireland accompanied by a brewer, St. Brigid and St. Columban are two great Irish saints known for performing beer miracles and for brewing to serve the Church. Brigid brewed for the diocese surrounding her monastery and performed beer miracles on at least four occasions. She also gave us the greatest beer prayer/toast, quoted earlier in this chapter. St. Columban spread the tradition of Celtic brewing during his missionary travels across the European continent. His disciples established many monasteries, which became not only centers of learning and prayer, but also of brewing. We earlier noted the three beer miracles he performed: preserving the spilled cellar beer, multiplying beer in the fields, and destroying the beer meant to honor the pagan god, Oden. St. Columban also mentions specific penances in his *Rule* for monks who spill large measures of beer: they must make up for it by drinking only water![18] In his *Instructions*, he used the image of drinking, seeing Christ Himself as the true spiritual drink:

> Merciful God, righteous Lord, grant that I may reach that fountain. There let me join the others who thirst for you, drinking living water from the living stream that flows from the fountain of life. Overwhelmed by its sweetness let me cling close to it and say "How sweet is the spring of living water that never runs dry, the spring that wells up into eternal life!" O Lord, you yourself are that spring, always and for ever to be desired, always and for ever to be drunk from. . . . You are everything to us, our life, our light, our health and strength, our food, our drink, our God.

We know that Columban and his monks regularly consumed beer as part of their monastic diet. Therefore, his monks would understand the analogy of Christ sustaining and inebriating us with His drink that is both eternally satisfying and drawing us to thirst for more.

---

[18] Nelson, *Barbarian's Beverage*, 93–94. Nelson mentions other early medieval saints known for beer miracles: St. Mochuda, St. Cronanus, St. Aidan of Connaught, St. Arnulf, and the Abbess St. Sadalberga (ibid., 96–97).

## ST. AMAND (584–675)

Though a patron saint of beer, St. Amand did not have much of a connection to beer during his life. He is known as the Apostle of Flanders, a major beer-producing region, which may explain the attribution. From a noble family of Gaul, he ran away to become a monk at Tours, one of the great monastic centers of France. He then moved to Bourges where he lived in a cave on only bread and water. At the age of thirty-three he was ordained a bishop and was sent as a missionary to Ghent and Flanders, founding many monasteries there and embarking on missionary endeavors to the Slavs and Basques. As a father of the faith and of monasteries in Belgium, he has been linked to the hospitality and drinks they provided. We could say he is simply the patron saint of fun, with patronage over beer, brewers, innkeepers, bartenders, vine growers, vintners, merchants, and even of Boy Scouts.

## ST. ARNOLD (ARNULF) OF METZ (582–640)

St. Arnold, another patron of beer, has more direct connections to the drink, especially given the quotation attributed to him: "From man's sweat and God's love, beer came into the world." He had a remarkable life at the center of politics in the Frankish Kingdom, both as a layman and as a bishop. He served at the Merovingian court and was a military leader. He was married, and through his son Ansegisel, he was the great-grandfather of Charles Martel and thus the great, great, great-grandfather of Charlemagne. It was quite a family as his son Ansegisel's wife Begga also became a saint, herself a daughter of Bl. Pepin and Bl. Ita. Arnold and his wife agreed to pursue the religious life, after which he became a priest and the bishop of Metz, where he continued to serve the Frankish king. He later retired as a hermit and founded a monastery.

There are two main beer stories associated with his life. In the midst of a plague, he told his people, "Don't drink the water, drink beer," and he blessed the brew kettle with his crucifix. Following his advice, they survived. Another miracle occurred in 642 after his death, as the people of Metz were bringing his bones to the city from the monastery of Remiremont. Those carrying the relics became exhausted in the summer heat. One of them prayed: "By his powerful intercession the Blessed Arnold will

St. Arnold at the St. Arnold Brewery.

bring us what we lack." The small amount of beer they carried supplied the entire group until they arrived in Metz the next day. It is fitting that the patron saint of beer should have a brewery named for him. The St. Arnold Brewing Company in Houston, Texas, was founded in 1994 and uses an icon of the saint as their logo. They brew seasonal beers for their Icon, Bishop's Barrel, and Divine Reserve Series.

## BL. CHARLEMAGNE (742–814)

Although Charlemagne has not been officially beatified, the title "blessed" traditionally refers to a holy figure whose cult (devotion) was locally recognized by the Church, but who has not been canonized (except by a German antipope, but alas, that does not count).[19] Approval for this local devotion was confirmed by Pope Benedict XIV in the 1700s. Charlemagne was undefeated in his annual campaigns against pagan Germanic tribes, the Lombards, Huns, Slavs, and Spanish Moors. In addition, he did much to enhance European education, religious life, and liturgical reform, and he standardized early medieval script. In addition, he advanced brewing in conjunction with the Benedictine monks he so actively supported. Wanting to ensure quality, Charlemagne established

[19] Alfred the Great (849–99), another king with local devotion, listed the necessities of life as "land to dwell in and gifts and weapons and meat and ale and clothes" (quoted in Nelson, *Barbarian's Beverage*, 87).

the first brewing regulations in Europe in his *Capitulare de Villis*. In these regulations governing estates, he called for "good workmen" and "brewers." He stipulated that "each steward, when he is on service, shall have his malt brought to the palace; and with him shall come master-brewers who can make good beer." He also insisted on cleanliness: "All these are made or prepared with the greatest attention to cleanliness."

One of his biographers, Einhard, relates his relative moderation, a serious feat for a Germanic warlord: "Charles was temperate in eating, and particularly so in drinking, for he abominated drunkenness in anybody, much more in himself and those of his household. . . . He was so moderate in the use of wine and all sorts of drink that he rarely allowed himself more than three cups in the course of a meal." He promoted moderation in others as well, calling for set days of abstinence from alcohol and regulating the monasteries in his empire. His Capitulary of 802 sought to curb excessive monastic drinking: "Let them altogether avoid drunkenness and feasting; for it is known to all that chiefly through them one comes to be polluted by lust." Charlemagne is known as a father of Europe, but could also be considered a father of Benedictine monasticism and medieval brewing.

## ST. ARNOLD (ARNULF) OF SOISSONS (1040-87)

Another major patron of beer named St. Arnold is more particularly known as the patron of hop-pickers and brewers, especially in Belgium. He is often depicted in images with a mash rake. Born in Brabant, Belgium, he became a solider in the French army of Henry I, later becoming a Benedictine monk, abbot, and finally bishop in Soissons in southern France. After he resigned the see, he founded the Abbey of St. Peter in Oudenburg back home in Belgium. It was here that his connections with beer were recorded.

Like the other Arnold, he told people to drink beer over water (a smart move in the Middle Ages) for the "gift of health." This saved the people from a cholera outbreak. Like St. Columban, he is also known to have multiplied beer. The roof of his monastery collapsed destroying the monks' supply of beer, but God allowed the remaining beer to stretch to meet the abbey's needs. He is depicted with bees because he is alleged to have used the straw cone beehives to filter the monastery's beer, a great

innovation for the time. He may not have a brewery named after him, but
St. Arnold is honored by the Belgian Brewers' Guild (The Knighthood of
the Brewers' Paddle) in Brussels each year the first weekend in September.

## ST. HILDEGARD OF BINGEN (1098–1179)

Hildegard was a Renaissance woman before her time — abbess, mystic,
papal-authorized preacher, composer, artist, and herbalist. Beer factors
into this last skill, as we saw in chapter two. She recommended beer
and hops for various ailments. We can also see drink entering into
her mysticism, as her prayer to the Holy Spirit speaks of tasting God.

> Fire of the Spirit, life of the lives of creatures,
> spiral of sanctity, bond of all natures,
> glow of charity, lights of clarity,
> taste of sweetness to sinners, be with us and hear us.
>
> Composer of all things, light of all the risen,
> key of salvation, release from the dark prison,
> hope of all unions, scope of chastities,
> joy in the glory, strong honour, be with us and hear us. *Amen.*

The prayer also shows her artistic bent, speaking of God as a composer.
Her own compositions have been recorded recently in a number of CDs.
Another poem, "God's Word Is in All Creation," shows how God's glory
shines forth in all His creatures:

> No creature has meaning without the Word of God.
> God's Word is in all creation, visible and invisible.
> The Word is living, being, spirit, all verdant, all creativity.
> This Word flashes out in every creature.
> This is how the spirit is in the flesh —
> the Word is indivisible from God.

Her vision shines forth as a model of the integration we need in Catholic
culture, uniting prayer, art, and even medicine. She is a true doctor, a Doctor of the Church and an herbalist, who has prescribed beer for our diet!

## ST. THOMAS MORE (1478–1535)

More is not only a Catholic hero, giving his life for the faith at the hands of King Henry VIII, but also a model of moderation. He wore a hair shirt and was known for his strong devotion and meditations on the Passion. Michael Foley's *Drinking with the Saints* points out that More drank small beer, that weak beer usually reserved for women and children.[20] Small beer provided a sanitary and nourishing drink, and fit with More's life of simplicity and penance. Erasmus described how he had "never seen any person less fastidious in choice of food. As a young man, he was by preference a water-drinker, a practice he derived from his father. But, not to give annoyance to others, he used at table to conceal this habit from his guests by drinking, out of a pewter vessel either small beer almost as weak as water, or plain water."[21] Foley points out that other than 3.2 percent beer sold in grocery stores in some states, Anchor Brewing in San Francisco brews the only "small beer" marketed as such in the United States.

More's simplicity and penitential practices must have helped him to prepare for his coming martyrdom. His witness calls us to prepare for the day our master comes: "But if that servant says to himself, 'My master is delayed in coming,' and begins to beat the menservants and the maidservants, and to eat and drink and get drunk, the master of that servant will come on a day when he does not expect him and at an hour he does not know, and will punish him, and put him with the unfaithful" (Luke 12:45–46). Thomas More provides a strong example of a faithful servant — father, politician, saint — who watches for the return of the master with sobriety.

## ST. CONRAD OF PARZHAM, OFM, CAP. (1818–94)

Our list would not be complete without a Bavarian, and Capuchin brother St. Conrad fits the bill. He was a porter at the convent near the Marian shrine of Altötting and his duties entailed the supremely important task of supplying pilgrims with beer. This got him into trouble with some after his death though, as his biography attests:

[20]  Foley, *Drinking with Saints*, 163.
[21]  Quoted in Foley, ibid.

The fact is we come across a few but precious stories of his "holy levity." In serving beer to the pilgrims, at least on one occasion, he lost his patience. After all, is it unthinkable that the "holy porter" should sometimes use strong language or come out with a gruff Bavarian remark?

. . .

One member of the tribunal [for his canonization] asked whether it was very "saintly" for the Brother to serve a Bavarian girl two steins of beer and thereby risk the danger of getting her tipsy. Cardinal Michael Faulhaber of Munich came to the defense of the porter saying that if the lady in question could get drunk on only two steins she was certainly not a Bavarian farm girl. . . . Others questioned the propriety of his hearty invitation, "Come, have another stein." But like the gospel cup of cold water, the stein of beer given by a saint was a gesture of holiness that would not go without its reward. . . . So as to have enough beer to serve his poor and the other people who came, he asked Br. Deodat Ring, the friary brewmaster, "Make a lot of beer." He was never happier than when he had plenty of bread and beer for his poor.[22]

May we share Br. Conrad's holy levity with plenty of beer and enough to share.

## BL. PIER GIORGIO FRASSATI (1901–24)

Pier Giorgio, a young man from Northern Italy dedicated to the poor, embodies the moderate pleasure of enjoying alcohol festively with friends. One of his biographers, Cristina Siccardi, describes how "his sanctity gets through to young people today because of the concreteness of his life; Pier Giorgio faced the everyday problems of all young men: the weariness of study, the joy and enthusiasm of being with friends, playing sports, communing with nature . . . and then his healthy appetite, his desire to sing and have fun, his way of being authentic without pretense and hypocrisy, with a pipe in his mouth, and a billiard cue in his hand, and

[22] Fr. Costanzo Cargnoni, OFM Cap., "St. Conrad of Parzham," in *The Capuchin Way: Lives of Capuchins* (North American Capuchin Conference, 1996), 2:180–206. I'm grateful to Fr. Blaine Burkey for pointing me to this source and to St. Conrad.

a glass of beer."[23] He knew how to have a good time, buying his friends a round of beer after a vigorous rowing expedition and rolling a large barrel of wine down the street for a celebration. A group of young people are petitioning for his canonization and collecting signatures. "In one of the US testimonies, a young person named Melanie said she decided to come back to the Church when she discovered the life of this man who 'was . . . funny! And liked beer! And played pranks on people, and climbed mountains, and was in love with a beautiful girl.'"[24] Frassati embodies the well-rounded and robust Catholic culture we need to rebuild today.

## G. K. CHESTERTON (1874–1936)

Preliminary investigation is underway to consider the canonization cause of this larger-than-life Catholic writer. It would be hard to imagine Chesterton being raised to the altar without his bosom buddy and author

G. K. Chesterton at work. (Wikimedia Commons)

[23] Cristina Siccardi, *Pier Giorgio Frassati: A Hero for Our Times* (San Francisco: Ignatius, 2018), 251.

[24] "Could the Canonization of Bl. Pier Giorgio Happen Next Year?" *Catholic News Agency*, August 23, 2017, https://www.catholicnewsagency.com/news/could-the-canonization-of-bl-pier-giorgio-happen-next-year-19833. For the website collecting petitions, see https://www.piergiorgioletter.org.

of the Pelagian drinking song, Hilaire Belloc. H. G. Wells described how the two of them, known collectively as Chesterbelloc, "have surrounded Catholicism with a kind of boozy halo." If Chesterton's cause advances, the Catholic drinker will surely have found his perfect patron! The priest researching his possible cause, Fr. John Udris, was asked if Chesterton's temperance toward food and drink will be a point of investigation. He responded: "The short answer to your query is YES—obviously any investigation into his sanctity will entail answering doubts in this regard."[25] A decision on whether or not to open his cause is expected by the Diocese of Northampton, England, in the fall of 2018. As we will see later, Chesterton clearly articulated a Catholic approach to beer: giving glory to God in moderation. For his extensive writing on this topic, I consider him the unofficial patron saint of Catholic drinking!

## ST. MICHAEL THE ARCHANGEL (ÆVITERNAL)

Michaelmas Day, September 29, marked the beginning of the Bavarian brewing season, lasting until the feast of another warrior saint, St. George, on April 23. Especially when we drink beer we should be prepared for spiritual warfare. Not only do we have to be on guard against the weaknesses of our own flesh and the peer pressure of the world, but also the "principalities and powers," the evil spirits, that are "prowling like a lion looking for someone to devour" (Eph. 6:12; 1 Pet. 5:8). As we have seen in this chapter, many holy figures are associated with beer and even secular brewers have continued the tradition of naming beers after saints. However, there are also many beers named for the enemy, the most famous of which is *Duvel* (devil) from Belgium. There are also some brewers who use monks and saints in mocking ways. I strongly recommend avoiding any labels that have demonic or sacrilegious images.

It is important to remind ourselves that we are always in the middle of a turf battle and have to fight to rightly order all things to the glory of God. As an old Anglo-Saxon poem recounts, the devil can use beer (*beor*) to tempt us:

[25] Steven Drummel, "Chesterton's Lack of Temperance Could Block His Canonization," *The Catholic Household*, November 18, 2014, http://www.catholichousehold.com/chestertons-lack-temperance-block-canonization/.

> I have led on some by my counsels
>> and brought them into discord,
> So that suddenly, drunk on *beor*,
>> they renewed old grievances; I have
> Served them strife from out of the cup,
>> so that by resorting to swords
> Within the wine hall, being stricken with wounds,
>> they released their souls to flit doomed away from their body.[26]

Drunkenness is a spiritual disorder; one that undermines the joy and fellowship that God intends for the use of alcohol. As we drink, we should keep the devil's attacks in mind and invoke our guardian angels and the great prince of the Church, St. Michael the Archangel.

---

[26] Cynewulf, "St. Juliana," quoted in Nelson, *Barbarian's Beverage*, 87.

PART III

EXPERIENCING
BEER

# CHAPTER 9
## *Developing Taste*

Due its hoppy bitterness, beer is an acquired taste. Even the ancient writer Xenophon recognized this of the Scythian beer consumed with straws, which he encountered in his military campaigns: "The beverage without admixture of water was very strong, and of a delicious flavor to certain palates, but the taste must be acquired."[1] Developing a sense of taste goes beyond beer, however. As part of our efforts to restore culture, we need to awaken all of our senses and our mind to the truth, goodness, and beauty of creation and rightly ordered culture. Beer, once again, discloses one small opportunity to encourage this awakening.

### IMPOVERISHMENT OF TABLE

Beer is the world's third most popular drink, after water and tea. None-theless, I think that most people have not really tasted beer. Charles Dickens relates this experience in his novel, *The Old Curiosity Shop*:

> "Did you ever taste beer?"
> "I had a sip of it once," said the small servant.
> "Here's a state of things!" cried Mr. Swiveller, raising his eyes to the ceiling. "She never tasted it — it can't be tasted in a sip!"

Returning with a much-needed meal as well as some purl (beer flavored with wormwood), they ask the servant:

> "Well, is it good?"
> "Oh! isn't it?" said the small servant. Mr. Swiveller appeared gratified beyond all expression by this reply, and took a long draught himself.

Like Mr. Swiveller (who beyond this act of generosity is not to be

[1] Xenophon, *Anabasis*, V.

imitated), I have had the experience, many times, of giving people their first *real* taste of beer. Many times, people have told me, "I don't like beer," but are completely shocked by the flavor of higher quality beer. Like the small servant, many people have taken only a sip of their dad's beer and are used to the flavor of the mass-produced lager beers that dominate the beer market. As part of a graduate class I taught at the Augustine Institute, "The New Evangelization and Culture," we would have a Trappist beer tasting, paired with monastic cheese. The response, both to the beer and the cheese, was overwhelmingly positive, as it opened my students to a whole new level of taste and experience.

As one more symptom of the general impoverishment of our culture, we are experiencing a food crisis. Watching the documentary *Food, Inc.* was quite an eye-opener for me, and started a long process of learning more about the food industry and genetic engineering, and what we should do about them. The great prophet of our agricultural and food crises, Wendell Berry, speaks of "counterfeit foods and beverages."[2] Think about some of our favorite drinks—they are artificial, with high levels of sugar and other harmful ingredients, and do not promote our health. They are part of a massive system that puts profit before the common good. Berry explains that "in the food industry—as in any other industry—the overriding concerns are not quality and health, but volume and price."[3]

Beer, in moderation, is healthier than artificial, sugary drinks, but it too has become part of our food crisis. We will return to the problem of consumerism later; for the time being we will look at the general impoverishment of taste in our country. I call this our "Bud Light" culture (though we could just as easily call it our "McCulture"). It applies to much more than beer, as we prefer food and drinks that are cheap, easy, and bland. This may indicate that we have produced a flat-souled culture, immune and numb to the ordinary wonder and complexity of life. When we make everything fast and easy, we are less able to appreciate the beauty of reading a long novel, patiently contemplate a great painting, sit through an entire symphony, have a long and serious conversation, and make time for silent prayer.

---

[2] Wendell Berry, "Feminism, the Body, and the Machine," in *The Art of the Commonplace: The Agrarian Essays of Wendell Berry*, ed. Norman Wirzba (Berkeley, CA: Counterpoint Press, 2003), 79.

[3] Wendell Berry, "The Pleasures of Eating," in *The Art of the Commonplace*, 324.

Pieter Claesz, *Herring with Bread and Beer* (1636). (Wikimedia Commons)

If we focus on the goods things of the earth too much it leads us into sin and even idolatry; but if we become dulled and unable to appreciate the goodness and beauty of things, our imagination becomes empty. That in turn makes it hard to appreciate higher goods, missing their order toward the goodness of the Creator. Foodies may go overboard, but they do show us how to be attentive to the complexity of taste and the artistic dimension of cooking. A really good beer enjoyed with friends should create some *joie de vivre* and slow down our distracted pace.

Part of developing a normal and healthy drinking culture entails consuming beer and food together. In addition to making beer part of our daily sustenance, pairing beer with food opens up a deeper appreciation of it by expanding the palate. Randy Mosher points us to "the cuisines of beer-drinking countries," which "offer many great beer and food combinations. Beer and cheese from the same region or even the same monastery may be an obvious choice."[4] The pairings themselves become a form of art and experimentation, a way to learn how to appreciate tastes and how they work with or against each other.

---

4  Mosher, *Tasting Beer*, 192.

## DEVELOPING AN AESTHETIC SENSE

Can good beer help push us past the "Bud Light" culture created by
mass-produced beer? Just as Wendell Berry argues for "food esthetics,"
I would argue that attending to the intricacies of good beer can help
us develop a deeper aesthetic sense.[5] When it comes to food and drink
we call this sense a palate, a discriminating sense of what is good, bad,
and truly excellent. A good palate can discern styles and flavors and
pick up notes missed by the average person. We have to learn how to
sense again — how to look, feel, and taste — and how to contemplate
this experience. "Beer is really quite beautiful," Randy Mosher tells us,
and we "have been singing the praises of its deep, clear color and white,
creamy foam for thousands of years."[6] Appreciating beer involves all of
our senses and helps us to develop an aesthetic sense.

Annie Swynnerton, *The Sense of Sight* (1895). (Wikimedia Commons)

[5] Ibid.
[6] Ibid., 56.

Wine may surpass beer for its subtlety, but beer certainly offers a greater variety of flavors, making good use of our complex faculty of taste. Jean Anthelme Brillat-Savarin aptly described how "the number of tastes is infinite, since every soluble body has a special flavor which does not wholly resemble any other. Tastes are modified, moreover, by their combinations."[7] Beer has a greater range of color, texture, strength, and taste than any other drink—with tastes (many only from the combination of malt and yeast) ranging from chocolate to bananas. Flavors come not only from distinct ingredients, but also from different types of barley and hops, the mineral makeup of the water, strains of yeast (which make an enormous impact), and the intensity of roasting the malt (from pale to black, giving the beer its color and malt flavor). Attending to these diverse flavors expands our palate and sensibilities and thus helps us to attend more to all our senses. As Gisela Kreglinger explains, "God was generous in endowing us with such a multitude of taste buds. . . . The complexity of flavors in our world is a gift of abundance; yet if often goes unnoticed and does not move us. This is a great loss."[8] Appreciating taste and the complexity of styles should overflow into other areas, helping us to appreciate art and beauty and awakening us to the overlooked details of everyday life.

Eduard von Grützner (1846–1925), the "beer-monk" painter, portrays this attention to the detail of flavor. The Munich-based artist specialized in genre paintings of monks and other religious drinking alcohol, and produced dozens of poses. Interestingly, he painted during a time when monasticism in general was in decline, but was resurging among the Benedictines (spearheaded by the Wolter brothers at Beuron, Germany). His paintings give the impression that Grützner (who was an unbeliever) may have had an agenda of trying to make monks look silly and even corrupt. Nonetheless, we are drawn to his paintings today (prints are still in demand), as they portray religious figures with discriminating good taste. These monks know a good drink when they see one! Grützner artistically presents the religious palate in action, discerning what is good, but hopefully also rightly ordering it. My favorite, *Brotzeit*, shows a simple monk sitting down for a beer and some cheese. Other images, however, show the monks breaking St. Benedict's directives against boisterous laughter.

---

7  Quoted in Kreglinger, *Spirituality of Wine*, 100.
8  Kreglinger, *Spirituality of Wine*, 101.

Grützner, *Brotzeit* (1908). (Wikimedia Commons)

Grützner, *Drei Mönche bei der Brotzeit* (1885). (Wikimedia Commons)

The novelist Thomas Hardy, in *The Trumpet Major*, also provides us with an artistic glimpse of beer's beauty and potency:

> It was of the most beautiful colour that the eye of an artist in beer could desire; full in body, yet brisk as a volcano; piquant, yet without a twang; luminous as an autumn sunset; free from streakiness of taste; but, finally, rather heady. The masses worshipped it, the minor gentry loved it more than wine, and by the most illustrious county families it was not despised. Anybody brought up for being drunk and disorderly in the streets of its natal borough, had only to prove that he was a stranger to the place and its liquor to be honourably dismissed by the magistrates, as one overtaken in a fault that no man could guard against who entered the town unawares.[9]

Beer is a form of art, broadly understood. Art is something fabricated, a work of culture, a product of what the Greeks called *techne* and the Romans *ars* (the origin of our English "art"). To appreciate the workmanship of any art, we need to learn how to look; in this case we also need to smell and to taste. The most basic way to learn how to appreciate the beauty of things is through poetic knowledge, a knowledge that comes by experiencing things directly. Our education has become abstract, focusing on ideas over things. We experience reality through screens, rather than through our experience and senses. In *Poetic Knowledge*, James Taylor describes an alternative way to enter into and know reality. Poetic knowledge "sees in delight," "gets us inside the thing experienced," and "derives from the love of a thing."[10] Taylor articulates a vision of the poetic as one that "reverberates . . . throughout the body and mind as a kind of real experience of the concept."[11] The famous Thomist, Jacques Maritain, further describes this way of knowing as "that intercommunication between the inner being of things and the inner being of the human Self which is a kind of divination."[12]

---

9  Hardy's lovely description of this complex English ale, a strong Dorchester beer, inspired local brewers to name a barley wine for the novelist, Thomas Hardy's Ale, which lives up to the description!

10  James Taylor, *Poetic Knowledge* (New York: SUNY Press, 1997), 6–7.

11  Ibid., 21.

12  Jacques Maritain, *Creative Intuition in Art and Poetry* (New York: Mass Market, 1957), 3.

The poetic offers an intuitive way of knowing through our experience, which inspires us to learn more by conversation, discursive reasoning, and contemplation.[13]

Hilaire Belloc, in *The Four Men: A Farrago*, used beer as an image of poetic knowledge, a means of coming alive to the reality of things. A critical moment of the story comes when "the Poet threw beer at a philosopher to baptize him and wake him into a new world." What was the philosopher's sin from which he needed washing? "Denying cause and effect." This form of skepticism, denying the intelligent order of the world and descending into relativism, has become too common today. Belloc offers a cure for those who suffer from this kind of weakened human knowledge:

> Now this kind of man can be cured only by baptism, which is of four kinds, by water, by blood, and by desire: and the fourth kind is of beer. So watch me and what I will do.

And here this natural sacrament was imparted, after the philosopher admitted his sin:

> On hearing this reply the Sailor, very quickly and suddenly, hurled over him all that was in the pint pot of beer, saying hurriedly as he did so, "I baptize you in the name of the five senses..."

An argument floats words, but a pint to the head imparts a good dose of reality! Roger Scruton describes how taking a drink in the evening "transfigures the world . . . illuminating that which is precisely most mysterious in the contingent beings surrounding you, which is the fact that they *are*—and also that they *might not have been*."[14] Beer brings us into contact with the fruits of the earth, the smell and taste of something real, and a cold glass in the hand, as we sit with friends and argue about reality. Intuitively, it brings us to assent to the truth of the five senses: we recognize the world as it is and know that it is good.

Some dismiss beauty as a subjective experience, as something only in

[13]  See Senior, *Restoration of Christian Culture*, 115.
[14]  Scruton, *I Drink*, 115.

the eye of the beholder. Aquinas did define beauty as that which pleases when seen, but he also pointed to the inherent qualities that please us: integrity, proportion, and clarity. The objective elements we perceive in the object of contemplation help us to become attuned to its beauty. Our subjective appreciation deepens as we learn to attend to the objective qualities of things. When we approach beer as a form of art, we deepen our capacity to perceive subtlety and complexity.

## APPRECIATING BEER

I am often asked, "What's your favorite kind of beer?" And I answer, "a good one." Not only do I not have a preferred style, but even within a given style there is a wide range of quality, as with anything we produce. Some people get annoyed by "beer snobs," but attention to quality is not inherently snobbish because taste is a rational exercise.[15] Animals may know when something has spoiled and is unsuitable for eating, but they have no sense of quality. In this section, we will discuss how to judge quality and appreciate the distinctive features of beer.

There is an underlying tension between the two poles of appreciating beer. On the one hand, when we judge beer we look for consistency of flavor and style. If you were to go to the liquor store and buy a pilsner, and it poured dark and malty, rather than light and bitter, you would want your money back! We have an expectation of how a certain style should taste and we look for excellence within our standards. On the other hand, we are drawn to innovation, especially within the American brewing scene. We get excited by innovative flavors, combinations, and even new styles. However, we have to know what to expect to appreciate innovation, so let us look at some basics for tasting beer.

Appreciating beer involves all our senses. First, we look at the beer bottle, which gives the first indication of what to expect. Who made the beer and what style is it? Where was it made? What ethos does the bottle's decoration suggest? Then we pour, which provides the initial sense of color and aroma (and should involve pleasant sounds as well). It should produce a good head of foam. (The fizziness indicates freshness from the carbon dioxide produced during fermentation.) After the pour we

---

[15] See, for example, Scruton, *I Drink*, 126.

Johann Wilhelm Preyer, *Münchner Bockstilleben* (1839). (Wikimedia Commons)

hold the glass up to the light to get a better sense of the color, ranging across a spectrum of yellow, orange, amber, brown, and black. Next, we hold the glass up to our nose while swirling it a bit to release more of the aroma. Finally, we engage the senses of taste and touch as the liquid enters our mouth and we evaluate flavor and texture. The clinking of glasses as we toast provides another opportunity to involve the sense of hearing, as a culmination of the drinking process.

Flavor is influenced by taste and aroma. Our sense of smell influences flavor more than we realize, which is why we should drink beer from glasses to give more access to our noses. Some of the main factors that influence taste are the age of the beer (most beer should be consumed within three to four months); temperature (there are preferred temperatures for different styles); and even the shape of the glass, which influences our perception, the foam, and how much aroma reaches us.

Learning to appreciate beer forms our palate, the ability to appreciate differences of taste and quality. Learning to detect flavors requires practice. Being attentive to color, smell, and taste awakens the senses to the reality of the goodness of what you are consuming and the fellowship that comes with it. Find a drinking partner with whom you can explore and discuss new beers. Because flavor is complex, discussing it with others and comparing perceptions helps to develop the palate. Taste requires attention, evaluation, and experience and is not completely objective and clear-cut.

Here are the basic steps toward appreciating beer. First, find a quality beer. Many people think beer tastes like the major pilsners that dominate the American market. To appreciate more of what beer has to offer, it is important to try new brewers and styles. Find a liquor store with more variety and look especially for local brewers. You can probably also find some beers with connections to the Catholic tradition, which will be described in a later chapter. Once you make your decision, some basic questions will guide what to look for in taste and quality. First, is the beer light or dark in color? The darker the color, the more heavily roasted was the barley malt. This will significantly influence the taste. Second, is the taste bitter or malty? The level of bitterness indicates how thoroughly it has been flavored with hops. If the beer is malty it means that it is lightly hopped and you are tasting the malted barley more strongly. Third, what flavors can you perceive? Is the beer acidic, spicy, smoky, toasty, sweet, hoppy, floral, dry, earthy, or sour? Do you perceive any hints of fruit, chocolate, coffee, resin, banana, clove, oak, citrus, bread, and alcohol?

Beer appreciation begins with knowledge of the main styles. The two most basic types are lagers and ales, distinguished by different brewing methods. Ales are brewed with yeasts that ferment in the top of the tank at warmer temperatures. Lagers, based on a brewing method developed relatively recently, over the last five to six centuries, has bottom-fermenting yeasts at cooler temperatures. Some of the basic styles include the following:

**Pilsner:** This is the most popular beer in the world, the crisp and light lager with a strong but not overbearing hop profile. They are popular for their drinkability and refreshing quality.

**German Lager:** A light German lager presents like a pilsner, but Germans also produce lager styles such as the darker dunkel, the stronger bock and doppelbock, and the black schwarzbier.

**Pale Ale and India Pale Ale (IPA):** These are lighter ales with a strong hop profile, especially in the IPA version, which was originally brewed with extra hops to preserve it for the long journey between Britain and India. The strong bitterness has become popular in the United States and has inspired similar styles, such as the American Pale Ale.

**Red Ale:** Red styles are popular in Ireland and Scotland, with a reddish to brown hue, medium body, and maltier taste.

**Brown Ale:** An English style, using darker, brown malts, with a mild, malty flavor. They can have nutty, chocolate, or caramel tones.

**Stout:** This is a dark, even black, ale, which is thick and moderately hopped, and may call for unroasted barley. Porter is a related style, a British dark ale, with stout originally standing for its strongest variety (though other distinctions emerged over time).

**Wheat:** Most beers are made solely with malted barley, but wheat beer includes the additional grain alongside barley. Wheat beers are generally lighter in color and texture and sweeter than other beers. Belgian Wits and German hefeweizens are two major wheat styles.

**Belgian:** Belgium has a unique brewing culture that includes the Trappist and Abbey beers, naturally fermented lambics, saisons, blond ales, sours, fruit-flavored ales, and many other innovate styles. This range of styles offers a great opportunity to branch out and expand your palate.

There are, of course, many other styles that you can explore! In chapter twelve, we will provide more detail on discovering beers related to the Catholic tradition.

# CHAPTER 10
# The Economics of Homebrewing

In the Middle Ages, trades were regulated by guilds, which oversaw who could exercise the trade and how they conducted business. Brewing, however, began as an exception, as anyone had the right to brew and many women brewed in their homes. Richard Unger points out that "everyone in the towns had a right to brew. . . . There were no apprenticeship requirements, no monopoly rights, no limitations of entry into beer making."[1] Not until the later Middle Ages did guilds and brewing organizations emerge, the last of all the guilds to form. Beer became more regulated over time to generate tax revenue and to prevent shortages of grain. As we saw in the first section, as breweries industrialized, homebrewing decreased and was even made illegal in the United States and other countries. Since the late 1970s there has been a huge resurgence in homebrewing.

About five years ago, a friend of mine challenged me, noting that I had been speaking and writing about beer, but had not actually made any! He invited me and my kids over to his house for my first brewing experience, while we watched the documentary with the exaggerated title, *How Beer Saved the World*. I then proceeded to buy my own brewing equipment and with the help of my Italian brother-in-law, made a delicious saison. It took up the good portion of a day and some attention over the next few weeks, but my first creation was a resounding success. This experience convinced me that people are telling the truth when they say it is fairly easy to start homebrewing!

---

[1] Unger, *Beer in the Middle Ages*, 48.

## THE IMPORTANCE OF HOME ECONOMICS

Within modern culture we have become dependent on the mass state, in which economics and politics are conducted on a large scale with the individual as subordinate and dependent. Agriculture itself has become industrialized and subjected to the manipulation of its crops at the genetic level. Brewing is one small way to break absolute dependence upon "the system." This kind of relative self-sufficiency is a crucial element of subsidiarity, the principle by which things should be done on the lowest level without intervention from above, unless necessary. Most people in human history lived with more self-sufficiency. There are many ways that we can become more self-reliant and live a more human lifestyle.

We may need more self-reliance, but we should also avoid the opposite extreme, or we will find ourselves in another modern problem, the isolated self. Rather than focusing on oneself, we should create works of culture as acts of love for God and others. God has given us a cultural vocation so that we can contribute to the common good by serving our families and society. We can get so caught up in our desires and ambitions that we lose sight of the most basic elements of our life and vocation. Work fosters humility by drawing us outside of ourselves and into the dirtiness and difficulty of the work and the care for others it entails. Work keeps us "grounded" and provides to us rational beings a way to express ourselves creatively, sharing in God's own creation by continuing to shape it through culture.

God commanded man to subdue the earth and exercise dominion over it, leading Adam to till and cultivate the Garden. We should ask ourselves how well we have exercised these first and fundamental commands. We are meant to be cultural creators who produce things and exercise creative oversight over the world. David Clayton notes that Catholic educators have been "good at forming *consumers* of Catholic culture, but not good at forming *creators*."[2] Pope St. John Paul II speaks of our general vocation to become artists, to fashion things, which lies at the heart of human identity. In his *Letter to Artists*, he describes how

[2] David Clayton, *The Way of Beauty: Liturgy, Education, and Inspiration for Family, School, and College* (Kettering, OH: Angelico Press, 2015), 61.

the opening page of the Bible presents God as a kind of exemplar of everyone who produces a work: the human craftsman mirrors the image of God as Creator. This relationship is particularly clear in the Polish language because of the lexical link between the words *stwórca* (creator) and *twórca* (craftsman). What is the difference between "creator" and "craftsman"? The one who creates bestows being itself, he brings something out of nothing—*ex nihilo sui et subiecti* as the Latin puts it—and this, in the strict sense, is a mode of operation which belongs to the Almighty alone. The craftsman, by contrast, uses something that already exists, to which he gives form and meaning. This is the mode of operation peculiar to man as made in the image of God. . . .

God therefore called man into existence, committing to him the craftsman's task. Through his "artistic creativity" man appears more than ever "in the image of God", and he accomplishes this task above all in shaping the wondrous "material" of his own humanity and then exercising creative dominion over the universe which surrounds him.[3]

There are many ways to exercise this role of craftsman, but the return of microbrewing and homebrewing provides one opportunity to return to this fundamental vocation of partnership with the Creator.

Homebrewing also presents an opportunity to return to smaller scale and local economics. We live in a society of mass production. Our goods are cheaply produced across the world, displacing the functioning of culture in our own community. Shifting our economic efforts to the local level constitutes an important part of rebuilding culture. With the relatively recent popularity of homebrewing, we can recognize the cultural impact of pouring ourselves into producing something of quality on a small scale. In fact, this movement takes us back to the very beginning of economics and the origin of beer production as a household commodity, providing essential nutrients to the daily diet.

The word "economics" comes from the Greek *oikonomos*, meaning literally the law (*nomos*) of the household (*oikos*). Throughout history, we find economic activity rooted in the family, involving and uniting

3 John Paul II, "Letter to Artists" (April 4, 1999), https://w2.vatican.va/content/john-paul-ii/en/letters/1999/documents/hf_jp-ii_let_23041999_artists.html.

Jost Amman, *Der Bierbreuwer* (1567). (Wikimedia Commons)

all the members in a common enterprise. Just as we need to reclaim the meaning of the word "economics," we need to uncover the meaning of the words "husband" and "husbandry." The root of "hus" is "house" in Old Germanic languages and "band" comes from *bondi*, the tiller of the soil. This meaning was preserved in the use of "husbandry" for farming or homesteading. The husband acts as head of the household economy. He is the master of the house and ensures its proper functioning. Wendell Berry helps us to recognize what happens when we lose the original plan for the economics of the family:

It is possible, then, to be liberated from the husbandry and wifery of the old household food economy. But one can be thus liberated only by entering a trap (unless one sees ignorance and helplessness as the signs of privilege, as many people apparently do). The trap is the ideal of industrialism: a walled city surrounded by valves that let merchandise in but no consciousness out. How does one escape this trap? Only voluntarily, the same way that one went in: by restoring one's consciousness of what is involved in eating; by reclaiming responsibility for one's own part in the food economy.[4]

Berry's solution is to "participate in food production to the extent that you can." Homebrewing is a small but easy first step. It is also an enjoyable one, for as Berry says, "there is pleasure in the growing, preserving, cooking, and eating of the good food that the family's own land provides."[5] If you are really ambitious you may even be able to grow some of your own brewing ingredients and harvest your own yeast.

Anthony Esolen, writing about cultural renewal in his work *Out of the Ashes*, situates brewing within a broader reflection on home economics. He notes that Prohibition contained a fundamental flaw, because "it made illegal an activity which, though it can be abused, in itself is not wicked or destructive of the common good."[6] It "outlawed something that could readily be made by ordinary people in their homes; they could let apple juice hang out in the sun to turn into hard cider.... Prohibition turned what was essentially a local, domestic, and personal problem into a national concern."[7] In fact, beer had been a household commodity from the dawn of civilization. In general, Esolen seeks to champion "all the things that human

[4] Berry, "The Pleasures of Eating," in *The Art of the Commonplace*, 324. Berry also notes the economic sense of this: "Starting with the economies of food and farming, we should promote at home, and encourage abroad, the ideal of local self-sufficiency. We should recognize that this is the surest, the safest, and the cheapest way for the world to live" ("Thoughts in the Presence of Fear," *Orion Magazine* accessed Aug. 4, 2018, https://orionmagazine.org/article/thoughts-in-the-presence-of-fear/).

[5] Wendell Berry, "Farmland without Farmers," *The Atlantic*, March 19, 2015, https://www.theatlantic.com/national/archive/2015/03/farmland-without-farmers/388282/.

[6] Anthony Esolen, *Out of the Ashes: Rebuilding American Culture* (Washington, DC: Regnery, 2017), 114.

[7] Ibid.

beings do with their hands, putting their minds and their hearts into the work, so that they become more human by it, not less; more like artists themselves, and less like the output of a Human Resource Machine."[8] Homebrewing can allow anyone to become a craftsman and an artist, and to return to a basic form of home economics.

## OVERVIEW OF THE HOMEBREWING PROCESS

If you want to know how to brew, you are asking an age-old question. And what better answer could we find to this age-old question than that found in an age-old epic? The Finnish poem *The Kalevala*, preserved orally through the centuries, contains a section on "The Brewing of Beer." The epic poem describes how to prepare the needed drink for a wedding feast.[9] First you need the right ingredients:

> Spake an old man from his corner:
> "Beer arises from the barley,
> Comes from barley, hops, and water,
> And the fire gives no assistance."

The poem describes the planting and harvesting of the ingredients so their forces can be combined. After they are gathered, the goddess of beer, Osmotar, sets forth the brewing process.

> Osmotar, the beer-preparer,
> Brewer of the drink refreshing,
> Takes the golden grains of barley,
> Taking six of barley-kernels,
> Taking seven tips of hop-fruit,
> Filling seven cups with water,
> On the fire she sets the cauldron,
> Boils the barley, hops, and water,
> Lets them steep, and seethe, and bubble,
> Brewing thus the beer delicious,

[8] Ibid., 140.

[9] Although the poem clearly preserves some ancient brewing practices, it also includes some newer additions, such as hops.

In the hottest days of summer,
On the foggy promontory,
On the island forest-covered;
Poured it into birch-wood barrels,
Into hogsheads made of oak-wood.

Reinheitsgebot commemorative stamp. (Wikimedia Commons)

Yet, one more thing was needed: How may it "ferment and be delightful?" After trying many things, it is found that honey would cause the fermentation, as (we now know) it naturally contains yeast:

Osmotar, the beer-preparer,
Placed the honey in the liquor;
Kapo mixed the beer and honey,
And the wedding-beer fermented;
Rose the live beer upward, upward,
From the bottom of the vessels,
Upward in the tubs of birch-wood,
Foaming higher, higher, higher,
Till it touched the oaken handles,
Overflowing all the cauldrons;
To the ground it foamed and sparkled.

But what to do as it ferments? Of all things, a robin sings the answer, while also reassuring the brewer about the quality (as any brewer needs):

> Do not grieve, thy beer is worthy,
> Put it into oaken vessels,
> Into strong and willing barrels
> Firmly bound with hoops of copper.

And then wait:

> Finally the beer was ready,
> Beverage of noble heroes,
> Stored away in casks and barrels,
> There to rest awhile in silence,
> In the cellars of the Northland,
> In the copper-banded vessels,
> In the magic oaken hogsheads,
> Plugs and faucets made of copper.
>     . . .
> Stronger grew the beer imprisoned
> In the copper-banded vessels,
> Locked behind the copper faucets,
> Boiled, and foamed, and sang, and murmured.

Finally, it is ready to drink!

To get started in brewing, there's not much more to it than that! Today, however, we add packets of yeast instead of honey. We also now have a more detailed and scientific understanding of the brewing process.

There are many ways to learn how to brew at home. I recommend visiting the American Homebrewers Association website (www.homebrewers association.org) or consulting a book such as John Palmer's *How to Brew: Everything You Need to Know to Brew Great Beer Every Time*.[10] To orient you to what homebrewing entails, here is a general overview of the steps for brewing an ale (a lager requires a longer and more complicated process).

[10] John Palmer, *How to Brew: Everything You Need to Know to Brew Great Beer Every Time* (Boulder, CO: Brewers Publications, 2017).

First, of course, you need the right equipment (which I will discuss below); the ingredients of milled grain (or extracts), hops, and yeast; and the right sanitation for your equipment, as bacteria and other contaminants will ruin your beer. You begin brewing by mashing, a process of soaking the grain in hot water, which activates the enzymes in the grain to change starches into sugars. The process of lautering then separates the newly produced clear liquid wort from the residual grains and may include sparging, sprinkling hot water over the residual grains to capture any remaining sugars. At this point, hops are added while the wort is boiled to stabilize it and to remove unwanted bacteria. With the boil complete, the temperature of the wort must be brought down quickly so that yeast can be introduced. Special wort chillers can be purchased, though beginners may start by giving the brew pot a cold bath. Then the wort is transferred to a fermentation container, a glass carboy or plastic container, and the yeast is pitched into it. So far the process has only taken a few hours, but fermentation will take weeks as the newly emerging beer sits at a stable temperature of 68 to 72°F. It is common to transfer the beer to another container for secondary fermentation, called racking, which helps the beer to clarify as fermentation completes. Finally, the beer is bottled, while adding priming sugar to create carbonation.

You can find ingredients and equipment at a local homebrewing store. Brewing does not require an extensive amount of equipment, but will require some purchasing to begin. Here is a list of the basic equipment you will need:

- large pot that holds at least four gallons
- special cleaner and sanitizer
- thermometer, stirring spoon, strainer, and measuring cup
- brew bag (for holding grain during the mash) or mash tun
- fermentation bucket with a hole in the lid for airlock and stopper, or a glass carboy
- syphon and tubing for transferring wort and beer
- bottles
- bottle caps, capper, and bottling wand
- bottle brush for cleaning wort chiller and hydrometer for measuring gravity (optional)

Again, this is a broad overview of the brewing process. Consult homebrewing guides for more detail and to learn techniques (such as measuring the gravity of the beer) that can enhance the process.

## A CATHOLIC APPROACH TO HOMEBREWING

Brewing involves some technical expertise, but is there also a spiritual dimension to the brewing process? It may sound like an odd question, but the first time I presented at Theology on Tap (a program of lectures sponsored by dioceses and held in informal gathering spaces such as bars), I was asked, "is there a charism of homebrewing?" My initial response was "no," but upon further reflection, brewing could fall under the charism of hospitality, because you can include others in the brewing process and then share the product. We might find an even clearer connection to the charism of craftsmanship. Sherry Weddell's *Fruitful Discipleship* defines the charism of craftsmanship as empowering "a Christian to be an effective channel of God's goodness to others through sacred or secular artistic creativity that beautifies and orders the physical world."[11] Weddell describes how "the power of the charism of Craftsmanship speaks to the hearts of individuals, but it can also be exercised as a form of pre-evangelization that shapes a whole culture in a way that fosters human flourishing and sets the stage for people to encounter God. Craftsmanship helps build bridges of trust, evokes spiritual curiosity, and helps people to move to openness."[12] Beer clearly can serve that role by opening people to conversation and providing a bridge to other elements of Catholic culture. No matter your charism, you must brew with the right spiritual disposition to exercise your role as co-creator and craftsman — giving thanks to God and friendship, hospitality, and service to others.

Now that we've investigated the relationship between monks and brewing, we can ask with Stan Hieronymus, "Could you brew like a monk? Should you? Would you?"[13] Hieronymus provides insights on how to brew like the Belgian Trappists, though he makes clear that his

[11]  Sherry Weddell, *Fruitful Discipleship: Living the Mission of Jesus in the Church and World* (Huntington, IN: Our Sunday Visitor, 2017), 178.

[12]  Ibid., 179–80.

[13]  Hieronymus, *Brew like a Monk*, 8.

book is not for beginners. He guides those with some brewing experience through some of the unique monastic and Belgian techniques: overcoming difficulties with attenuation, using candi sugar, refermenting in the bottles, and matching Trappist ingredients and techniques. He offers many recipes to mimic Trappist and abbey styles, which entail practice and finesse. The finished product probably will not be an exact match, but will result in your own version of the classic beers. Quoting another brewer, Hieronymus rightly points out, "you could have every recipe from every brewery, every detail, their mashing, their fermentation temperatures, and you wouldn't have their beer."[14] Nonetheless, the great brewing achievements inspire us to venture into our own creations.

There are alternatives to brewing like a monk. You could brew like a priest (if there is much of a distinction). Fr. Jeff Poirot, pastor of Holy Family Catholic Church in Fort Worth, Texas, won the Ninkasi Award for best homebrew in 2017 from the American Homebrewers Association. He won with a Belgian Trappist Quad, concocted with his brewing partner Nick McCoy. Speaking to his local paper, Fr. Poirot related, "for me, I always want to balance [brewing] with being a priest, because being a priest is primary, first and foremost for me."[15] He was inspired to brew like a monk, visiting the Trappist abbeys of Belgium, and earning the title of one of the nation's premier beer nerds.[16] Unfortunately, his bishop was not amused, missing the great evangelization potential, and told him to stop brewing.[17]

So far, we have seen that to begin homebrewing, you need the right equipment and ingredients, the right spiritual dispositions of hospitality and craftsmanship, as well as the inspiration of tradition. Next, it helps to brew with others, reaching out to friends with experience to guide you as you learn the brewing process. I first brewed at a friend's house, and was

---

[14] Ibid., 217.

[15] "Holy Homebrew: Catholic Priest Wins Brewing's Highest Honor," *Catholic News Agency*, July 15, 2017, https://www.catholicnewsagency.com/news/holy-homebrew -catholic-priest-wins-brewings-highest-honor-56515.

[16] Matthew Martinez, "Holy Homebrew: Fort Worth Priest Jeff Poirot Is One of Nation's Premier Beer Nerds," *Star Telegram*, July 1, 2017, http://www.star-telegram. com/entertainment/restaurants/brew/article159284719.html.

[17] Mathew Martinez, "Father Jeff Was a Master Brewer—Until the Bishop Turned off the Tap," *Star-Telegram*, September 29, 2017, http://www.star-telegram.com/news/ local/community/fort-worth/article176075481.html.

Rochefort Brewery. (Wikimedia Commons)

blessed to take a class on homebrewing at Holy Name of Jesus Parish in Denver, CO, led by another friend, Chris Lanciotti, a consecrated member of the Sodalitium Christianae Vitae and Formation Director for Creatio, an outdoor ministry. Chris gave a great presentation and led us through the first steps of brewing. The Catholic Drinkie, Sarah Vabulas, rightly points out that "while it's fun to brew alone, it's more fun to brew with friends!" In part because, "there is a unique joy in sharing the hobby of home-brewing with someone who has never done it before. . . . There is an art and a finesse to home-brewing that requires patience and some math. I love to invite friends over who have never brewed before and teach the magic."[18]

You will also need to choose a recipe for the style of beer you want to brew. The Catholic Drinkie offers some innovative homebrew recipes, such as "Not G. K. Chesterton's Tea":

> This traditional English Style Bitter (ESB) has a little something extra added to it: Earl Gray tea. This brings a different flavor (and color) to the beer. It adds a citrus flavor and aroma derived from

---

[18] Sarah Vabulas, *The Catholic Drinkie's Guide to Home Brewed Evangelism* (Liguori, MO: Liguori Publications, 2015).

the addition of oil extracted from the rind of the bergamot orange, a fragrant citrus fruit. . . . Grab a pipe and toast to everyone's favorite English theologian.[19]

Vabulas has many other great recipes, such as "If St. Brigid Had a Lake of Beer...," an Irish blond, which includes a pinch of Irish moss. As you gain experience in brewing, you develop as an artist, experimenting with recipes and techniques. Randy Mosher tells us that "if you do it right, brewing is about ideas. A big impression can be made with brute force, but sometimes a whisper speaks louder than a shout. In the end, all great beers tell a story."[20]

Homebrewing is one way to revive the economics of the home. It will save you some money, but more importantly it will give you the satisfaction of making your own brew while you produce something beautiful and enjoyable.

[19] Ibid.
[20] Mosher, *Tasting Beer*, 77.

CHAPTER 11

# Brew Evangelization

Within the crypt of the basilica church of San Carlo al Corso in Rome, located along one of the city's main thoroughfares, there is an unusual parish establishment. The Diocese of Rome runs a "Pub Giovanni Paolo II," a bar dedicated to the great saint who inspired the New Evangelization, St. John Paul II. The pub offers live music, films, speakers, and alcohol in moderation to facilitate "evenings of fun and gatherings, but also of culture and spirituality."[1] Known as GP2, the pub teaches youth about John Paul II and his legacy, exemplifying the Pope's desire to find new ways to reach people in a secular culture.

Since Benedictines have been brewing for fifteen hundred years, it makes sense to look to them as models for evangelizing through culture. Rod Dreher's *The Benedict Option* caused a media sensation by proposing the Benedictine tradition as a model for building Christian culture in the midst of a hostile, secular environment. He drew from Alasdair MacIntyre's statement in *After Virtue* that we are waiting for "another — doubtless very different — Benedict." Dreher was inspired by a group of mostly American Benedictines (introduced in chapter four), living in the Apennine mountains outside of St. Benedict's hometown, Norcia, Italy. These monks inspired the Benedict Option, but also the Beer Option — advancing the New Evangelization by uniting prayer, work, and brewing.

## MONKS AND THE NEW EVANGELIZATION

Pope St. John Paul II launched the New Evangelization as a call to reevangelize the Western world and those Christians who were baptized but no longer practice the Catholic faith. The culture constructed by monks

---

[1] "Roma apre il primo local per Cattolici: sotto la basilica di S. Carlo," *Corriere*, October 11, 2010, https://roma.corriere.it/notizie/cronaca/10_ottobre_11/pub-oratorio-giovanni-paolo-roma-1703924594990.shtml.

during the Middle Ages has been hijacked and turned against the Christian faith of its origin. Christians now live within a secularized culture, which seeks to remove God from our everyday life, making it difficult to live the Christian faith in the world. Therefore, John Paul called Catholics to "commit all of the Church's energies" to this evangelization, new not in content but in ardor, method, and expression.[2] We will examine how beer could be part of the new method and expression of the Church's efforts to evangelize, enabling us to speak of a "Brew Evangelization."

Evangelization is the direct proclamation of the Gospel, seeking to lead all people to accept the salvation offered to us by Christ. However, it has become ever clearer that we need to also evangelize — spread the good news — about the goodness and integrity of nature, which, like the Christian faith, has been rejected by our culture. Both God and nature have become constraints to our modern understanding of freedom. This rejection of natural realities applies most fully to the goods of marriage and sexuality, but also to the simple aspects of life that have been eclipsed by technology. We have become so removed from the basic production of goods that reemphasizing simple things forms a necessary task for cultural renewal.

Rod Dreher describes how the Benedictines, known for their brewing, can be a model for reevangelizing culture:

> What these orthodox Christians are doing now are the seeds of what I call the Benedict Option, a strategy that draws on the authority of Scripture and the wisdom of the ancient church to embrace "exile in place" and form a vibrant counterculture. Recognizing the toxins of modern secularism, as well as the fragmentation caused by relativism, Benedict Option Christians look to Scripture and to Benedict's *Rule* for ways to cultivate practices and communities. Rather than panicking or remaining complacent, they recognize that the new order is not a problem to be solved but a reality to be lived with. It will be those who learn how to endure with faith and creativity, to deepen their own prayer lives and adopting practices, focusing on

---

[2] See Pope John Paul II, *Redemptoris Missio*, encyclical letter, Vatican website, December 7, 1990, http://w2.vatican.va/content/john-paul-ii/en/encyclicals/documents/hf_jp-ii_enc_07121990_redemptoris-missio.html, §3.

families and communities . . . and building churches, schools, and
other institutions within which the orthodox Christian faith can
survive and prosper through the flood.[3]

Christians must do now what the Benedictines did in the Dark Ages:
begin the long process of evangelizing and rebuilding culture. The Norcia
monks, a model of the Benedict Option, connect this vision explicitly to
beer. Their beer made a splash; when only in its second year it was served
at the Papal Conclave that elected Pope Francis. Some may question the
prudence of serving beer at a conclave. However, Cardinal George Pell,
when blessing the monks' expanded brewing equipment in 2014, held
up their brewery as an "example of the new evangelization." One of the
monks described the monastery's rationale in brewing:

> Father Nivakoff said the monks began brewing August 15, 2012, with
> three goals: contributing to the monastery's self-sufficiency; solidify-
> ing bonds with the town; and reaching out to people who are "turned
> off by religion." For those who wouldn't think of going to Mass, he
> said, the monastery gift shop gives them contact with the monks
> "in a setting and over a product they feel comfortable with. There's
> a spiritual gain for them, even though they aren't looking for it."[4]

Drawing visitors to the monastery shares the Gospel without needing
to preach. Fr. Nivakoff explained further: "The beer is a catalyst . . . for
making people comfortable and beginning conversations. Brewing
monks seem more accessible to the average person! Plus, the monks
show how to rightly order beer . . . : If the prayer doesn't come first, the
beer is going to suffer."[5] Visitors may be attracted to the beer, but they
encounter the witness of the monks, who put God first.

Brewing also accomplishes the goal of tying the monastery more
strongly to the surrounding community. It attracts visitors to Norcia, and
"as part of the monks' campaign to rebuild [from the 2016 earthquake],

---

3  Dreher, *Benedict Option*, 18–19.
4  Cindy Wooden, "Beauty and Beer: Monks Outreach Is Part of the New Evangelization," *Catholic News Agency*, August 21, 2013, http://www.catholicnews.com/services/
englishnews/2013/beauty-and-beer-monks-outreach-is-part-of-new-evangelization.cfm.
5  Ibid.

the brewery is giving 15 percent of all proceeds to charitable causes. They will also give a portion of all funds raised to the people of Norcia."[6] This partnership attracted the attention of National Public Radio: "These monks came to Norcia to observe a contemplative life of prayer. But now they're also full-fledged members of the town — contributing to its economy and becoming its spiritual and cultural point of reference."[7] Fr. Nivakoff again explains how the impact of a monastery visit influences the surrounding culture: "Because they can't take a monk home, to take something that the monks make is a way of bringing a little bit of monastic life into their homes. . . . To bring home a wine or a beer or a product that monks or nuns make sort of sanctifies their home for them."[8] The monks model the Beer Option by using their Birra Nursia to foster an encounter with God and others and to stimulate cultural renewal.

The rebuilding of Norcia signifies the revitalization we need in our culture more broadly. The combination we see there of monks renewing the monastic life and creating a more dynamic engagement with culture has the potential to inspire a Brew Evangelization. The New Evangelization requires a renewed proclamation of the treasury of the Christian faith to meet the needs and challenges of modern culture, especially for those Christians who have fallen away from the faith. The revival of brewing has recovered a small part of monastic tradition, which shored up culture in the past, particularly after the collapse of the Roman Empire. Monastic brewing provides an example of how Catholics must reassert their presence and influence in modern culture.

Pope Benedict spoke of the role of Benedictines in the New Evangelization, singling out both their spiritual tradition and cultural patrimony: "I know and deeply appreciate the generous and competent cultural and formative work carried out by so many of your monasteries, especially for the young generations, creating an atmosphere of brotherly acceptance

---

[6] Inés San Martín, *Crux*, "Beer-producing monks set on rebuilding through praying and brewing" August 26, 2017, https://cruxnow.com/global-church/2017/08/26/beer-producing-monks-set-rebuilding-praying-brewing/.

[7] Sylvia Poggioli, *National Public Radio*, "Beer-Brewing Monks Are Helping Rebuild Earthquake-Devastated Town in Italy" September 3, 2017, https://www.npr.org/sections/parallels/2017/09/03/545599850/beer-brewing-monks-are-helping-rebuild-earthquake-devastated-town-in-italy.

[8] Ibid.

that favors a unique experience of the Church."[9] One Benedictine monastery took up this project in earnest: the Monastery of the Immaculate Conception, a community of female Benedictines in Indiana, together with the independent St. Benedict's Brew Works, held a beer-brewing retreat in November of 2016 and March of 2017. They advertised the event as follows: "Brewery owners Vince Luecke and Andy Hedinger will share the history of beer and reflections on Gospel parables about grain, earth, yeast, and water. Participants will sample beers, learn beer terminology, and make craft beer."[10] They also offered a Monastery Beer Festival in 2017, which included a monastery-themed meal and beer pairings, live entertainment, a beer tasting with more than 100 beers, tours of monastery grounds and church, and Mass.

Monastery of the Immaculate Conception. (Wikimedia Commons)

9   Pope Benedict XVI, "Address at Castel Gandolfo" (Sep. 20, 2008).

10   Roseann Derk, "'Monastic Beer Experience' Coming to Fredinand," *Courier & Press*, September 11, 2017, https://www.courierpress.com/story/news/local/2017/09/11/monastic-beer-experience-coming-ferdinand/105508940/.

## CATHOLIC BEER EVENTS

The broader Church has increasingly been imitating the Benedictines'
use of beer to evangelize. The evangelization part may be new, but beer
in fact has a long connection to the parish. E.A. Wasson describes a
part of this history:

> In medieval England an "ale" was synonymous with a parish fes-
> tival, at which this was the chief drink. The word was frequent in
> composition. Thus, there were Whitsun-ales, clerk ales, church-ales,
> brid-ales (now bridals). The "bridal" is the bride plus ale, or wedding
> feast. The parish ales were of much ecclesiastical importance in
> England. The chief purpose of the church—and of the clerk (that
> is, clergy)—ales was to facilitate the collection of parish dues or to
> make an actual profit from the sale of the beverages by the church
> wardens. These "ale" profits kept the parish church in repair or were
> distributed as alms to the poor.[11]

I am sure many women would be happy to know the true etymology
of "bridal" as "bride's ale"! The function of the parish festival seems
to maintain the custom and purpose of the medieval ales as a time to
gather parishioners and other locals to raise money for the parish in
a spirit of festivity. Some parishioners have brewed for special parish
events and some couples have rediscovered the meaning of bridal by
brewing special beers for their wedding reception.

Catholic apostolates have arisen to harness beer for the work of evangelization. Theology on Tap emerged in the 1980s in the Archdiocese of
Chicago as a ministry for young adults, and since 2003 has been licensed
by RENEW International throughout the country. It has become the
model for evangelizing with beer: host a speaker on a Catholic topic, at
a comfortable venue, followed by conversation over beer. RENEW International describes its mission "to provide an opportunity for Catholic
parishes and groups to share the richness of Catholic faith with young
adults, and offer a setting where people of similar values and faith can
gather in a peer community," but also clarifies that "RENEW Theology on

---

[11]  E. A. Wasson, *Religion and Drink* (New York: Burr Publishing, 1914), 160.

The author presenting at Theology on Tap. Photograph courtesy of *The Gazette,* Colorado Springs.

Tap does not promote drinking, but strives to meet young adults where they are, and many gather in bars and restaurants to eat, drink, and socialize."[12] The point is, evangelizing through beer does not focus on the beer, but on the message and fellowship facilitated by gathering over a pint.

Another apostolate, the Catholic Beer Club, arose when Benedictine College graduates decided to share with others the fellowship they built during their college years:

> Like many great ideas, Catholic Beer Club was discovered by accident. One evening, a couple of friends simply decided to grab a beer. As they sat together discussing higher things and the beauty of relationships, they decided that this experience must be shared. A gathering of like-minded people, the absence of an agenda, a cold beer, and the underlying principles of the Catholic faith, built a foundation for a great community.[13]

[12] "RENEW Theology on Tap FAQs," Theology on Tap, accessed June 4, 2018, https://www.renewtot.org.

[13] "Evangelization through Community: Why Catholic Beer Club is Different," Parish Catalyst, March 14, 2016, https://www.parishcatalyst.org/evangelization-though-community-why-catholic-beer-club-is-different/. See www.catholicbeerclub.com.

Like Theology on Tap, the Catholic Beer Club has spread throughout the country with over twenty chapters. "It is about setting a concrete time and place to give individuals an opportunity to build friendships [and] relationships, and [to] be a witness to their faith. If the contagious laughter of a CBC event brings joy to the waitress serving the groups, or an apprehensive newcomer finds a welcoming atmosphere to call home, the night was a success." While Theology on Tap's format is to host speakers on Church teachings, the Catholic Beer Club has no specific format. Rather, it simply focuses on the encounter of the moment. In both apostolates, however, beer has helped create the conditions for relational evangelization.

The concept of Brew Evangelization has caught on across many parishes and dioceses as well. When I was a high school seminarian, the Diocese of La Crosse hosted "Beer and Brats with the Bishop" at the Leinenkugel's brewery, with the then bishop of the Diocese, Cardinal Raymond Burke. Bishops in Minnesota and Iowa have hosted similar gatherings. My own parish, Our Lady of Lourdes in Denver, offers "Pint with a Priest," hosted in front of the beautiful outdoor grotto, and a family-friendly Oktoberfest to raise money for the school. My friend, Fr. John Riley, chaplain of the Augustine Institute, has also modeled the integration we need to evangelize, holding "Prayer, Penance, and Pub Nights" at St. Thomas More Parish. Sam Guzman wants to foster greater fraternity with priests over beer, promoting on his website, *The Catholic Gentleman*, "International Buy a Priest a Beer Day" on September 9. Hopefully, this movement will catch on.

The Catholic apologist Matt Fradd has furthered the theology and beer concept with his book (and follow up podcast), *Pints With Aquinas: 50+ Deep Thoughts From the Angelic Doctor*. The book begins:

> Do you have a beer? You're going to need a beer. If you could sit down with St. Thomas Aquinas over a pint of beer and ask him any one question, what would it be? In this book we'll ask him over 50 questions (don't worry he's a patient guy) having to do with God, faith, virtue, the sacraments, and much else besides.

The Order of the Angelic Doctor itself has recently launched an initiative for the eight hundredth anniversary of the founding of the Dominicans in the Netherlands. The Order of Preachers, whose founder St.

Dominic converted his first heretic by talking with him all night in a pub, is returning to its roots. In addition to university debates and a radio program, the Dutch Dominicans sponsored a special beer and conversation event in the pub:

> The campaign consists of several elements. First there is the beer called *Sunday*, a special brew of a small brewery called De Hemel (Heaven) — what's in a name? It is a blond and tasteful beer and it goes with special beer mats. On these mats are quotes from famous Dominicans as Meister Eckhart, Catharine of Siena, Thomas Aquinas and Edward Schillebeeckx. With the quotes come questions to deepen the encounter, such as "What is God?" or "What do you hope for?" or "What are you grateful for? And how do you know that?"[14]

Does theology really pair well with beer? I have found that it does. Just as we saw in the chapter on friendship, beer draws people together for a good theological conversation and provides inspiration, which results from leisurely and thoughtful conversation. The pub provides an ideal location to ask questions and discuss new ideas.

In September 2015, in my home state of Pennsylvania, brewers themselves took the initiative to welcome Pope Francis to the World Meeting of Families in Philadelphia. They produced a number of Pope-themed beers, such as:

> Papal Ale (Manayunk Brewing), Belgian-style amber, 6.7 percent
> Papist Ale (Vault Brewing), India pale ale, 8.7 percent
> Pater Noster (2nd Story Brewing), patersbier, 4 percent
> Holy Wooder (Philadelphia Brewing Company), Belgian tripel,
>     9.75 percent
> White Smoke (Forest and Main), saison, 4.5 percent
> YOPO a/k/a You Only Pope Once (Cape May Brewing), pale ale,
>     5.2 percent[15]

---

14 "Dutch Dominican Launches Family Jubilee in the Pub," Order of Preachers, accessed May 20, 2018, https://www.op.org/en/content/dutch-dominican-family-launches-jubilee-campaign-pub.

15 John Kell, "Pope-Themed Beers to Bless Philadelphia's Faithful," *Fortune*, August 28, 2015, http://fortune.com/2015/08/28/pope-beer-philadelphia/.

(Courtesy of the Philadelphia Brewing Company)

These papal beers demonstrate the intuition of brewers to mark a holy occasion and to use beer for hospitality. They also show that the secular culture still takes interest in large Catholic gatherings and may not be immune to public moments of evangelization.

## FORMING CATHOLIC BEER CULTURE

Although the Church has not hesitated to turn to beer to reach people, in the eyes of many the Church remains far removed from their everyday lives. Christians should not accept the dualism of faith and culture, which separates belief from experience. William Blake expressed the dualism that many find between the Church and the pub in his poem "The Little Vagabond."

Dear Mother, dear Mother, the Church is cold,
But the Ale-house is healthy & pleasant & warm;
Besides I can tell where I am use'd well,
Such usage in heaven will never do well.
But if at the Church they would give us some Ale,
And a pleasant fire, our souls to regale;
We'd sing and we'd pray, all the live-long day;
Nor ever once wish from the Church to stray,
Then the Parson might preach & drink & sing.
And we'd be as happy as birds in the spring:
And modest dame Lurch, who is always at Church,
Would not have bandy children nor fasting nor birch.
And God like a father rejoicing to see,
His children as pleasant and happy as he:
Would have no more quarrel with the Devil or the Barrel
But kiss him & give him both drink and apparel.

Staff members of a Welsh pub also could not imagine the integration of church life and pub life. They kicked a group of seminarians out of their pub for wearing cassocks (black robes). The staff thought they were up to no good, dressed up as priests as a prank:

How does a pub make up for mistakenly trying to kick out a group of celebrating seminarians? By naming a beer after them and calling it the "Thirsty Priests." Tim Lewis is the PR Manager for Brains, the company which owns the City Arms Pub in Cardiff, Wales. He said that re-naming one of the seminarian's favorite beers was a small thank you for the group's good humor in being mistaken as a bachelor party and nearly kicked out of City Arms Pub. "Thirsty Priests," with the added slogan "saving souls and satisfying thirsts." The seminarians took the error in good humor, and were warmly received by staff and customers for the rest of their time at the pub. The whole affair was amusing, noted the seminarians, and the men were encouraged by the positive interaction with the community—which also enabled the locals to engage the seminarians in questions about the Church.[16]

16  "Welsh Pub Renames Beer after Seminarian Mix-up," *Catholic News Agency,*

Though the staff initially thought that seminarians did not belong in a pub, the incident created a positive interaction with the local community. The world needs the witness of Catholics outside of church to bring faith back into the fabric of society.

Catholics also need to re-create a positive and holy drinking culture, which integrates alcohol with friendship, hospitality, and evangelization. Alcohol must be redeemed. Our drinking habits should flow from our participation in the sacraments and be placed within a robust Catholic culture. Sean Daily contrasts Catholic and Protestant drinking in "The Lost Art of Catholic Drinking."[17]

> Protestant drinking tends to occur at one extreme or another: either way too much or none at all, with each being a reaction to the other. Some people, rightly fed up with the smug self-righteousness of teetotalers, drink to excess. And teetotalers, rightly appalled at the habits of habitual drunkards, practice strict abstinence. It seems to occur to neither side that their reaction is just that: a reaction, and not a solution.

Catholic drinking, Daily argues, should be distinguished by conviviality: "When friends get together for a drink, it may be to celebrate, or it may be to mourn. But it should always be to enjoy one another's company." In chapter thirteen, we will look at how a Catholic drinker needs to navigate between the two extremes of hedonism and puritanism. Drinking should also be ecumenical, as we strive to overcome sectarian beverage divisions. Rod Dreher provides the example of Eighth Day Books in Wichita, Kansas, which hosts events and symposia and a Hall of Men, where in a "kind of Christian speakeasy next to the bookstore, Catholic, Orthodox, and Protestant men have been coming together . . . to pray, to discuss and debate the works of a great figure of Christian history, then to sit around the table drinking pints of beer and enjoying each other's company."[18]

Engaging with the things of the world does not mean giving in to their misuse. As we form a Catholic beer culture again, colleges are the perfect

---

August 7, 2017, https://www.catholicnewsagency.com/news/welsh-pub-renames -beer-after-seminarian-mix-up-48412.

[17] Sean P. Daily, "The Lost Art of Catholic Drinking," *Crisis Magazine*, April 13, 2012, https://www.crisismagazine.com/2012/the-lost-art-of-catholic-drinking.

[18] Dreher, *Benedict Option*, 137.

place to begin. Colleges are places where alcohol is most misused, and college students need to be formed to sensibly fit alcohol into their lives. Good Catholic colleges aim to educate students in virtue, and this includes situating alcohol within Christian culture to teach students (of the appropriate age) to drink well. The University of Mary, for instance, requires students (twenty-one and older) to complete an alcohol training seminar before they can enjoy drinking at Chesterton's, the campus pub. The University says it "is committed to educating students on the responsible and moral use of alcohol. Student members participate in thorough training which includes cultural, legal, and health perspectives."[19] Benedictine College also provides a place for fellowship on campus, the Haverty Center, which "contains a coffee house/pub area, poet's corner with fireplace, the Monte Cassino Inn, the Raven Store, and a student workout facility."[20] This center demonstrates a proper integration of university life, which situates "the pub" in a public place on campus where people can gather.

We have the opportunity to create a new, integrated Catholic culture, which includes the moderate use of alcohol, and which aims to create a merry, wholesome, and familial environment. From an evangelistic perspective, we need to create opportunities for encounter, particularly by reclaiming the Lord's Day. Sunday, a day meant for leisure, provides the prime opportunity to encounter others over a drink. An early Church Father even wrote to hermits that "I prescribe that, at least on Sundays and feast days, they drink wine or beer."[21] The drink was an essential part of affirming the goodness of God's creation and entering into the festivity of the holy day. Though St. Paul affirmed those who wanted to abstain, he noted that those who ate did so to give thanks (Rom. 14:6). Eating and drinking with one another on the Lord's Day extends the Eucharistic thanksgiving of the Mass further into the world. The family meal truly serves as a sacramental for thanks and communion, making the Lord present where two or more are gathered in His name.

[19] "Chestertons," The University of Mary, accessed May 5, 2018, https://www.umary.edu/student-life/campus-activities/chestertons.php.

[20] "Haverty Center," Benedictine College, accessed June 4, 2018, https://www.benedictine.edu/about/facilities/buildings/haverty-center.

[21] Pseudo-Augustine, *Sermones ad Fraters in Eremo Commorantes*, Sermon 28, quoted and trans. Joseph Strickland, "Beer, Barbarism, and the Church," 31. Although the work had been attributed to Augustine, due to its anti-Manichaean focus, Strickland proposes a Gallic connection due to the early use of *cervisia*.

Sunday may be a good day to drink beer, as part of the leisure of the Lord's Day, but a medieval miracle reinforced that it was not a day to brew:

> Beer, however, was not to be brewed on Sunday, and when the people of Wisa once tried to celebrate the martyred Saints Chrysanthus and Daria they were unable to draw beer (*cervisia*) out of the barrel (*cupa*) no matter how many times it had been tapped, so it was claimed, since it had been made on a Sunday and God did not allow them to drink it. After pledging that this would never happen again and that they would give the beer to paupers the beer flowed out normally.[22]

The miracle reinforced not only the need to observe the Lord's Day with rest and leisure, but also the need to serve and include the poor as well. Carving out time each week for the Lord and for others fights against the trends of our secular culture to focus only on oneself and one's own entertainment. John Paul II spoke of living Sunday distinctly as one way of bringing our faith into the world: "It is with this strong conviction of faith, and with awareness of the heritage of human values which the observance of Sunday entails, that Christians today must face the enticements of a culture which has accepted the benefits of rest and free time, but which often uses them frivolously and is at times attracted by morally questionable forms of entertainment."[23]

One particular environment created for the leisure of the Lord's Day can be found in German beer gardens, which created an outdoor, family friendly environment for Sunday picnics. We tend to think of alcohol as an antifamily force, but in the Catholic cultures of northern Europe this was not the case. Following their example, we need to re-center drinking within a Christian and familial environment. Beer had a central place in family gatherings, served with food and in the context of fellowship and Sunday festivity. Pope Francis speaks of the family as a leaven that can transform the world: "If we were — beginning with the Church — to center our attention on the family that listens to and practices the Word of God,

---

[22] Nelson, *Barbarian's Beverage*, 97.

[23] See John Paul II, *Dies Domini*, apostolic letter, Vatican website, July 30, 1998, http://w2.vatican.va/content/john-paul-ii/en/apost_letters/1998/documents/hf_jp-ii_apl_05071998_dies-domini.html.

we would become like the good wine of the wedding feast of Cana, we would ferment like the leaven of God."[24] The family provides the surest foundation for rebuilding a complete and integrated Christian culture.

The Dutch genre painter, Jan Steen (1626–79), whose father was a brewer, gives us a glimpse of a healthy drinking culture and the kind of environment we could form. We see people gathering over drinks and music with their families. The setting clearly points to the opportunities for groups of families to have fellowship and to encounter each other, rather than simply remaining isolated within their own home.

Jan Steen, *Merrymaking in a Tavern* (1674). (Wikimedia Commons)

---

[24] Pope Francis, General Audience, "Evangelization" (September 2, 2015), http://w2.vatican.va/content/francesco/en/audiences/2015/documents/papa-francesco_20150902_udienza-generale.html.

Jan Steen, *Tavern Garden* (1660). (Wikimedia Commons)

We need more places for families to gather and celebrate together, places that are more wholesome environments than bars. Bars emphasize electronic entertainment, pairing off and hooking up, and excessive drinking. Gardens and picnics with multiple families emphasize the community, outdoor leisure and recreation, and the proper balance of eating and drinking.

Within my own community in the Archdiocese of Denver, there are a number of positive signs of an emerging Catholic beer culture. There are a few beer gardens; one that I visited with my children included outdoor games. Here are some other initiatives that are creating a positive beer culture:

- Theology on Tap is sponsored by the Office of Evangelization and Family Life Ministries of the Archdiocese of Denver (where I work). It meets monthly at the Irish Snug downtown, with almost two hundred attendees. Denver also has an active Catholic Beer Club.
- A brewing group at Holy Name of Jesus Church serves beer for parish events, including a robust Oktoberfest to help "reconnect inactive Catholics to their faith and . . . [to help] non-Catholics decide to join the faith inquiry program at their local Catholic parish."[25]
- Dominican and Capuchin Franciscan friars brews for parish and city events, such as Oktoberfest. A Dominican friar has also blessed local breweries.
- The Jesuit university, Regis, offers a certificate in Applied Craft Brewing, directed by Matthew Peetz, a local Catholic who co-founded Inland Island Yeast Laboratories, which supplies yeast to many of the major craft brewers in Colorado.
- A classics professor at the University of Colorado, Travis Rupp, serves as the resident beer archeologist at Avery Brewery in Boulder. He designs an ongoing series called Ales of Antiquity, recreating ancient styles, including a Beersheba style to correspond with the traveling Dead Sea Scrolls exhibit in 2018. He also visited the monks in Norcia in 2017 for inspiration to create a monastic-style beer.
- A group of young families visit breweries after Sunday Mass, calling their gathering "Breweries and Babies."
- A new Catholic-owned brewery, De Steeg, opened in Denver in 2013 and has recently expanded to produce Blind Faith Beer.

I had the opportunity to meet the owners of De Steeg and Blind Faith and hosted a wonderful evening with them to promote a beer pilgrimage. Ken Klispie and Tom Martinez met as members of the Knights of Columbus at Our Lady of Fatima in Lakewood, Colorado, and started brewing for parish events. They decided to focus on brewing for charitable events and raised money to purchase ultrasound machines, four of which were sent to the Congo. As they continued to brew successfully, they decided to start their own brewery, and in the fall of 2017, they purchased De

---

[25] Kevin Jones, "Colorado Parish Cultivates 'New Evangelization' Spirit," *Catholic News Agency*, October 25, 2013, https://www.catholicnewsagency.com/news/colorado-parish-cultivates-new-evangelization-spirit.

Steeg (The Alley) brewery and added another line of beers called Blind
Faith Brewing. They told me they seek to emulate monastic brewing,
not just with their Belgian style beers, but with hospitality, offering high
quality, nutritious beers and a welcoming place to gather.

The *Denver Catholic* newspaper featured Blind Faith Brewing, so
called because Martinez lost his sight while they were working to start
their own brewery:

> This step of trust and faith strengthened the vision they had for the
> brewery, one that followed the monastic tradition of beer quality and
> evangelization through hospitality. "We see [our work] as a way to
> evangelize. We do it through the way we run our business, the way
> we name the beer and the conversations we have," Martinez said.
> "Every single day we end up talking about the faith with someone
> that comes in. Friendships lead to conversations about God and the
> Church." Both men hope to increase capacity without compromising
> quality to get the beer out to the market and expand to a bigger
> location. They also hope to become well-known to the Catholic
> community in town and one day be the official beer sponsors of the
> Archdiocese of Denver.
>
> "I always remind myself of those opportunities where we can
> actually show the community what we are all about and be evange-
> lists in a subtle way," Martinez said. "So that when people leave our
> taproom, for some reason they may not be able to put their finger
> on, they say, 'That was a good experience. Those guys made me
> feel good. I want to get some more of that.' Then we open a door to
> [talk about the faith]. People grow in interest of what we're all about
> because of what they've experienced."[26]

Through all of these initiatives, Catholics in Denver have used beer
to create encounters with others. In the midst of one of the most vibrant
beer cultures in the country, Denver has also seen the rise of a new
Catholic beer culture, using beer to promote a renewal of fellowship
and evangelization.

[26] Vladimir Mauricio-Perez, "Blind Faith Brewing: The New Catholic Taproom in Town," *Denver Catholic*, March 1, 2018, http://denvercatholic.org/
blind-faith-brewing-new-catholic-taproom-town/.

## CHAPTER 12

# A Pilgrimage through Monastic Beer

The famous Colorado beer, Fat Tire, is named for an epic bike ride that Jeff Lebesch, co-founder of the New Belgium Brewery, took through the Belgian countryside. He took the trip for inspiration and to sample the great beers, including the Trappists'. Three young ladies from Texas felt inspired to hop on a plane to do their own epic tour of all the world's Trappist breweries, spanning Belgium, the Netherlands, Austria, Italy, and the United States. They recount their travels and describe all eleven breweries in *Trappist Beer Travels: Inside the Breweries of the Monasteries*.[1] In the fall of 2018, I will be leading a beer pilgrimage, called "Saints, Monks, and Beer," through France and Belgium, visiting two Benedictine brewing monasteries and three Trappist ones. The pilgrimage will offer a holistic experience of Catholic culture: we will visit Gothic churches and the Louvre, pray with the monks, venerate relics of saints, and sample monastic beer.

The Beer Hunter, Michael Jackson (not the singer), served as my first docent through the world of beer with his *Great Beer Guide: 500 Classic Brews*. The book helped me to discover my first monastic beers and to sample a variety of styles from around the world. For those who cannot travel on an actual beer pilgrimage, here I present thirty good beers with connections to monks and the Catholic tradition. Not all of them still have monks as their brewers, but most have at least historical connections with Benedictines, Norbertines, Augustinians, or Franciscans. Many of these beers have dates representing the oldest breweries in the world, but there are some new ones as well. I focus mainly on beers that are accessible in the United States, but have included some that are more difficult to find.

---

[1] Caroline Wallace, Sarah Wood, and Jessica Deahl, *Trappist Beer Travels: Inside the Breweries of the Monasteries* (Atglen, PA: Schiffer, 2017).

## TYPES OF MONASTIC BEER

Before beginning this tour of monastic beer, we need to lay out some terms. Not all of the beers on my list are brewed by monks, but many are. Two of the styles require an official certification: Trappist and Belgian Abbey beers. In addition to these official designations, I will also present beers brewed directly by monks, others brewed in a cooperative with monks, some with a historical connection to a monastery, and a few that simply have a monastic theme.

The most famous of the monastic beers, of course, are the Trappist beers, and any tour of Catholic beer must begin with them. The Trappists are considered by many beer experts to be the best brewers in the world. "Trappist" is the nickname for the Cistercians of the Strict Observance,

Trappist beers. (Wikimedia Commons)

a reform movement begun at the Abbey of La Trappe, France, in 1664 (separating from the broader group of Cistercians in 1892). The original Cistercians were a Benedictine reform movement, begun at Citeaux in France by Robert of Molesme and Stephen Harding (though St. Bernard launched the reform across Europe). Thus, both Trappists and Cistercians are part of the Benedictine family of monks. The great Trappist brewers are rooted in Belgium, but additional Trappist abbeys in Europe and the United States have recently begun brewing.

Although the Trappist monks themselves generally do not brew, "they play an active role in the brewery operation. They sit on the board of administrators, hold all the shares of the separate brewing company, and control the investment of charitable decisions."[2] They follow the general principles of limiting production, preserving traditional recipes, and using

---

[2]  Hieronymus, *Brew like a Monk*, 69.

"low profile" advertising.[3] The one Trappist abbey where the monks do all the brewing themselves is the highly admired Westvleteren brewery. An Authentic Trappist Product is an official and trademark-protected designation, requiring that the product, beer or otherwise, be made within the monastery walls, controlled by the monastery (policies and the means of production must follow Catholic social teaching), and used to support the monastery and other charitable causes. In 2011, only seven Trappist breweries existed in Belgium and the Netherlands, but five additional breweries have sprung up in the Netherlands, Austria, Italy, the United States, and England.

Following the introduction of a Trappist certification, the Belgian Brewers trade organization introduced the trademarked title, "Certified Belgian Abbey Beer." The beer must "have a link with an existing or former abbey, pay royalties for charities or to protect the cultural heritage of the abbey, or... benefit an institution that represents a former abbey. The abbey or existing institution has control over advertising material."[4] This certification comes with a logo for the beer label and applies to about eighteen beers. The beer can be brewed directly by a non-Trappist abbey or by an independent brewery that has obtained a license from an abbey. There is also a requirement that the abbey have a history of brewing.[5]

There are also a number of monastic beers in Germany, the Czech Republic, England, and the United States that are brewed directly by monks. The monks may or may not conduct all of the brewing themselves, but they control an on-site brewery or form a cooperative with an established secular brewery, with varying levels of involvement by the monks.

Similar to some of the Belgian Abbey beers there are also secularized monastic breweries with historical ties to monks. Sometimes the secular brewery uses the same name and brewing location as the monastery, and claims the entire history of the monastic brewery as their own. There are a large number of these breweries in Germany, which use the name Klosterbrauerei.

3 Ibid., 70.
4 Ibid., 95.
5 See "Collective Marks," Belgian Brewers, accessed Aug. 5, 2018, http://belgianbrewers.be/en/beer-culture/the-art-of-beer/article/collective-marks.

There are also a large number of brewers, particularly in Belgium and the United States, that name their beers after monastic themes or breweries. They make a deliberate connection to Catholic and monastic history. We also find some reconstructed medieval monastic recipes on the market from secular brewers.

A decent liquor store will have a good number of these beers, but an online store specializing in monastic products, Monastery Greetings, sells some of the harder-to-find beers with limited distribution (BelgianStyle-Ales.com).

## A TOUR OF THIRTY MONASTIC BEERS

The following list presents my personal ranking of the top thirty beers with a connection to the monastic brewing tradition. These beers present the full range of countries, religious orders, levels of monastic involvement, styles, and ages of breweries (stretching from the Middle Ages to the last few years). As a whole, they tell the story of the evolution of the monastic brewing tradition and invite you to enter it through your senses.

### 30. ABITA ABBEY ALE
ABITA BEER, COVINGTON, LOUISIANA

In Louisiana, known for its Catholic culture, Abita Abbey Ale brings brewing and monasticism together. The Abbey Ale is brewed in the Belgian monastic tradition and supports a local Benedictine Monastery. The brewery describes the beer as part of its effort to give back to the community:

> Abita Abbey Ale honors the ancient traditions of monks who perfected the art of brewing beer to support the monastery. Abita offers up their support and thanks to the brothers at nearby St. Joseph's Abbey and Seminary College in Covington, Louisiana with a 25-cent donation with every bottle sold of this heavenly brew. The program has raised thousands of dollars for the local monastery, which has provided educational, cultural and spiritual support to those in need for over 100 years.[6]

---

[6] "Giving Back," Abita, accessed March 18, 2018, https://abita.com/about/giving-back#.

The beer is bottle-conditioned and has an aroma of caramel, fruit, and cloves. A famous Benedictine oblate of St. Joseph's, Walker Percy, would be pleased, even though he may have preferred a Gin Fizz.

## 29. LEFFE BLOND
### AB INBEV, LEUVEN, BELGIUM

Leffe is one of the best known and most widely distributed Certified Belgian Abbey Beers. The Norbertine Abbey Notre Dame de Leffe in Dinant entered into one of the first formal licensing agreements with a commercial brewery in 1952.[7] Brewed alongside Stella Artois, it is currently owned by the world's largest brewer, AB InBev, giving it a wide profile. The blond is described as smooth and subtle with a slightly high ABV (alcohol by volume) at 6.6 percent. The beer dates to the 1950s when Father Abbot Nys decided to resurrect the abbey's brewery (which had been closed by the French Revolution) and created this beer that he thought, with its golden color, shone brighter than the sun.

## 28. KORBINIAN
### WEIHENSTEPHANER, FREISING, GERMANY

Weihenstephaner makes the list simply as the oldest brewery in the world, dating from at least 1040, though probably dating back farther, especially since hops were mentioned there already in 768. It was secularized in 1803 and remains in the possession of the Bavarian state. This beer honors the bear-riding bishop St. Corbinian (d. 730), who established the Benedictine monastery outside of Freising. The brewery, which still operates in the old monastery buildings, describes this beer as a "full-bodied, dark Doppelbock with light brown foam, [which] wins beer-lovers over with a balance of fruity hints of plums and figs, a dark malt aroma — reminiscent of toffee, nuts and chocolate.... Brewed according to our centuries-old brewing tradition on the Weihenstephan hill."[8] For Pope Benedict's eightieth birthday, the Auxiliary Bishop of

---

7  Hieronymus, *Brew like a Monk*, 96.
8  "Korbinian," Weihenstephaner, accessed March 18, 2018, https://www.weihenstephaner.de/en/our-beers/our-korbinian/.

Munich brought him eighty bottles of this beer![9] It was a good choice as Pope Benedict honored St. Corbinian by placing the bear he rode over the Alps on his coat of arms when he was chosen as Archbishop of Munich-Freising, succeeding the saint in this see.

## 27. 1554
NEW BELGIUM, FT. COLLINS, COLORADO

The beer 1554, modern yet built with a medieval recipe, has a fascinating story:

> In 1997, a Fort Collins flood destroyed the original recipe our researcher, Phil Benstein, found in the library. So Phil and [our] brewmaster, Peter Bouckaert, traveled to Belgium to retrieve this unique style lost to the ages. Their first challenge was deciphering antiquated script and outdated units of measurement, but trial and error (and many months of in-house sampling) culminated in 1554, a highly quaffable dark beer with a moderate body and mouthfeel.[10]

Stan Hieronymus describes how there is even more to the story, with Bouckaert, now of Purpose Brewing, bringing his own heritage to the beer: "'Belgian born and raised' [he] was destined by his parents to be either a priest or a brewer. Beyond the ancient recipe of this beer, he describes it as 'trying to create a piece of beauty,' based on 'Knowledge, Experience, and Creativity.'"[11] New Belgium has led the charge to bring Belgian and monastic style beers to prominence in the United States.

## 26. AMPLEFORTH ABBEY BEER
AMPLEFORTH ABBEY, ENGLAND

Benedictine monasticism received a deathblow during the English Reformation, when Henry VIII confiscated monastic lands. English monks

---

[9] "80 bottles of beer for Benedict XVI," *Welt*, March 14, 2007, https://www.welt.de/regionales/muenchen/article761037/80-Flaschen-Bier-fuer-Benedikt-XVI.html.

[10] "1554," New Belgium, accessed May 16, 2018, http://www.newbelgium.com/beer/1554.

[11] Hieronymus, *Brew like a Monk*, 207.

regrouped in France and Belgium, including the monks of Ampleforth who brewed a *bière anglaise* in De Dieulouard, France. They returned to England in 1802 (fleeing Napoleon and welcomed back home by his enemies), though it took them until 2012 to get the brewery going again. The monks worked with a Dutch company, Wim van der Spek, and created a dark, bottle-fermented, Trappist-style ale with a connection to their historic recipe. Though it is only available locally, it has earned a wider reputation through its many awards.

## 25. AFFLIGEM BLONDE
### HEINEKEN, OPWIJK, BELGIUM

Former knights turned Benedictine monks founded the monastery of Affligem in 1074, which has a long history of brewing and hop production.[12] In 1580 the abbey suffered destruction from Protestant forces under William of Orange. Much later, during World War II, the monks' brewing kettles were stolen by German troops. After the war, the monks turned to the De Smet Brewery for help, where the abbey beer was produced until it was taken over by Heineken, who more than tripled sales in the first three years of ownership.[13] The abbey ensured that the recipe was a "renovated" version of the medieval ones, and now uses the proceeds of the beer to support a youth farm. The Blonde ale is unfiltered and bottle-conditioned, aiming to be balanced and refreshing, with notes of banana, yeasty spice, and a hoppy aroma.

## 24. VAL-DIEU GRAND CRU
### BRASSERIE DE L'ABBAYE DU VAL-DIEU, AUBEL, BELGIUM

Val-Dieu claims to be the only Certified Abbey Beer still brewed within a living monastery in Belgium. Once a full-fledged Cistercian Abbey, the buildings now host a secular (lay) group affiliated with the Cistercians known as the Christian Community of Val-Dieu. Some members of this small community live on-site and others work at the abbey, where they continue praying the Liturgy of the Hours. The abbey dates to 1216,

---

[12] Ibid., 97.
[13] Ibid., 95.

reclaiming an area known once as the Valley of the Devil, but renamed the Valley of God — Val-Dieu in French. The abbey survived the French Revolution and the on-site brewery uses traditional recipes. The term Grand Cru has been borrowed from highly regarded vineyards and in the beer lexicon refers to higher quality and elaborate styles. Val-Dieu's Grand Cru is a rich and powerful dark ale with 10.5% ABV, offering complex aromas and a tangy taste. Val-Dieu offers regular tours of its basilica, brewery, and gardens, runs a restaurant, and also makes cheese and cider.

## 23. SAINT-WANDRILLE
### ABBAYE ST. WANDRILLE, FRANCE

Wandrille has an ancient history, dating back to 649, and is rich in holiness, having formed thirty saints. I have already noted that one of the oldest recorded mentions of hopped beer occurred here and its medieval cloister displays the plant in a stone relief. Therefore, it seemed natural for the abbey to return to brewing in 2016, producing a "deeply coloured pale ale with a good hoppy flavour, smooth and refreshing, made at the abbey from cereals and hops grown only in France. This is the only beer in France to be produced by monks within their monastery."[14] Two monks were trained as master brewers, though other monks served as taste testers to fine tune the recipe.

## 22. GRIMBERGEN ROUGE
### ALKEN-MAES, ALKEN, BELGIUM

This Certified Belgian Abbey Beer arose when the Alken-Maes brewery approached an extant Norbertine abbey at Grimbergen and proposed brewing an abbey beer together. St. Norbert founded the monastery himself in 1128, which exhibited a long tradition of brewing, lasting at least until 1797. Although Alken-Maes has grown since being acquired by Heineken, the monks plan to go small and return to their roots by starting a microbrew in the old monastic brewery by 2020, though they are still searching their records for an original recipe. The beer has a monastic

---

[14] "A Beer Brewed by Monks," Abbey Saint Wandrille, accessed May 16, 2018, https://st-wandrille.com/en/32-english/the-abbey/74-beer-brewed-by-the-monks.

motto *Ardet nec consumitur*, "burned but not destroyed," symbolized by a phoenix. The Rouge beer is colored with red fruit, but balances its strawberry aromas with flavors of clove and spiciness.

## 21. MAREDSOUS 8 (BRUNE)
### MOORTGAT, PUURS, BELGIUM

Maredsous is a Benedictine abbey founded in 1872 during the Benedictine rival of the late nineteenth century. This beer is close to my heart because of the great abbot Bl. Columba Marmion. Marmion, a Dublin-born diocesan priest, received an extraordinary call to this Belgian abbey, becoming not only its abbot but an internationally renowned retreat director and writer. *Union with God*, one of my favorite spiritual books, contains excerpts from his letters of spiritual direction that combine practical advice with a deep Christ-centered spirituality. In 1963, the family-owned brewery Duvel Moortgat obtained a license from Maredsous to begin brewing abbey beer. Ironically, *Duvel*, one of Belgium's most popular beers, is named after the devil, as an early taster remarked, "It was a devil of a beer." One of Maredsous's monks, Fr. Atout, formulated the current recipes, using records from the abbey library. Maredsous Brune (brown) is a dark abbey-style beer and has a creamy head, a dark burgundy color, and a caramel bouquet with fruity touches.

## 20. EDELSTOFF
### AUGUSTINER-BRÄU, MUNICH, GERMANY

Although now under secular control, Augustiner-Bräu is the oldest monastic brewery in Munich, founded by the Augustinians in 1328. It was secularized in 1803 and purchased by the Wagner family, who renovated the monastery buildings and built a large beer hall, the "Zum Augustiner." The brewery retains traditions such as oak-barreled draft beer and traditional floor malting (done by turning over a thin layer of barley every eight hours on a limestone floor). The brewery also strives to maintain a traditional vision: "We are concerned with the outstanding quality of our beer, with tradition and with our roots in Munich. Our restaurants and beer gardens — including the 'Augustiner Keller' and the 'Hirschgarten' — are places of the conviviality and the comfort that are long since typical of Munich."[15] Edelstoff is their export beer, described as both "sparkling" and "fresh," and an example of "the old Bavarian brewing art."

## 19. SINT STEFANUS BLONDE
### VAN STEENBERGE, ERTVELDE, BELGIUM

Another ancient example of Augustinian brewing dates back to 1295 and can be found in Ghent, Belgium, with St. Stefanus. There is still a connection to an existing monastery, though this Certified Belgian Abbey Beer is brewed by the family-owned Van Steenberge Brewery, just north of Ghent. The beer has traditionally been called Augustijn, though it has been marketed as Sint Stefanus to avoid a trademark dispute with Augustiner-Bräu. The abbey and the brewery claim a strong relationship with and a commitment to preserving traditional brewing methods, including using a wild yeast. Sint Stefanus is a strong golden ale that, already cellared at the brewery, can continue to mature in the bottle. Speaking of the bottle, it has a beautiful cap with Augustine's heart transfixed by an arrow and an attractive label with the brewer's signature.

## 18. BENEDIKTINER WEISSBIER NATURTRÜB
### ETTAL ABBEY AND LICHER BRAUEREI, LICH, GERMANY

Ettal Abbey was founded in 1330 by the Emperor Louis IV. In the late Middle Ages, it operated a brewery in the Bavarian village of Oberammergau, founding its own monastery brewery in 1609. The abbey continues to brew on its grounds for German and Austrian distribution and partners with Licher Brauerei for other exports. The monastery uses its traditional recipe as well as its Ettaler cellar yeast that imparts a fruity taste. The monks are directly involved in the brewing both on-site and at Licher, conducting taste tests with the "monk glass." The monastery specializes in wheat beers and its Naturtrüb is a hefeweizen, known for its cloudiness. The monks describe it as making *dem Himmel so nah* (heaven so close).

---

[15] "About Us," Augustiner-Bräu München, accessed May 17, 2018, https://www.augustiner-braeu.de/en/home/about-us.html.

Christ in the Desert Monastery. (Wikimedia Commons)`

## 17. MONKS' ALE
### ABBEY BREWING COMPANY, ABIQUIU, NEW MEXICO

In 2003 the monks of Christ in the Desert Monastery became the first American brewing monks since Prohibition. They have since stepped back from the Abbey Brewing Company, but a small brewery remains on their property. Most of the beer is now brewed through an alternating proprietorship, allowing Abbey Brewing to control the brewing process at a larger brewer's facilities. Their main beer, Monks' Ale, is a patersbier, a style traditionally reserved for the monks' consumption. The beer strives for balance and drinkability, "with a distinct aroma of cloves and moderate fruity esters (particularly stone fruits). The yeast lends a note of clove and, in combination with the malts, hints of plum and apricot. The malts provide a distinct honeyish quality up front and [a] round, full middle. The malts and yeast leave a clean, crisp, dry finish."[16]

---

[16] "Monks' Ale," Abbey Brewing Co., accessed May 17, 2018, https://www.abbey-brewing.biz/monks-ale/.

## 16. BLACK HABIT ALE
BENEDICTINE BREWERY, MOUNT ANGEL ABBEY, OREGON

Mount Angel is one of the few monasteries in the United States to brew beer, beginning in 2014 with their flagship beer, Black Habit, a Belgian strong dark ale (7.8% ABV). It has been described as sweet and fluffy (think oatmeal), with a hint of maple syrup. The monastery began brewing at Seven Brides Brewery with the help of beer writers Jeff Alworth (*The Beer Bible*) and Stan Hieronymus (*Brew Like a Monk*). The monks now have a new brewery on-site, next to hop fields. The abbey runs a seminary, has beautiful hiking nearby (especially Silver Creek Falls), and hosts annual cultural events such as the Abbey Bach Festival and the Saint Benedict Festival in July.

Weltenburg Abbey and beer garden. (Wikimedia Commons)

## 15. WELTENBURGER KLOSTER BAROCK DUNKEL
WELTENBURGER KLOSTERBRÄUEREI, KELHEIM, GERMANY

Weltenburg Abbey sits at the entrance of a beautiful gorge on the Danube River, offering a popular guest house for boaters. It was founded by Irish monks sent by St. Columban in 600, making it Bavaria's oldest monastery. St. Boniface brought the *Rule of St. Benedict* there in the eighth century. The first documentation of the monastery's brewery comes from 1050, making it the world's oldest monastic beer, and a mere ten years younger than the secularized Weihenstephaner. Their baroque dunkel (dark), a classic Bavarian style, won the World Beer Cup for best dunkel in 2004, 2008, and 2012. It is a dark lager with a low alcohol content of 4.7 percent, which should be enjoyed in the beer garden next to the monastery's baroque buildings! The kloster (cloister) beer is brewed both at the abbey and in Regensburg by the Bischofshof Brewery.

## 14. LA TRAPPE QUADRUPEL
### KONINGSHOEVEN BREWERY, BERKEL-ENSCHOT, NETHERLANDS

La Trappe is one of two Trappist beers in the Netherlands, brewed by the Koningshoeven Abbey, but named for La Trappe Abbey in France, the first Trappist monastery. The brewery dates to 1884, but between 1969 and 1979 the abbey had a partnership with Stella Artois. It returned to brewing again in 1980 and now produces more beers than any other Trappist brand, including a doppelbock named Ora et Labora. Between 1999 and 2005, however, the Authentic Trappist label was temporarily revoked due to an arrangement with the Bavaria Brewery to run the abbey's brewery. La Trappe is best known for its quadrupel, introducing this style for the first time in 1991. It has an alcohol level of 10 percent and is described as "the heaviest ale of La Trappe Trappist ales and is eponymous of this ale style. A full, warming and intensive taste. Malty with the sweet tones of date and caramel."[17]

## 13. ENGELSZELL GREGORIUS
### STIFT ENGELSZELL, ENGELHARTSZELL AN DER DONAU, AUSTRIA

The Stift Engelszell, a Trappist abbey in Austria, began brewing in 2012 and names its beers for the abbey's former abbots: Benno (a dubbel), Gregorius (a strong dark ale), and Nivard (a Belgian dark ale). The abbey, located along the Danube river, dates to 1293, but its beautiful rococo church was completed in 1764. The monks have insisted on creating unique beers that represent their *terroir* and ecological commitment. For instance, the Gregorius "presents itself with a deep dark chestnut color. Honey from the region and the vinous character of the French-Alsacian wine yeast create stunning sweet-sour notes on the palate. A slightly tart chocolate-fragrance is accompanying the warming

---

[17] "La Trappe Quadrupel," La Trappe Trappist, accessed May 18, 2018, https://www.latrappetrappist.com/en/our-trappist-ales/la-trappe-quadrupel/.

Abbey Church of Engelszell. (Wikimedia Commons)

finish of this solid Trappist beer."[18] With its herbal and licorice aroma, the monks describe it as deep and thoughtful. Another more amber colored beer seeks to mirror the "stunning reflection of the amazing colors of a sunny day in autumn in the Danube valley."

## 12. ANDECHSER VOLLBIER HELL
### KLOSTER ANDECHS, GERMANY

Benedictines came to the oldest pilgrimage church on Bavaria's Holy Mountain in 1455. The monastery has preserved its traditional methods to this day, especially multiple mashing and a two-tank method, but have also continually modernized, adding steam power in 1871, building a new and larger brewer at the foot of the hill in 1984, and adding state-of-the-art technology and greater efficiency in 2006. A Helles Vollbier literally means a "bright, full beer." Andechs's version presents with a bright straw yellow color and is imbued with floral hoppiness.

---

[18] "Stift Engelszell," Authentic Trappist Product, accessed May 18, 2018, http://www.trappist.be/en/pages/trappist-beers-engelszell.html.

"Its light and soft body leaves a pleasant, tangy taste in the mouth. The mild sweetness marries well with the velvety bitterness of the hops. It concludes on a rounded, harmonious note."[19] The abbey describes their beer as a "delight for body and soul."

Cardinal Ratzinger, his brother Georg (left), and the Abbot of Andechs. KNA. Used with permision.

## 11. SPENCER TRAPPIST ALE
### SPENCER BREWERY, ST. JOSEPH'S ABBEY, SPENCER, MASSACHUSETTS

In 2014, St. Joseph's Abbey launched the first Trappist beer in the Americas and has since built a fairly large brewery on the grounds. They began with a simple Trappist-style patersbier or enkel (single), used by the monks for their own consumption and generally not sold to the public. The abbey describes the beer as follows: "These sessionable beers are brewed by the monks for their dinner table and are typically only available at the monastery. Spencer is a full-bodied, golden-hued ale with fruity accents, a dry finish, and light hop bitterness. The beer is unfiltered and unpasteurized, preserving live yeast that naturally

19 "Andechser Vollbier Hell," Kloster Andechs, accessed May 18, 2018, http:// andechs.de/en/brewery/our-beer-specialities/vollbier-hell/.

A Brewing Monk of St. Joseph's Abbey. Photograph courtesy of Spencer Brewery.

carbonates the beer in the bottle and keg and contributes to the beer flavor and aroma."[20] We can be grateful to Spencer for bringing Trappist beer across the Atlantic!

## 10. TRE FONTANE TRIPEL
### TRE FONTANE ABBEY, ROME, ITALY

Tre Fontane was raised on the spot where St. Paul was beheaded, and marks the burial places for the martyrs St. Zeno, St. Vincent, and St. Anastasius. It is one of the oldest Benedictine sites in the world, with monks dwelling there since 626. It has historical associations with Charlemagne, the monks of Cluny, and St. Bernard, who brought it into the Cistercian movement. The now Trappist abbey also has the distinction of raising the lambs whose wool is used to make the pallium for archbishops throughout the world. In 2015, the monks added brewing to this illustrious history, making a beer with their trademark ingredient eucalyptus, which adds fruity and herbal notes. It has a high alcohol content at 8 percent, and has a stiff bitterness and dry finish. The abbey also makes a beer jelly, combining ricotta, honey, burrata, gorgonzola, and beer to produce it.

---

[20] "Spencer Trappist Ale," Spencer Brewery, accessed May 18, 2018, https://spencerbrewery.com/index.php/our-beers/spencer-trappist-ale.

## 9. OVILA WHITE ALE
SIERRA NEVADA, CHICO, CALIFORNIA

One of the most successful craft brewers in the United States, Sierra Nevada, has entered a collaboration with New Clairvaux Trappist Abbey in California to brew a series of monastic-style beers. The proceeds are helping to reconstruct the chapter house of the medieval Spanish monastery of Óvila on New Clairvaux's grounds. Sierra Nevada has been experimenting with various monastic styles, such as the dubbel and quadrupel and has on occasion infused them with fruit, such as plum and peach. In 2018, they featured a Belgian wit, the white, wheat style flavored with coriander and orange peels (popularized in the US by Coors's Blue Moon). In my opinion, Ovila, "blending Old World tradition and modern-day mastery," is the best monastery-related beer in the United States. The abbey also runs New Clairvaux vineyards, working with a local vintner to continue the Cistercians distinguished wine-making tradition.

## 8. SALVATOR DOPPELBOCK
PAULANER BRAUEREI, MUNICH, GERMANY

Paulaner is named for St. Francis Paola, the Italian founder of the Franciscan Friars Minim, a strict reform movement. Strictness notwithstanding, the friars began brewing in 1634, holding to the maxim that liquids do not break the fast. Salvator (Latin for "savior") was developed as a bock style Lenten beer to strengthen the friars during the fast. It is the most traditional and strongest of all the Paulaner beers at 7.9% ABV. It has a chestnut brown color, exhibits a chocolate flavor, with a balance of maltiness and sweetness. For centuries, the first batch of the Lenten season has been ceremonially presented for approval to the head of the Bavarian state (once the royal family but now the Minister President) during the Holy Father Feast, which lasts from the feast of St. Joseph on March 19 to the feast of St. Francis Paolo on April 2. Salvator is served in a distinctive earthenware beer stein, which depicts this annual beer ceremony (and can also be seen on the Salvator label).

Eduard Ille, *Frater Barnabas Offers Salvator Beer to Elector Karl Theodor* (c. 1890). (Wikimedia Commons)

## 7. BIRRA NURSIA EXTRA
### IL MONASTERO DI SAN BENEDETTO, NORCIA, ITALY

The monks of the Monastery of St. Benedict in Norcia, Italy, have featured prominently in this book for reviving monasticism in St. Benedict's hometown, preserving traditional monastic and liturgical practices, and using monastic brewing for evangelization. Their plans have shifted in light of a major earthquake and they are now reestablishing themselves in the mountains outside of Norcia while working to build a new brewery. Br. Augustine Wilmeth, the brewmaster, verifies that the brewery is operated exclusively by monks. The monks brew both a Blonde and an Extra. The Extra is a Belgian strong dark ale, at 10 percent alcohol, and is described on birranursia.com, where it can be purchased, as having "a beguiling dark brown hue with luminous ruby reflections and a creamy, frothy head. Its aroma is characterized by notes of fresh yeast, dark berries and stone fruits, embellished with a touch of cocoa. It is a well-structured beer dominated by malty flavors with hints of caramel and liqueur, rounded off by a warm, dry and peppery finish."[21]

## 6. ST. BERNARDUS ABT 12
### ST. BERNARDUS BREWERY, WATOU, BELGIUM

St. Bernardus has a strong link to the Trappist tradition. From 1945 until 1992 it brewed the St. Sixtus Beers for the Trappist abbey that now brews the world-famous Westvleteren beers. The brewery sought to continue that link by depicting a Trappist monk on its bottles, but were forced by the International Trappist Association to switch to a non-descript habited monk as their logo. St. Bernardus Abt 12 is probably the most highly regarded of any of the Belgian abbey beers, due to its direct continuity with Trappist beer, though it is not a Certified Belgian Abbey Beer. The brewery describes the Abt 12 as their *nec plus ultra*, a dark, strong ale at 10% ABV, calling it "a very balanced beer, with a full-bodied taste and a perfect equilibrium between malty, bitter and sweet."[22] It is rightly considered one of the best beers in the world and an easier way to get close, at least, to the elusive Westvleteren 12.

---

[21] "Purchase," Birra Nursia, accessed June 4, 2018, https://birranursia.com/purchase/.

[22] "St. Bernardus Abt 12," St. Bernardus Watou, accessed May 19, 2018, http://www.sintbernardus.be/stbernardusabt12.php?l=en.

## 5. ROCHEFORT 10
ROCHEFORT BREWERY, ABBEY OF NOTRE-DAME DE SAINT-RÉMY, ROCHEFORT, BELGIUM

The abbey was founded originally for Cistercian nuns in 1230, though monks later replaced them and began brewing in 1595. The monastery's motto, *Curvata Resurgo*, refers to its perseverance through the ravages of the Reformation and French Revolution, continuing to arise, even when bent down. The motto still applies as the abbey recently rebuilt after a devastating fire in 2010. Their three beers are unique in that they employ a traditional method to brew the same style of beer in three different strengths. They refer to the three beers with distinct numbers: 6, 8, and 10 (marked by caps of red, green, and blue, respectively). The numbers refer to the original gravity of the beers in Belgian degrees. Rochefort 10, or Blue Cap, was first brewed around 1950, and has been consistently considered one of the best beers in the world. It has a high alcohol content at 11.3 percent, a dark brown color, a firm body, vigorous and complex flavor, and a bouquet reminiscent of port wine, leather, apricots, oak, and spice.

## 4. WESTMALLE TRAPPIST TRIPEL
WESTMALLE BREWERY, ABBEY OF OUR LADY OF THE SACRED HEART, WESTMALLE, BELGIUM

Westmalle pioneered innovative styles in the Trappist tradition to create our featured Tripel in 1931. Since then, the brewery has helped to establish and support many other Trappist breweries. The name "tripel" probably referred to the fact that it was the monastery's third beer, but the names single, double, and triple traditionally refer to strengths, which were indicated by the symbols X, XX, and XXX. The abbey was founded in 1794 (a year after the reign of terror) as a refuge for monks fleeing the French Revolution, though they still had to flee Napoleon. The monks began brewing in 1836 and innovated many Trappist brewing techniques, such as using pure liquid Belgian candi sugar to increase alcohol content. The Westmalle Tripel is the exemplar of the style: a strong pale ale, at 9.5% ABV, with an herbal and candied orange aroma and a rich malt sweetness.

## 3. CHIMAY GRANDE RÉSERVE (BLUE)
CHIMAY BREWERY, NOTRE DAME DE SCOURMONT ABBEY, CHIMAY,
BELGIUM

Chimay is the best known and easiest to find of all the Trappist beers. The abbey was founded in 1850, with a farm, dairy, and brewery following. Their flagship beer, the Blue, was created by the famous Père Théodore as a Christmas beer in 1948, but its popularity encouraged the monks to produce it year-round. Fr. Théodore (who worked with the brewing scientist from the Catholic University of Louvain, Jean de Clerck, to revive the brewery) also isolated the Chimay yeast strain, displaying his Benedictine patience. Chimay has a history of helping other monasteries, and Fr. Théodore and de Clerck were kept busy across Belgium. Today Chimay remains the most successful of the Trappist breweries, with over two hundred employees.

I usually introduce people to monastic beers through Chimay Blue (Grande Réserve) and I have not yet found anyone who has not liked it. It is described as a dark and strong ale (9% ABV), with rich flavors of mulling spices and caramel, a smooth palate, and warming finish. Other Chimay beers include Gold, Red (Première), White (Cinq Cents), as well as a barrel-aged version of the reserve. The Chimay website has an entire section describing gastronomy, offering recipes that call for its beer. It recommends using the Blue to make crêpes. You can also pair it with Chimay cheese, made using the beer, which can be purchased in the United States as well. Chimay offers advice for enjoying them together:

> An ideal tasting experience in 4 steps:
> 1. Take a slow sip of your ale to enjoy its flavor.
> 2. Next taste a piece of cheese without its rind.
> 3. Try another piece of cheese, this time with its rind.
> 4. Finally, take a generous mouthful of the ale to mix the two products in your mouth . . . and enjoy the flavors![23]

---

[23] "Ale and Cheese Pairings," Chimay, accessed May 19, 2018, http://chimay.com/us/jumelage-bieres-et-fromages/.

## 2. ORVAL TRAPPIST ALE
ORVAL BREWERY, ABBAYE NOTRE-DAME D'ORVAL, ORVAL, BELGIUM

Orval is a Trappist abbey in the south of Belgium, founded in 1070. The abbey's symbol, a fish with a ring in its mouth, points to its founding by the Countess Mathilde of Tuscany. (The countess had lost her ring in a fountain, which was miraculously recovered by a trout.) Medieval ruins remain today and make a dramatic backdrop for the beautiful modern monastic buildings, constructed in 1926 to revive the presence of monks after the monastery's closure. Orval is a unique beer among the abbey and Trappist beers, particularly for its use of the wild Brettanomyces yeast. The bottle also has a unique shape, designed by the abbey's architect to hold in yeast when pouring.

In addition to a small beer for its own consumption, the abbey distributes a strong golden ale with a strong hop aroma created by the method of dry hopping. Its distinctive taste stems from its brewing process: "The various stages of fermentation — combined fermentation with the original yeast and with wild yeast, followed by fermentation in the bottle — mean the beer must age for some time and requires numerous quality controls.... Orval beer is a high-fermentation beer. The ageing process adds a fruity note, which strikes a subtle balance between the beer's full-bodied yet complex flavour and bitterness."[24]

Medieval ruins next to Abbaye d'Orval. (Wikimedia Commons)

---

[24] "Orval Brewery," Orval Abbey, accessed May 19, 2018, http://www.orval.be/en/8/Brewery.

## 1. WESTVLETEREN 12
### WESTVLETEREN BREWERY, SAINT-SIXTUS ABBEY, VLTEREN, BELGIUM

Westvleteren, one of the world's most consistently top-rated beers, is brewed by St. Sixtus Abbey in Belgium. It is also the hardest to obtain, as they brew only enough to support their basic needs and sell only limited quantities to individuals who come to the monastery. St. Sixtus is the only Trappist brewery where only monks brew directly and then only on seventy-two days of the year, with only a few lay workers for secondary tasks. Occasionally distributors attempt to stockpile bottles sold to them by monastery visitors, though the abbey has threatened legal action against this to curb any commercial resales. In a rare exception, to raise funds for a roof, they issued a special release just for the United States, selling a pack of four 750 ml bottles of their most popular beer, Westvleteren 12, a quadrupel style, for $85. People camped outside stores for the beer.

All three Westvleteren beers are highly regarded: Blonde (5.8% ABV), 8 (8% ABV), and the most famous, 12 (10.2% ABV). Westvleteren 12, with its burgundy-brown color, warrants a longer description of its merits:

> Very full, creamy smooth and round-bodied aroma, average to good carbonation. Tart dark fruit, raisins, caramel sweetness, warming alcohol, tobacco and leather. Very lush and sincere beer, good malt flavor. Balanced taste, exceptionally complex with an aftertaste that lasts and ends with a dry finish. A taste and experience that is as individual as the person drinking it.[25]

The beer should be aged in order to grow stronger and more complex over time.

Many wonder why St. Sixtus Abbey brews one of the world's most popular beers in such limited quantities. During the dedication of their new brewery, the abbot answered this question:

[25] "Westvleteren 12," Beer Tourism, accessed May 19, 2018, https://belgium.beer-tourism.com/belgian-beers/westvleteren-12.

As every man we must be able to live, so we have to try to earn our living and let others share in what we have to abstain from. Indeed, we have to live "from" and "with" our brewery. But we do not live "for" our brewery. This must be strange for business people and difficult to understand that we do not exploit our commercial assets as much as we can. We are no brewers. We are monks. We brew beer to be able to afford being monks.[26]

Another monk, the brewmaster Br. Joris, responded to the beer's top rating by pointing out that "the first Benedictine value . . . is humility. . . . Humility begins with not comparing oneself with another."[27]

We have made it through a pilgrimage of thirty major beers with some relation to monasticism. These beers are made by monks directly, in a direct partnership with them, or by using the traditions of secularized or defunct monasteries. Hopefully, this list will help you to experience the monastic brewing tradition directly: growing in friendship with drinking companions while relishing the aesthetics of complex, wonderful beers.

## OTHER MONASTIC OR CATHOLIC-RELATED BEERS

These beers did not make my top thirty list, but still have some connection to the monastic or Catholic tradition. Some have a direct connection to Catholic religious orders, while others are just inspired by Catholic brewing history. Some are accessible in the United States, but others are available only in their local areas. Although not exhaustive, the list seeks to include as many monastic-related beers as possible, as well as other beers with a Catholic connection thought worth noting.

**Abadía de Los Toldos** is the beer of the Benedictine monastery of Santa Maria de Los Toldos in Argentina. They brew both a blond and a

---

[26] "Brewing to Live," The Abbey of St. Sixtus of Westvleteren, accessed May 18, 2018, https://web.archive.org/web/20130703084129/http://www.sintsixtus.be/eng/brouwen.htm.

[27] Noelle Knox, "Monks Who Make World's Best Beer Have a Message," *USA Today*, October 3, 2005, https://usatoday30.usatoday.com/money/industries/food/2005-10-03-beer-usat_x.htm. The message was: don't buy our beer unless you come to the abbey.

dark. The monastery was founded in 1948 with the help of St. Meinrad Archabbey in Indiana.

**Abbaye de Bonne Espérance**, a Certified Belgian Abbey Beer, is brewed in Quenast, Belgium by Lefebvre Brewery. The abbey, now defunct, was affiliated with the Norbertines.

**Abbaye de Cambron** is also a Certified Belgian Abbey Beer, representing a defunct Cistercian abbey, brewed in Silly by Brasserie de Silly.

**Abbaye de Forest** is another Certified Belgian Abbey Beer, affiliated with a defunct Benedictine abbey of nuns, brewed by Brasserie de Silly.

**Abbaye de Saint-Martin** is a Certified Belgian Abbey Beer, related to a defunct Benedictine monastery dating to 1096. It is brewed near Tournai by Brasserie Brunehaut.

**Abdij Dendermonde** is an existing Benedictine monastery in Belgium. They sponsor a Certified Belgian Abbey Beer, brewed in Merchtem by Brouwerij De Block.

**Achel Trappist** is brewed by the Abbey of St. Benedict (Achelse Kluis), which borders the Netherlands. After its brewing was interrupted by the World Wars, it reintroduced Trappist beer in 2001. In the spring of 2018, due to a decrease in vocations, the monks gave their buildings to Fazenda da Esperança, a Latin American group dedicated to addiction recovery, but promise that the brewery will continue.

**Alpirsbach Klosterbrauerei** in the Black Forest of Germany is on the site of a former Benedictine monastery that was dissolved by the Reformation. Though used by Lutherans since then, Catholic worship has also returned to the old abbey church.

**Augustiner Bräu Kloster Mülln** is sponsored by the Benedictine Abbey of Michaelbeuern, near Salzburg, Austria, in partnership with private shareholders. As the name indicates, the beer originated with the Augustinians in 1621. The brewery runs the largest beer hall in Austria.

**Bornem** is a Certified Belgian Abbey Beer, named for a Cistercian abbey in the Archdiocese of Brussels, brewed by Brouwerij Van Steenberge.

**Břevnovský Benedict** is brewed at the Brevnovsky Klaster, a Benedictine abbey in Prague founded by St. Aldebert in 993 as the first Benedictine Monastery in Bohemia. It claims to be the oldest brewery in the Czech Republic, though it only began brewing again in 2011. It also brews Praha 993 in South Korea.

**Cardeña** is the beer of the Trappist Monasterio de San Pedro de Cardeña in Burgos, Spain, brewed for them by the MarPal Brewery, which means it will not be an official Trappist product until it is brewed within the monastery itself. Cardeña is one of the oldest monasteries in Spain, founded in 534 by monks sent from Monte Cassino by St. Benedict himself. Two hundred of its monks were martyred in 953 at the hands of the Muslim rulers.

**Corsendonk** is an unofficial Belgian abbey beer brewed by Brasserie Du Bocq, associated with the defunct Corsendonk Priory, now a hotel.

**Eschweger Klosterbrauerei** is a family-owned brewery on the site of an Augustinian brewery dating to 1278, though the monastery was dissolved during the Reformation.

**Ename Abbey**, a defunct Benedictine abbey, now gives its name to a Certified Belgian Abbey Beer, brewed in Oost-Vlaanderen by Brouwerij Roman, which provides funds for the continued excavation of the abbey's ruins.

**Floreffe Abbey** is a defunct Norbertine monastery. Lefebvre Brewery produces four styles of Certified Belgian Abbey Beers with the Floreffe name and uses a portion of the proceeds to fund a school housed in the former monastery. The brewery dates to 1250 and can still be visited today on the beautiful abbey grounds.

**Four Saints**, a brewery in Asheboro, North Carolina, is named after Saints Wenceslaus, Nicholas, Luke, and Augustine — four of the many patron saints of brewing. Their website describes how "Four Saints Founders Joel McClosky and Andrew Deming are carrying on the brewing tradition in the hopes of future sainthood, or at least to make some really good beer."

**Highland Brewing** in Asheville, North Carolina, has brewed a number of beers for Belmont Abbey, including a doppelbock brewed with the help of Brother Tobiah for his fellow Monks at Belmont Abbey. These beers have been served at Belmont Abbey College events.

**Hoegaarden**, the famous Belgian white beer, traces its recipe back to 1445, when Benedictine monks put coriander and orange peel into beer for the first time. Long after the monastery closed, a local milkman, Pierre Celis, kept the brewery from closing in the 1950s. It is now owned by AB InBev.

**Kapuziner Schwarz-Weizen** is a secularized Capuchin beer, brewed by Kulmbacher Brauerei in Bavaria.

**Keizersberg** is a Certified Belgian Abbey Beer, licensed from an extent Benedictine abbey north of Leuven, Belgium, and brewed by Brouwerij Van Steenberge.

**Kreuzberg Kloster**, a Franciscan monastery in Franconia, Germany, has a restaurant and brewery on the monastery grounds. The site has a long history, since St. Kilian established it as a place of pilgrimage in 686, making it known as the Holy Place of the Franks.

**Mallersdorf Kloster**, a Franciscan female monastery in Bavaria, brews beer for its own consumption and for local sale. Sister Doris Engelhard, a certified master brewer, has been brewing for over forty years. She may be the only master brewer nun in the world. Sr. Doris related, "I really love my job, and I love the smell when I'm making beer. I love working with living things: yeast, barley, and the people who enjoy beer. Beer, actually, is the purest of all alcoholic beverages, and it is really very healthy, as long as you do not pour it down senselessly."[28]

**Mont des Cats** is a Trappist certified beer of the Abbey of St. Marie de Mont des Cats in Northern France. The monks brewed in the late nineteenth and early twentieth centuries, but were forced to stop due to the anticlerical laws of the Third French Republic. The abbey continued making cheese, but in 2011 the Abbey of Scourmont and its Chimay Brewery agreed to brew a beer for Mont des Cats.

**Mosteiro** is the beer of the Benedictine abbey of São Bento in San Paulo and was launched on the feast of St. Benedict, July 11, 2017. The monastery was founded in 1598, but didn't begin brewing until Belgian and German monks came to the monastery in 1903. The beer's bottle label is embedded with augmented reality technology to project an animated image of the abbey church and Gregorian chant to cell phones.

**Neuzelle** is a recently revived Cistercian abbey in Germany. The beautiful baroque abbey boasts of martyrs from the Hussite Wars and resistance to the Reformation. The site also preserves the secularized Klosterbrauerei Neuzelle, which brews Dark Monk and Black Nun.

**Notre Dame des Mokoto** was a Trappist monastery in Congo, destroyed by civil war in 1996. Although now defunct, I include it in

---

[28]  Daneil Esparza, "Sister Doris Engelhard: The Master Brewer of Mallersdorf Abbey," *The Atlantic*, August 12, 2016, https://aleteia.org/2016/08/12/sister-doris -engelhard-the-master-brewer-of-mallersdorf-abbey/.

hopes that monastery brewing will return to Africa. The founder of Mariannhill Trappist Abbey in South Africa, Abbot Francis Pfanner, an Austrian, originally brought Trappist beer to Africa in the 1800s.

**Postel** is a Certified Belgian Abbey Beer, brewed in Opwijk by Brouwerij De Smedt (now owned by Heineken). Postel is a Norbertine abbey, which began contracting its brewing in 1953, though brewing on-site dates back to 1611.

**Ramée** is a Certified Belgian Abbey Beer brewed in Purnode by Brasserie du Bocq and named for a defunct women's Cistercian abbey that was secularized following the French Revolution.

**Reutberg Kloster** is a Franciscan monastery in Sachsenkam, Bavaria, which survived secularization. Brewing resumed in 1954 and is currently conducted on-site through a cooperative with a brewer.

**Riedenburger** brewery is dedicated to brewing organic beers and promoting ecology. It brews four monastic beers through a cooperative with the Benedictine Abbey of Plankstetten. The abbey itself has a long brewing tradition and runs an organic farm. Together they hold a Maibockfest on the abbey grounds. The brewery holds that the cooperative reflects their "shared ethics of sustainability and belief in the integrity of creation."[29]

**San Miguel** is one of the most popular beers in Asia. It is based in Manila, the capital of the Philippines, but it has run a successful brewery in Hong Kong for some time. It is named for a district of Manila named after St. Michael and was brewed for the first time in 1890 on his feast day (the traditional day to begin brewing in Bavaria).

**Sankt Gallen** is a brewery in Atsugi, Japan, founded in 2001. It is an example of how the European monastic tradition continues to inspire brewing worldwide. The brewery is named for the Monastery of St. Gallen in Switzerland, which received the first brewing license in the world.

**Schlägl Stiftsbrauerei** in Austria is one of two examples of brewing within the walls of a Norbertine monastery. On-site brewing dates back to 1580; a modern brewery was built in 1974.

**Scheyern Klosterbrau** is the brewery of the Benedictine Abbey of Scheyern in Bavaria. Founded in 1119, it was the medieval burial site

[29] See https://www.riedenburger.de/en/homepage/brewery/history.html.

for the Wittelsbach family, the royal family of Bavaria. It claims to be the third oldest brewery in the world and underwent a major upgrade in 2006, though they only distribute the beer locally.

**Shiner Bock** is brewed by the Spoetzl Brewery in Shiner, Texas. Michael Foley describes how the beer began as a seasonal Lenten beer, before being brewed year-round as one of Texas's most popular beers.[30]

**St. Arnold Brewery** is a popular craft brewer in Houston, Texas, named for the Belgian patron saint of beer.

**St. Benedict's Brew Works** opened in 2015 on the grounds of the monastery of the Sisters of St. Benedict in Ferdinand, Indiana. Their motto is Pray-Work-Brew, and the brewery cooperates with the sisters to offer a number of evangelization opportunities such as beer retreats.

**St. Feuillien** is named for the Irish missionary Foillan, who came to Belgium in 655. The Norbertines eventually built a monastery at the site of the saint's martyrdom, though it was suppressed following the French Revolution. A guild preserves the traditions of the monastery and its beer: "All members are connected to the town of Le Roeulx, all wish to help develop the bonds of friendship between the people of Le Roeulx, all are protectors of the town's venerable traditions, all are champions of the beers of Saint-Feuillien Abbey both inside and outside the walls of Le Roeulx."[31] The Brasserie St-Feuillien was founded in 1873 and remains a family-owned and independent brewery.

**St. Marienstern Klosterbrauerei** operates at the Cistercian monastery in a small Saxon city of Oberlausitz. It ran from 1700 until closing in Communist East Germany in 1973. After the fall of Communism, the monastery was returned to the Cistercians who converted its premises into a shelter for disabled people. The brewery reopened in 1993 using traditional recipes and is run by the Stadtbrauerei Wittichenau.

**Strahov Klášterní Pivovar** is a brewery operating in the ancient Norbertine monastery in Prague. Centrally located in the old city, the brewery has helped to restore the beautiful structure and to create a setting for monastic hospitality.

**Steenbrugge** is a Certified Belgian Abbey Beer, brewed in Brugge by Palm Breweries. The beer was originally brewed by the Benedictine Abbey

---

30  Foley, *Drinking with Saints*, 405.
31  See http://www.st-feuillien.com/en/la-brasserie/confrerie-st-feuillien/.

of Saint Peter in Steenbrugge. Significantly, the monastery, now defunct, was founded by the patron saint of brewing, St. Arnold of Soissons.

**Tongerlo** is a Certified Belgian Abbey Beer named for a Norbertine monastery and brewed in Boortmeerbeek by Brouwerij Haacht. The monastery produced martyrs during the Reformation and houses the Da Vinci museum with a replica of the Last Supper worked on by Da Vinci himself.

**Tripel Karmeliet** is brewed by Bosteels Brewery. It does not have a current connection to a religious order, but the recipe dates to 1679 from the Carmelites of Dendermonde, Belgium.

**Tynt Meadow** is the new Trappist beer from Mount Saint Bernard Abbey, released in June 2018. The abbey provides the following description of its new brew: "Being part of the great Trappist tradition, we've chosen to produce a strong dark ale, but one with a clearly English character. Tynt Meadow is mahogany-coloured, with a subtle, warm red hue, and a lasting beige head. Its aroma carries hints of dark chocolate, liquorice, and rich fruit flavours. The beer is full-bodied, gently balancing the taste of dark chocolate, pepper, and fig. It leaves a warm and dry finish on the palate."[32]

**Urban Artifact**, a Cincinnati-based craft brewer, specializes in wild beers using local wild yeast. The name refers to the location of the brewery in a shuttered Catholic parish, St. Patrick's, which the brewery owners are preserving as an artifact of Northeast Cincinnati culture. They use the building's rose window as their logo, seek to continue fostering local community life, and have used St. Joseph's Trappist Seville Orange Marmalade in one of their beers, Flash Lamp.

**Ursberg Klosterbrauerei** is a hotel and brewery located alongside the Franciscan Friary (formerly Norbertine) of Ursberg, Germany.

**Urstoff Kloster** was brewed until recently by the Augustinian monastery in Munnerstadt, Bavaria. They contracted the brewing until 1995, when Rother Brau acquired exclusive rights to brew it.

**Weissenohe Kloster** is the site of a Benedictine monastery dating to 1050. The abbey was not resurrected following secularization in 1803,

---

[32] "Tynt Meadow English Trappist Ale," Mount St. Bernard Abbey, accessed Aug. 4, 2018, http://www.mountsaintbernard.org/tynt-meadow-ale. See Simon Caldwell, "Inside Britain's First Trappist Brewery," *Catholic Herald*, July 20, 2018, http://catholicherald. co.uk/issues/catholic-herald-app-2018-07-20/inside-britains-first-trappist-brewery/.

though a family-owned brewery and beer garden have remained on the grounds.

**Klášter Želiv** is a Norbertine monastery in the Czech Republic, which brewed until a fire closed down the monastery brewery in 1903. The Communists used the monastery as a prison for over four hundred priests and religious. The Norbertines returned after the fall of Communism, and the Želivský klášterní pivovar (monastery brewery) opened in 2003 in cooperation with lay brewers. The venture failed, however, and the Norbertines opened a new brewery themselves in 2010.

**Zundert** is the second Dutch Trappist beer, introduced only in 2013, and is brewed by the Abbey of Maria Toevlucht. The monks call the beer "a bit stubborn," meaning it requires leisure to fully appreciate its complexity. Two of the abbey's monks assist in the brewing process. The town of Zundert is also the birthplace of Vincent van Gogh.

**Zwiefalten** is a defunct Benedictine monastery in Baden-Württemberg, Germany. A family-owned klosterbrauerei continues the monastery's brewing tradition. The brewery has made itself into a so-called beer heaven destination, with brewing classes, a farmer's market, and a beer garden.

This list of beers reveals some interesting patterns. Brewers remember the past and still brew in honor of Celtic missionaries who arrived in their homeland almost fifteen hundred years earlier. They remember lost abbeys and even work to preserve their legacy. Religious from many different orders — primarily Benedictines, Franciscans, Norbertines, and Augustinians — all continue to participate in brewing in various ways: by brewing directly, operating cooperatives, or sponsoring beers. We also see that the Catholic brewing tradition has continued around the world — not just in Europe, but also in the United States, Latin America, and Asia.

PART IV

BEER

&

CULTURAL
PROBLEMS

# CHAPTER 13
# *Drunkenness and Temperance*

We looked earlier at the Bible's positive vision of alcohol as a sign of God's blessing. That is not the whole story, however. In fact, we find the first mention of alcohol in Genesis 9 when Noah plants a vineyard after the flood: "Noah was the first tiller of the soil. He planted a vineyard; and he drank of the wine, and became drunk, and lay uncovered in his tent" (Gen. 9:20–21). Although fundamentalists are wrong to claim that drinking is a sin in the Bible, it is true that it refers to drunkenness over seventy times — more often than it refers to alcohol's positive use. Any Catholic account of alcohol and beer, therefore, would be incomplete without speaking of their misuse. We will look at why drunkenness constitutes a sin and how moderation guides the proper consumption of beer.

## THE SIN OF INTOXICATION

Is drinking too much a sin? I have had some vigorous arguments on this point; it helps to first define sin. One way to think of sin is as a disordered attachment to the things of the earth, especially when we put them before God. The *Catechism of the Catholic Church* defines venial sin as a "disordered affection for created goods," which if deliberate and unrepented could lead to the point of "preferring an inferior good to [God]" — a mortal sin (CCC 1863; 1855). Augustine puts it in a similar way: "Lesser things should be subordinate to better things."[1] Sin represents a disorder by inordinately choosing a lesser good before a more important one.

In the case of alcohol, we can affirm its goodness as a foodstuff, which promotes nutrition and health, and which furthermore brings joy to the heart and fellowship among men. However, when we allow this good to impede more important goods, then sin enters into our drinking. We

---

[1] Augustine, *On the Free Choice of the Will*, trans. Peter King (New York: Cambridge University Press, 2010), 52.

must drink in the proper way, rightly ordered toward what is higher. In particular, the *Catechism* insists that we drink in moderation: "The virtue of temperance disposes us to avoid every kind of excess: the abuse of food, alcohol, tobacco, or medicine. Those incur grave guilt who, by drunkenness or a love of speed, endanger their own and others' safety on the road, at sea, or in the air" (CCC 2290). The misuse of alcohol can be grave, leading us into serious, mortal sin.

Velazquez, *Los Borrachos* (1628). (Wikimedia Commons)

St. Paul counsels several times against drunkenness. In fact, he speaks quite harshly about it, linking it to other serious sins that keep us from heaven: "Now the works of the flesh are plain: immorality, impurity, licentiousness, idolatry, sorcery, enmity, strife, jealousy, anger, selfishness, dissension, party spirit, envy, drunkenness, carousing, and the like. I warn you, as I warned you before, that those who do such things shall not inherit the kingdom of God" (Gal. 5:19–21). He contrasts drunkenness with the true inebriation of the Spirit: "And be not drunk with wine, wherein is luxury; but be ye filled with the Holy Spirit" (Eph. 5:18). We cannot be inebriated on both alcohol and God. God should consume us and lead us into a kind of ecstasy that exceeds reason, which is why, as we discussed earlier, we speak of sober inebriation.

Aquinas affirms the gravity of drunkenness: "To take more meat or drink than is necessary belongs to the vice of gluttony, which is not always a mortal sin: but knowingly to take too much drink to the point of being drunk, is a mortal sin."[2] Aquinas not only affirms the sinfulness of drunkenness, but points us to why it is a sin. Its sinfulness consists in impairing the good of rational nature:

> It may happen that a man is well aware that the drink is immoderate and intoxicating, and yet he would rather be drunk than abstain from drink. Such a man is a drunkard properly speaking, because morals take their species not from things that occur accidentally and beside the intention, but from that which is directly intended. In this way drunkenness is a mortal sin, because then a man willingly and knowingly deprives himself of the use of reason, whereby he performs virtuous deeds and avoids sin, and thus he sins mortally by running the risk of falling into sin.[3]

Deliberate drunkenness consciously impairs one's rationality, rescinding precisely what makes one human, the source of nobility and goodness. St. Alphonsus Liguori refers to drunkenness as "an injury to God, whose image one would disfigure."[4] To retreat to this non-rational state entails both a degradation of one's condition and also one's relation to others while in that impaired condition. Alcohol abuse flies from reason, seeking an anesthesia to our spiritual and cultural problems.

The serious and even deadly effects of alcohol abuse cannot be underestimated. The National Institute on Alcohol Abuse and Alcoholism provides some statistics:[5]

> In 2015, 26.9 percent of people ages 18 or older reported that they engaged in binge drinking in the past month; 7.0 percent reported that they engaged in heavy alcohol use in the past month.

---

2   *ST* II-II, q. 150, a. 2, ad. 2.
3   *ST* II-II, q. 150, a. 2, corpus.
4   Alphonsus Liguori, *Moral Theology*, vol. 1, bks. II–III, trans. Ryan Grant (Post Falls, ID: Mediatrix Press, 2017), bk. II, ch. 3, art. 5.
5   "Alcohol Facts and Statistics," National Institute on Alcohol Abuse and Alcoholism, accessed February 18, 2018, https://www.niaaa.nih.gov/alcohol-health/overview-alcohol-consumption/alcohol-facts-and-statistics.

... 15.1 million adults ages 18 and older (6.2 percent of this age group) had AUD [Alcohol Use Disorder]. This includes 9.8 million men (8.4 percent of men in this age group) and 5.3 million women (4.2 percent of women in this age group).

An estimated 88,000 people (approximately 62,000 men and 26,000 women) die from alcohol-related causes annually, making alcohol the third leading preventable cause of death in the United States. The first is tobacco, and the second is poor diet and physical inactivity.

In 2014, alcohol-impaired driving fatalities accounted for 9,967 deaths (31 percent of overall driving fatalities).

Unfortunately, alcoholism presents a problem even in the Church. Although there are no official statistics, it appears that priests have a higher-than-average rate of alcoholism.[6] A bishop spoke to me of his reluctance to endorse beer-related projects because of this concern. One Michigan-based ministry, Guest House, seeks to address this problem in a holistic way. Guest House provides "information, education, treatment and care needed to assure that Catholic clergy, men and women religious, and seminarians suffering from alcoholism, addictions and other behavioral health conditions have the best opportunity for quality recovery and overall health and wellness."[7] Priests who face isolation and high levels of stress need support so as not to fall into problematic coping methods.

Drunkenness arises from misusing the goods of beer and wine. Roger Scruton argued that drunkenness is to drinking as divorce is to a first kiss: the rupture of what should be a good and healthy relationship.[8] Misusing anything good leads to sin. The great beer drinker discussed in chapter three, Martin Luther, taught "infallibly" that we should not "suppose that abuses are eliminated by destroying the object which is abused. Men can go wrong with wine and women. Shall we then prohibit

[6] Fr. Alexander Lucie-Smith, "Why Are So Many Priest Alcoholics?" *Catholic Herald*, Aug. 25, 2014, http://catholicherald.co.uk/commentandblogs/2014/08/25/why-are-so-many-priests-alcoholics/.

[7] Guest House, accessed February 18, 2018, http://guesthouse.org.

[8] Scruton, *I Drink*, 124.

and abolish women?"[9] Although it is not nearly as common, even ordinary goods can be abused. For instance, if you drink too much water quickly, it will kill you. Not many are inclined to drink water to excess, whereas alcoholism has become a true social problem. The misuse of alcohol provides a clear example of how sin wounds us and can destroy lives. Paul's prohibition of alcoholism demonstrates how God's commands lead us to what is truly good for ourselves and society.

## TEMPERANCE OR TEMPERANCE MOVEMENTS

Many Protestants did not take Luther's advice and wanted to outlaw alcohol because of its abuse. Although the early Reformers supported the moderate use of alcohol, as the Reformation traditions developed, new sects such as Baptists and Methodists emerged that encouraged abstinence from alcohol. Virtues are the habits that perfect our actions, but when we remove the struggle completely we do not form virtue (though this may be necessary in cases of serious incontinence). Temperance is the virtue that concerns moderation of food and drink. All virtue, according to Aristotle, finds the mean between two extremes.

Temperance avoids both the excess of pleasure and the defect that rejects pleasure or is insensitive to bodily needs. Regarding drinking, these extremes appear as drinking or thirsting too much! In relation to alcohol, the excess is clearly drunkenness, while the defect may come from rejecting its legitimacy. We may think that people tend more toward excess, but some groups have traditions that tend toward extreme abstinence, such as in Islam, Mormonism, and puritanical Christianity (although even the Puritans of Massachusetts drank beer). If you can believe it, Aquinas said *not* drinking wine could be sinful if it were to harm one's health.[10]

In the first part of the book, we looked at the Catholic history of drinking, but there is also a Catholic history of encouraging abstinence

9 Quoted in Stephen Mansfield, *The Search for God and Guinness: A Biography of the Beer that Changed the World* (Nashville, TN: Thomas Nelson, 2014), 29.

10 Here is the full quote: "As the Philosopher says (*Ethic.* iii, 11), insensibility which is opposed to temperance 'is not very common,' so that like its species which are opposed to the species of intemperance it has no name. Hence the vice opposed to drunkenness is unnamed; and yet if a man were knowingly to abstain from wine to the extent of molesting nature grievously, he would not be free from sin," *ST* II-II, q. 150, a. 1, ad 1.

from alcohol. Even the great founder of the brewing monks, St. Benedict, said that "monks should not drink wine at all," though he acknowledged that he could not convince his monks of this. Therefore, he urged, "let us at least agree to drink moderately, and not to the point of excess." Some early fathers agreed with Benedict's ideal, such as Clement of Alexandria. Clement, the great catechist, wrote: "I therefore admire those who have adopted an austere life, and who are fond of water, the medicine of temperance, and flee as far as possible from wine, shunning it as they would the danger of fire."[11] He especially advised keeping wine from youth: "And we must, as far as possible, try to quench the impulses of youth by removing the Bacchic fuel of the threatened danger; and by pouring the antidote to the inflammation, so keep down the burning soul." Nonetheless, he also recognized that moderation is possible through the governance of reason, and gives three major laws for proper drinking during feasts. First, Clement counsels that "reason . . . be introduced to mix in the feast, to act the part of director (*pædagogue*) to wine-drinking." Second, that "its first manifestation be towards God in thanksgiving and psalmody." And third, that drinking should be directed "toward our neighbor in decorous fellowship." Clement recognizes that reason and faith can direct our drinking, ordering it to moderation and even praise.

The Christian tradition values abstinence and recognizes it as a path toward perfection, but it also recommends temperance as the general guide for most people. More recent Protestant reactions against alcohol, however, contained a different impetus. In the fifteenth century, monks began experimenting with the process of distilling and invented a number of spirits, which they used for medicinal purposes.[12] They called their experiments with distilled liquor *aqua vitae*—the water of life! As spirits spread in popularity in the early modern world, drinking habits altered drastically. Beer made up part of the daily diet; spirits were consumed for their intoxicating effects.

---

[11]   Clement of Alexandria, *The Pedagogus*, in *Ante-Nicene Fathers*, vol. 2, ed. Alexander Roberts, James Donaldson and A. Cleveland Coxe (Buffalo, NY: Christian Literature Publishing Co., 1885), II, ch. 2.

[12]   James Ross points to an exchequer document from 1484 for an early reference to *aqua vitae*: "To Friar John Cor, by order of the king, to make aquavitae, VIII bolls of malt," *Whisky* (London: Routledge, 1970), 158. Whiskey was of royal concern from the beginning. There had been some isolated usages of distillation earlier in the Middle Ages, but no consistent production until the fifteenth century.

Daniele Crespi, *Supper of St. Carlo Borromeo* (c. 1610). (Wikimedia Commons)

In early America, though, liquor had a greater prominence than beer. Many farmers made hard liquor instead because it did not spoil and it served as a currency in rural economies. Thus, a large number of Americans drank hard liquor on a daily basis and alcoholism became a national problem. It appears that the tendency of many American Protestants to emphasize "defect" (the rejection of drink) arose precisely due to the "excess" of regular consumption of spirits. Protestant groups drove the temperance movement and pushed for prohibition throughout the nineteenth century. Many pointed to beer as a solution to the drunkenness caused by the stronger spirits. The temperance movement, however, did not consider this solution and lumped beer and spirits together in the push for prohibition.

Jack London provides a unique voice for the temperance movement in his autobiographical novel, *John Barleycorn*, which describes his conversion from an alcoholic to a supporter of prohibition. In the novel, he describes his vote for prohibition supporters:

And that is the perfectest hell of it. John Barleycorn makes toward death. That is why I voted for the amendment to-day. I read back in my life and saw how the accessibility of alcohol had given me the taste for it. You see, comparatively few alcoholics are born in a generation. And by alcoholic I mean a man whose chemistry craves alcohol and drives him resistlessly to it. The great majority of habitual drinkers are born not only without desire for alcohol, but with actual repugnance toward it. Not the first, nor the twentieth, nor the hundredth drink, succeeded in giving them the liking. But they learned, just as men learn to smoke; though it is far easier to learn to smoke than to learn to drink. They learned because alcohol was so accessible. The women know the game. They pay for it — the wives and sisters and mothers. And when they come to vote, they will vote for prohibition. And the best of it is that there will be no hardship worked on the coming generation. Not having access to alcohol, not being predisposed toward alcohol, it will never miss alcohol. It will mean life more abundant for the manhood of the young boys born and growing up — ay, and life more abundant for the young girls born and growing up to share the lives of the young men.

The temperance movement reached worldwide and even drew in Catholics. Countries across the Christian spectrum such as Orthodox Russia, Lutheran Scandinavia, and Catholic Ireland faced serious issues related to drunkenness, in part due to their predominant consumption of liquor. When the Communists came to power, they banned alcohol in Russia (one of their many inhuman policies). From a Catholic perspective, Fr. Theobald Matthew made it his life's work to combat alcoholism among the Irish. He became known as the "apostle of temperance," and he worked not only in Ireland but traveled extensively across the United States. In the 1830s and 40s, he helped millions to make a pledge of total abstinence from alcohol.

One notable example of someone who took the pledge is Ven. Matt Talbot, who was an uncontrollable alcoholic in his early teenage years, but who stayed sober for over forty years after taking the pledge in 1884. Born into a poor, large family, Matt began working for a wine shop at age 12, which led to his alcoholism as he sipped the store's goods. Abandoned even by his friends, he turned to God, devoted his life to prayer and strict penance, and taught himself to read so he could study the great spiritual classics. He became a Third Order Franciscan, and faithfully served his fellow laborers, showing great sympathy for those suffering from alcoholism: "Never be too hard on the man who can't give up the drink. It's as hard to give up the drink as it is to raise the dead to life again. Both are possible and even easy for Our Lord. We have only to depend on him."[13]

Brad Miner describes how other Catholic movements, such as the Catholic Total Abstinence Union of America, focused primarily on discouraging the consumption of spirits and on personal temperance rather than on prohibition. Miner relates how both Leo XIII and Pius X supported the Union, though the latter specified the problem arose from "the abuse of strong drink" rather than beer or wine.[14] Catholics generally did not support prohibition, but rather encouraged moderate consumption of lower alcohol drinks. G. K. Chesterton sums up the Catholic view of beer as a moderate drink:

> Some statements I disagree with; others I do not understand. If a man says, "I think the human race would be better if it abstained totally from fermented liquor," I quite understand what he means, and how his view could be defended. If a man says, "I wish to abolish beer because I am a temperance man," his remark conveys no meaning to my mind. It is like saying, "I wish to abolish roads because I am a moderate walker."[15]

The prohibition of beer removed the moderate way of drinking alcohol.

## HOW TO DRINK PROPERLY

When we drink beer, we need to keep in mind the proper balance between the extremes we have examined. Temperance regulates our desire for food, drink, and bodily pleasure, and seeks to properly use material

---

[13] Meg Hunter Kilmer, "He Was a Drunk. And Now He's on the Path to Sainthood. Meet Matt Talbot," *Aleteia*, Sep. 14, 2017, https://aleteia.org/2017/09/14/he-was -a-drunk-and-now-hes-on-the-path-to-sainthood-meet-matt-talbot/.

[14] Brad Miner, "A Brief History of Catholic Prohibition," *The Catholic Thing*, September 23, 2013, https://www.thecatholicthing.org/2013/09/23/a-brief-history-of-catholic-prohibition/.

[15] G. K. Chesterton, "Science and Religion," in *All Things Considered* (London: Methuen & Co., 1908).

things for our flourishing. Aquinas lays out the basic principle: Our consumption of "meat and drink should be moderate in accordance with the demands of the body's health."[16] Food and drink should promote the human good in body, mind, and soul — as well as in our social life.

Traditionally, the beer used for daily consumption was lower in alcohol and was consumed throughout the day with almost every meal, helping the average person to consume enough calories to receive proper nutrition. The Middle Ages did see some excess on feast days, however. Drunkenness became a larger problem, as I discussed above, with the rise of distilled alcohol at the end of the medieval period. People did not consume this beverage as part of a normal diet and with regular meals, but found in it something more potent, drinking for drinking's sake. Therefore, some have argued that we should drink beer and wine regularly, to the exclusion of stronger alcohol. One famous example comes from Hilaire Belloc's *Path to Rome*, where he describes his resolution to avoid the devil in his drinking and to maintain the ideal of proper drinking (as represented, somewhat oddly, by Bacchus):

> I made up this rule for him to distinguish between Bacchus and the Devil. To wit: that he should never drink what has been made and sold since the Reformation — I mean especially spirits and champagne. Let him (said I) drink red wine and white, good beer and mead — if he could get it — liqueurs made by monks, and, in a word, all those feeding, fortifying, and confirming beverages that our fathers drank in old time; but not whisky, nor brandy, nor sparkling wines, not absinthe, nor the kind of drink called gin.
>
> This he promised to do, and all went well. He became a merry companion, and began to write odes.

Belloc describes how moderate drinking fostered his conviviality during his great walking pilgrimage across the Alps from France to Rome.

Now, I certainly enjoy a glass of scotch and would not follow Belloc's resolution wholesale (even though he made an exception for monastic liqueur), but I do think it makes sense to emphasize drinking beer and wine with meals on a regular basis while saving stronger drinks for

---

[16] *ST* II-II, q. 150, a. 2, ad 3.

Pilgrim's Inn, Glastonbury. (Wikimedia Commons)

special occasions and with strict moderation. Alcoholism arose when hard liquor became the daily, regular drink of choice.[17]

Here are several tips for drinking in the proper context to avoid excess and overattachment:

First, drink with food. This limits the absorption of alcohol, but more importantly, places drinking in the right context of one's diet — as foodstuff, not as a crutch.

Second, drink with others. Beer should bring us closer to others and facilitate conversation. Drinking with family or friends also provides a good check against drinking too much.

Third, have a strict limit, based on what you can reasonably consume without becoming impaired. An individual's limit varies by weight, sex, and age, but most people can consume two or three drinks per day.

Finally, don't drink too often. It is important for the spiritual life not to become too attached to anything. I have found it helpful to periodically fast from beer and alcohol. Lent is a natural time for this, as alcohol was included in the ancient fasting rules. Many men, including myself, have gone through Exodus 90, a ninety-day program of prayer and penance completed with the company of like-minded men.

[17] Phillips, *Alcohol*, 116.

We also need to examine our motivation for drinking. Are we drinking for the right reason? Chesterton put it best with his famous quotation from *Heretics*: "Drink because you're happy, but never because you are miserable." He also said: "We should thank God for beer and burgundy by not drinking too much of them." Combining these two points, we see that we should drink as an expression of our thanks for the goodness of life, as an affirmation of this good, and not as a negative expression of frustration and depression. When consumed with a negative intention, alcohol takes us down to further depths of darkness. When consumed with a positive intention, with others, and in moderation, it lifts us up.

Chesterton, our patron saint of Catholic drinking, captures the purpose and danger of drinking best:

> Let a man walk ten miles steadily on a hot summer's day along a dusty English road, and he will soon discover why beer was invented. The fact that beer has a very slight stimulating quality will be quite among the smallest reasons that induce him to ask for it. In short, he will not be in the least desiring alcohol; he will be desiring beer. . . .
>
> Doubtless, it is unnatural to be drunk. But then in a real sense it is unnatural to be human. . . . The real case against drunkenness is not that it calls up the beast [in man], but that it calls up the Devil. It does not call up the beast, and if it did it would not matter much, as a rule; the beast is a harmless and rather amiable creature, as anybody can see by watching cattle. There is nothing bestial about intoxication; and certainly there is nothing intoxicating or even particularly lively about beasts. Man is always something worse or something better than an animal; and a mere argument from animal perfection never touches him at all. Thus, in sex no animal is either chivalrous or obscene. And thus no animal ever invented anything so bad as drunkenness–or so good as drink.[18]

We must choose how to consume alcohol properly. We can gravitate toward the extremes of excess or defect, or find the proper mean of moderation, drinking in thanksgiving for the blessings God has given us.

---

[18] G. K. Chesterton, "Wine When It Is Red" in *All Things Considered* (London: Methuen & Co., 1908), 233–34.

## CHAPTER 14
# *Beer versus Marijuana*

When I first gave a talk on beer and Catholic culture, I was surprised by the number of questions and comments related to drugs. I guess I should not have been, because I was in Colorado. In 2012, when I voted against Amendment 64, which sought to legalize marijuana in Colorado, I laughed off the ballot measure, thinking it would not have a chance of passing. Since then, I have been disturbed by what's been happening in Colorado, as well as throughout the country. In fact, the legalization of marijuana stands as one link in a chain of cultural changes, all reflecting a withdrawal from reality, a breaking down of boundaries and natural limits, and a retreat from personal and social responsibility.

Dr. Vince Fortanasce, an internationally renowned Alzheimer's researcher, has bemoaned the fact that Catholics have pretty much accepted the rise of marijuana in our country without a fight.[1] Although he acknowledges that we need more research, he points out that there has been enough to conclusively point to marijuana's dangerous impact on the brain, especially for adolescents and young adults. The moderate consumption of alcohol has a strong place in the Catholic tradition and Catholics need to be able to distinguish this practice from the use of a drug; we should not equate it with the recreational use of marijuana. This chapter will explore the reasons why in more detail.

## IS BEER A DRUG?

Chesterton again makes an important point regarding the extremes of excess and defect when it comes to drinking: "The dipsomaniac and the abstainer are not only both mistaken, but they both make the same

---

[1] See a talk he gave for the Catholic Medical Association, "Marijuana," released by St. Joseph Media on CD (2018). See also his overview, "Marijuana & the Brain – The Modern Era of Medicine," Fortanasce-Purino Medical Center, accessed May 5, 2018, http://www.healthybrainmd.com/conditions-treat/marijuana-brain-modern-era-medicine/.

mistake. They both regard wine as a drug and not as a drink."[2] Those who push back against a Catholic critique of drugs claim that drugs are made from natural substances, and thus, like alcohol, can be seen as the fruit of God's creation. What is the difference in the enjoyment derived from them?, they ask. The need to answer this question now presses urgently upon us as the acceptance of drugs grows in our country.

The first distinction we need to make to reply to this objection comes from recognizing that beer and wine are foodstuffs. They come not just from natural substances (uranium is a natural substance), but from substances used for normal human consumption. Like the components from which they are made, beer and wine are naturally healthy and should be consumed as part of an overall healthy diet. As a foodstuff, Aquinas defends the consumption of alcohol as permitted within the Gospel's lifting of the prohibition against normal food and drink: "No meat or drink, considered in itself, is unlawful, according to Matthew 15:11, 'not what goes into the mouth defiles a man, but what comes out of the mouth, this defiles a man.'"[3] Though already considered "clean" in the Old Covenant, beer and wine would pass the muster set forth in Matthew's Gospel. Other natural substances, including plants used to produce drugs, would not pass this test; they are not foodstuffs and intrinsically harm the body.

Many people claim that both caffeine and alcohol are drugs because they alter the body and the functioning of the brain. If we followed this logic, we would have to admit that just about everything we consume is a drug, because all food and drink impact the body and brain in some way. If we look at the difference between caffeine, alcohol, and drugs, we can draw some distinctions:

- Caffeine does not impair normal brain functioning.
- Alcohol in moderate use does not impair normal brain functioning, but immoderate use does.
- Drugs in ordinary use impair normal brain functioning.

By "ordinary use of drugs," I mean that people use drugs, including marijuana, specifically to get high. I admit it is possible to use drugs in a

---

[2] G. K. Chesterton, *George Bernard Shaw* (New York: John Lane, 1909), writing against Shaw's puritanism.

[3] *ST* II-II, q. 149, a. 3, corpus.

moderate way if small amounts are consumed, but this falls outside ordinary usage and would apply only to a small number of cases, compared to the large number of people who ordinarily use alcohol in moderation.[4] Some components of drugs are used in pharmaceuticals, but we have discovered serious problems when these drugs are overused or abused. If we consider the moderate consumption of alcohol to be a usage of drugs, then we are equivocating. Drugs, as the word usually connotes, are substances that engender a feeling of being high, in a withdrawal from ordinary experience and consciousness. Anything we ingest alters us, but normally our food and drink do so in accord with our good, in harmony with the good of our rationality.

Barley and grapes, along with water, are the main ingredients of beer and wine, respectively. These are foods, which are part of a normal diet and the fermentation process does not fundamentally alter their nutrition. There is nothing intrinsically harmful in the chemical composition of beer and wine, including alcohol, except at higher dosages. In fact, the moderate use of alcohol has many health benefits, which have been confirmed by many scientific studies. Rod Phillips summarizes these findings: "All other variables being constant, moderate alcohol

Barley. (Wikimedia Commons)

4 One of these exceptions comes from the diminishment of THC from the cannabis plant, such as the Charlotte's Web Strain, and the strengthening of CBD, which can prevent seizures.

consumption is a healthier option than abstaining from alcohol."[5] Some of the particular benefits from the regular and moderate consumption of beer include better bone health, improved cholesterol, decreased stress, reduced risk of type-2 diabetes, and a healthy dose of fiber and vitamins.[6] Even St. Paul confirmed the healthfulness of alcohol: "Stop drinking only water, but use a little wine for the sake of your stomach and your frequent ailments" (1 Tim. 5:23).

The Catholic tradition affirms the moderate use of alcohol, with the support of divine revelation itself! Now that drugs are becoming more and more widespread, it is time for Catholics to mark the clear difference between alcohol and drugs. Drugs demand a negative response as they do not promote the human good, neither individually nor culturally. They offer anesthesia, a way to escape from a sick culture. But this sick culture desperately needs us to face it and transform it, to fill the black hole of God's absence. Gisela Kreglinger, in her book *The Spirituality of Wine*, notes that the rise of drugs has accompanied the decline of religious belief and practices. She points out that a decline in faith precludes the socialization and rituals surrounding alcohol that Christianity offers. She claims that it is less likely for alcohol to be abused and for people to resort to drugs when children are taught "the proper benedictions for food and drink," "drinking as an act of communion," and "drunkenness as profanity."[7] These religious practices show the communal and religious context for drinking, and link alcohol to the family and sacred meal. Alcohol becomes a normal and at times sacred element of life, not an individual revolt against family, society, and God.

Rod Phillips has speculated that a decline in drinking among young people, which at first may seem positive, may indicate a shift toward drug use.[8] The chemical differences alone between barley and grapes and the makeup of the cannabis plant reveal a problem with this shift.[9]

---

[5]  Phillips, *Alcohol*, 316.

[6]  See Brianna Steinhilber, "7 Science-backed Reasons Beer May Be Good for You," *NBC News*, March 16, 2018, https://nbcnews.com/better/health/7-science-backed-ways-beer-good-your-health-ncna788986.

[7]  Kreglinger, *Spirituality of Wine*, 190.

[8]  Phillips, *Alcohol*, 322. In fact, he points to the rise of reliable drinking water in the twentieth century as the reason for the decline of wine and beer as everyday — and even throughout the day — drinks. Coffee has now taken on this role in the United States.

[9]  Ironically, hops and hemp are both members of the Cannabaceae plant family.

Tetrahydrocannabinol, abbreviated as THC, is the main psychoactive chemical found in the cannabis plant. Cannabis has eighty unique chemicals, which can be contrasted with the much simpler chemical makeup of alcoholic drinks, particularly when we contrast THC with ethanol. The plant's flower buds, when dried, are used to smoke as marijuana; the resin of the plant is used to make hashish, which can be smoked or made into an extract oil. Significantly, THC levels in marijuana have risen from about 1 percent to between 20 and 30 percent in the last fifty years.

THC primarily affects the brain: euphoria, calmness, anxiety, paranoia, distorted sense of time, magical or random thinking, short-term memory loss, depression, distorted perceptions, difficulty with thinking and problem solving, and disrupted learning and memory.[10] It also has many physical effects, such as greater carcinogenic harm than smoking cigarettes. Unlike consuming a foodstuff in moderation, the consumption of cannabis immediately affects the functioning of the brain, an effect compounded over time, especially for adolescents. In fact, marijuana usage can permanently alter the brain, leading to a great risk of psychosis, psychological problems, and lower IQ scores.[11] Further, one of the most frightening discoveries shows that consuming marijuana alters DNA, creating harmful mutations that will be passed down to children and future generations. One doctor studying this phenomenon, Dr. Stuart Reece, concluded "that cancers and illnesses were likely caused by cell mutations resulting from cannabis properties having a chemical interaction with a person's DNA."[12] Smoking pot can have permanent health effects — and not just for the individual user.

---

Hops, however, lack the psychoactive qualities of cannabis and have no THC. The cannabis plant does have a positive use, not as food, but in its fibers, used to make hemp.

[10] See "What Is Marijuana?," *National Institute on Drug Abuse*, https://www.drugabuse.gov/publications/drugfacts/marijuana.

[11] For the mental health impact, particularly schizophrenia and depression, and many other important findings, see the National Academy for Sciences, Engineering, and Medicine, *The Health Effects of Cannabis and Cannabinoids: The Current State of Evidence and Recommendations for Research*, January 12, 2017, http://nationalacademies.org/hmd/reports/2017/health-effects-of-cannabis-and-cannabinoids.aspx.

[12] Lizzie Parry, "Smoking Cannabis ALTERS Your DNA 'Causing Mutations That Can Trigger Serious Illness, Including Cancer,'" *Daily Mail*, May 24, 2016, www.dailymail.co.uk/health/article-3607444/Smoking-cannabis-ALTERS-DNA-causing-mutations-trigger-illness-including-cancer.html#ixzz59IQdOnw9.

For these and similar reasons, the Vatican's pastoral handbook on drugs claims that to speak of marijuana as a soft drug "is a pure illusion" and cautions against its trivialization.[13] It also affirms that "cannabis is not an ordinary substance."[14] Beer is an ordinary substance, even if it can be abused. Writing on the differences between marijuana and alcohol, Roger Scruton notes that "obviously there are significant medical and physiological differences. Alcohol is rapidly expelled from the system and is addictive only in large doses — at least to those . . . whose genetic make-up has been influenced by the millennia of winemaking." Furthermore, "the effects of cannabis remain for days, and it is both more addictive and more radical, leading not just to temporary alterations of the mind but to permanent or semi-permanent transformations of personality, and in particular to a widely observed loss of moral sense."[15] The moderate use of alcohol, however, promotes health, friendship, and, as we have seen, finds divine sanction for its role in Christian worship.

## THE INTRINSIC PROBLEM OF MARIJUANA AND OTHER DRUGS: ESCAPE FROM REALITY AND REASON

Drugs represent one, and possibly the most pronounced, attempt to escape from reality, acting as an anesthetic against one's problems. The growing role of drugs reminds me of the use of "soma" in Huxley's *Brave New World*: "Why you don't take soma when you have these dreadful ideas of yours. You'd forget all about them. And instead of feeling miserable, you'd be jolly. *So* jolly." Accepting drugs represents an important step toward the dystopia that Huxley saw emerging in the world. Ultimately, drugs offer a spiritual dystopia, one that seeks to eliminate the Gospel's daily call to take up one's Cross, deny oneself, and to follow Christ. They lead us away from the reality that "it is necessary for us to undergo many hardships to enter the kingdom of God" (Acts 14:22). Drugs cover over our tribulations, seeking an escape hatch from our difficulties, though they generally create even more of them.

---

[13]  Pontifical Council for Health Pastoral Care, *Church: Drugs and Drug Addiction: A Pastoral Handbook* (Città del Vaticano: Liberia Editrice Vatican, 2002), 42; 57.

[14]  Ibid., 167.

[15]  Scruton, *I Drink*, 129.

Drugs stand at the heart of modern disillusionment with life. At the heart of this crisis lies the lack of a central unifying force for our culture. We have lost a sense of purpose and lack the inspiration needed to work hard in the messiness of reality. Ultimately, drug use reflects our spiritual crisis, as Pope Benedict describes:

> The new forms of slavery to drugs and the lack of hope into which so many people fall can be explained not only in sociological and psychological terms but also in essentially spiritual terms. The emptiness in which the soul feels abandoned, despite the availability of countless therapies for body and psyche, leads to suffering. There cannot be holistic development and universal common good unless people's spiritual and moral welfare is taken into account, considered in their totality as body and soul.[16]

To resign ourselves to a culture that accepts and embraces drugs caves into a position of spiritual despair, raising up an impediment that stops us from offering a more compelling vision through evangelization.

Alcohol, when abused, certainly provides a similar false escape from personal problems. It does not, however, deceive us by offering the possibility of entering some higher realm or false world. Both alcoholism and marijuana addiction isolate users, leading them to withdraw from the social setting set by fraternal drinking. Beer as a work of culture can be ordered toward the building up of culture, unlike drugs. Creating beer as the fruit of culture is an unlocking or perfecting of God's creation — a perfecting that He intended by making us rational beings. Drugs lead us into a dead-end, a satanic turn inward in rebellion against God and man. They lack beer's ability to promote human flourishing by integrating into a communal life and even holiness.

In order to evaluate the morality of drugs, we must return to Aquinas's teaching on drunkenness. Aquinas speaks of sobriety as needed for drinks "which by reason of [their] volatility [are] liable to disturb the brain (*caput*)."[17] We need to drink rationally, respecting the good of our nature

[16] Pope Benedict XVI, *Caritas in Veritate*, encyclical letter, Vatican website, July 7, 2009, http://w2.vatican.va/content/benedict-xvi/en/encyclicals/documents/hf_ben-xvi_enc_20090629_caritas-in-veritate.html, §76.

[17] *ST* II-II, q. 149, a. 1, corpus.

James Ensor, *The Drunkards* (1883). (Wiki Art)

and our end. Aquinas teaches us that virtue disposes us to the perfection of our nature.[18] Vice, on the other hand, does the opposite: "Now man derives his species from his rational soul: and consequently whatever is contrary to the order of reason is, properly speaking, contrary to the nature of man, as man."[19] Consequently, Aquinas defines sin as something contrary to right reason. This does not deny, but includes, the fact that sin ultimately contradicts the will of God, because God created the good of nature and His commands lead us to our own flourishing and happiness.

Aquinas's description of drunkenness provides a foundation for understanding why drugs harm human life and culture. Unlike alcohol they are not consumed moderately, but intrinsically involve surrendering full possession of reason. They provide a retreat from a rational and responsible confrontation with reality. Pope Benedict stated it even more strongly by arguing that they also represent an escape from the reality of the spiritual life that God presents to us: "The patient and humble adventure of asceticism, which, in small steps of ascent, comes closer to the descending God, is replaced by magical power, the magical key of drugs—the ethical and

---

18   *ST* I-II, q. 71, a. 1.
19   Ibid., a. 2.

religious path is replaced by technology. Drugs are the pseudo-mysticism of a world that does not believe yet cannot get rid of the soul's yearning for paradise."[20] Here we see drugs specifically as a distorted attempt to respond to our rational and religious nature, but in a way that ultimately undermines them.

The *Catechism of the Catholic Church* takes a different angle on drugs, demonstrating how they violate the commands of God, specifically the fifth commandment. It emphasizes the harm that drugs inflict on us, the basic threat they pose to human life: "The use of drugs inflicts very grave damage on human health and life. Their use, except on strictly therapeutic grounds, is a grave offense. Clandestine production of and trafficking in drugs are scandalous practices. They constitute direct co-operation in evil, since they encourage people to practices gravely contrary to the moral law" (§2291). The *Catechism* also implicates those who facilitate and encourage drug use.

Ironically, drugs first became legal in the United States under the rubric of health (with medical marijuana in California in 1996), but have quickly become legal in many states for recreational use as well. Recent statistics show that medical marijuana use in Colorado has decreased, while recreational use has increased.[21] The *Catechism* notes that drugs can be used for therapeutic reasons, but the need to alleviate pain must balance with the effects that such therapy has on the soul. The right use of reason and one's spiritual health trump physical concerns. In this light, consideration should be given to other options for care that respect our rational nature and support it, rather than work against it.

Culture should draw us together as we work to pursue the common good. This requires the proper formation of the faculty of reason (which

[20] Josef Cardinal Ratzinger, *Turning Point for Europe?* (San Francisco: Ignatius Press, 1994), 20.

[21] Miles Moraitis, "Medical Marijuana Licenses See Decrease in Colorado, While Recreational Ones Increase," 9News, September 1, 2018, https://www.9news.com/article/news/local/medical-marijuana-licenses-see-decrease-in-colorado-while-recreational-ones-increase/73-470056264. The decrease in the use of medical marijuana should not surprise us, as a "comprehensive 2015 scientific review found medical marijuana to be useful only for a small number of medical conditions. Writing in the *Journal of the American Medical Association*, an international team of researchers found scant evidence to support broad claims for the drug's effectiveness" (Tadeusz Pacholczyk, "The Smoke Over Medical Marijuana," *Denver Catholic*, July 3, 2018, https://denvercatholic.org/the-smoke-over-medical-marijuana).

should occur in education) and the exercise of that reason in service to others. Just as drug use provides a retreat from personal problems, it also provides a retreat from a common culture. Drugs stand as a "no" to common goods and self-transcendence and offer a retreat into oneself. Pope Benedict once again provides illumination: "The anti-culture of death, which finds expression for example in drug use, is thus countered by an unselfish love which shows itself to be a culture of life by the very willingness to 'lose itself' (cf. Lk 17:33 et passim) for others."[22] The contrast is between a culture of death where individuals selfishly withdraw from others, putting their feelings and pleasure first, and a culture of life that encourages the sacrifice of oneself for others.

## CONSEQUENCES OF MARIJUANA LEGALIZATION

Defenders of legalized marijuana claim that it is safe and healthy and benefits our country by taking pressure off law enforcement (although the crime rate has risen in Colorado[23]). This argument fits with our general understanding of freedom: let individuals make their own choices, especially if they are not harming anyone else. The embrace of this radicalized understanding of freedom, however, has come with a cost to both the individual and society. We can see already that legalized pot seriously damages health and presents a moral and physical danger to society.

Pope Francis responded to the growing trend toward legalization as follows:

> Let me state this in the clearest terms possible: the problem of drug use is not solved with drugs! Drug addiction is an evil, and with evil there can be no yielding or compromise. . . . Attempts, however limited, to legalize so-called "recreational drugs," are not only highly questionable from a legislative standpoint, but they fail to produce the desired effects. . . . Here I would reaffirm what I have

[22] Pope Benedict XVI, *Deus Caritas Est*, encyclical letter, Vatican website, December 25, 2005, http://w2.vatican.va/content/benedict-xvi/en/encyclicals/documents/hf_ben-xvi_enc_20051225_deus-caritas-est.html, §30.

[23] Scott McLean and Sara Weisfeld, "Colorado Governor Won't Rule Out Banning Marijuana Again. Here's Why," CNN, April 20, 2018, https://www.cnn.com/2018/04/20/us/colorado-marijuana-and-crime/index.html. Governor John Hickenlooper was a craft beer pioneer, cofounding Denver's Wynkoop Brewery in 1988.

stated on another occasion: No to every type of drug use. It is as simple as that.[24]

The question from a Catholic point of view really comes down to whether or not drugs promote the human good. If they do, they can be drawn into the life of virtue; if they do not, they are rather a part of vice and sin that undermine our lives.

When discussing the consequences of legalization, we must focus on the common good rather than on the importance of individual choice. The transfer of drug use from a strong subculture into American mainstream culture will affect the entire nation. Aquinas explains how this is so. Today we understand law's purpose as securing personal rights. But Aquinas explains that law is meant to lead the individual beyond the self to an exterior and shared good: "The proper effect of law is to make those to whom it is given, good."[25] Whatever the law legitimates comes to be seen as good. This has happened in our country with contraception, abortion, euthanasia, and gay marriage. While it is unfortunately true that some immoral things have to be tolerated, this cannot be used as an excuse to permit things that undermine goodness and happiness on a fundamental level. If drugs attack the faculty that leads to happiness, our reason, then there are legitimate grounds to think that it will threaten the maintenance of society and consequently hurt others. We have to ask what kind of citizen we want in our country. Our laws should reflect that ideal, although we do not generally have a shared ideal of citizenship today.

We have already seen a number of damaging effects of marijuana legalization in Colorado. The *Denver Post* noted that legalizing marijuana immediately encouraged some Coloradans to rethink their position on pot and to try it for the first time because it became "easy, convenient and legal."[26] By legalizing marijuana, states are saying they no longer see it as fundamentally detrimental to human life and society. But despite

[24] Pope Francis, "Address to Participants in the 31st International Drug Enforcement Conference" (June 20, 2014), https://zenit.org/articles/pope-s-address-to-conference-against-drugs/.

[25] *ST* I-II, q. 92, a. 1.

[26] Colleen O'Connor, "Colorado's New Pot Buyers Are Curious, but Some Worry about Stigma," *Denver Post*, January 4, 2014, https://www.denverpost.com/2014/01/04/colorados-new-pot-buyers-are-curious-but-some-worry-about-stigma.

Denver. (Wikimedia Commons)

marijuana's growing acceptance, there has been a documented rise in health and social problems. Following the legalization of marijuana, Colorado formed a Retail Marijuana Public Health Advisory Committee, which released a report on January 30, 2015. The Committee found a general increase in health problems: "In general, there were large increases in poison center calls, hospitalizations, and emergency department visits observed after medical marijuana was commercialized in 2010 and additional increases after retail (recreational) marijuana was legalized in 2014."[27] The increase in hospitalizations applies to children as well, as Colorado noted that one in six children entering the hospital for lung issues had been exposed *to marijuana.*[28]

Although defenders of legal pot claim that there has not been an increase in youth consumption, schools have dealt with a sharp increase in marijuana-related problems:

> An investigation . . . shows drug violations reported by Colorado's K-12 schools have increased 45 percent in the past four years, even as the combined number of all other violations has fallen. . . . The investigation found an increase in high school drug violations of 71 percent since legalization. School suspensions for drugs increased

[27] Ibid.

[28] John Daley, "Colorado Study: 1 In 6 Kids Hospitalized for Lung Issue Exposed to Pot," *CPR News*, May 13, 2016, https://www.cpr.org/news/newsbeat/colorado-study-1-6-kids-hospitalized-lung-issue-exposed-pot.

45 percent. The National Survey on Drug Use and Health found Colorado ranks first in the country for marijuana use among teens, scoring well above the national average.[29]

Legalization has led to even easier access to marijuana for youth. Colorado has also experienced increased car crashes that involve people impaired by the influence of marijuana. The Advisory Committee cited above found "substantial evidence that risk of motor vehicle crash doubles among drivers with recent marijuana use. Additionally, we found substantial evidence for a positive relationship between THC blood level and motor vehicle crash risk—that is, substantial evidence that the higher the level of THC in blood, the higher the crash risk." In 2015 over one hundred thousand people moved to Colorado, with a large number coming for marijuana, driving up housing costs significantly. The roads quickly became congested (with potheads), leading to yearly increases of fatal crashes caused by marijuana's influence.[30] Other effects include a 4 percent rise in crime at the same time the rest of the country saw a decrease in crime—including an increase, not a decrease, in drug trafficking. The legalization of marijuana has provided a means for Mexican drug cartels to cover activity and has opened a new and easy means of transmitting pot across the United States.[31] Colorado has also seen an 8 percent spike in the homeless population.

Many state officials, not just in Colorado, have been positive on legalization. In part, this comes from what has been referred to as an "addiction to revenue" from taxing marijuana sales. For the 2014–15 fiscal year, ending last summer, Colorado collected seventy million dollars

[29] Gazette Editorial Board, "The Sad Anniversary of Big Commercial Pot in Colorado," *The Gazette*, November 9, 2017, http://gazette.com/editorial-the-sad-anniversary-of-big-commercial-pot-in-colorado/article/1614900.

[30] David Migoya, "Traffic Fatalities Linked to Marijuana Are Up Sharply in Colorado," *Denver Post*, August 25, 2017, https://www.denverpost.com/2017/08/25/colorado-marijuana-traffic-fatalities/.

[31] Sally Mamdooh, "Mexican Drug Cartels Are Taking Full Advantage of Colorado's Marijuana Laws," Denver ABC 7, April 7, 2016, https://www.thedenverchannel.com/news/local-news/marijuana/mexican-drug-cartels-are-taking-full-advantage-of-colorados-marijuana-laws; Dane Schiller, "Colorado Combats a New Breed of Drug Traffickers," *Seattle Times*, September 26, 2016, https://www.seattletimes.com/nation-world/colorado-combats-a-new-breed-of-drug-traffickers/.

in taxes on pot, even more than it collected from alcohol.[32] Given the social problems already mentioned, this revenue comes at a serious cost to Colorado citizens. Overall, the tone of the culture has shifted. One crazy example can be found in the International Church of Cannabis, which "claims cannabis as its primary sacrament."[33] The "church" was prosecuted by the County of Denver for the public consumption of pot, but the judge declared a mistrial because of the difficulty of obtaining jurors with an unbiased view of marijuana. Marijuana advocates have been pushing for greater access to public smoking.

When discussing Prohibition in chapter thirteen, I noted that it was wrong to equate beer consumption with the immoderate consumption of liquor. The temperance movement targeted both, unable to recognize that beer was the moderate alternative. Similarly, beer provides a moderate alternative to marijuana, one that promotes fellowship, and therefore links us to a common good that transcends the self. Drug use, like hard liquor, helps us to withdraw from society and even from the goods of our own nature. Many people have compared laws against marijuana to Prohibition. However, just as the prohibition of alcohol clearly failed in the eyes of Americans, I hope legalization of marijuana will do the same. Alcohol, as a foodstuff meant for moderate consumption, could not be banned successfully. Marijuana, which fails to meet the same criteria, should be banned for pushing the user too quickly beyond reason.

---

[32] Tanya Basu, "Colorado Collected More Tax Revenue from Marijuana than from Alcohol," *Time*, May 18, 2016, http://time.com/4037604/colorado-marijuana-tax-revenue/.

[33] Alex Pasquariello, "Judge Declares Mistrial for Cannabis Church Charges," *Denver Post*, March 2, 2018, https://www.thecannabist.co/2018/03/01/international-church-of-cannabis-mistrial-420/100191/.

# CHAPTER 15

# *Refermenting a Consumerist Culture*

In light of the crisis of the common good we saw in the previous chapter, we need to consider beer's place within a broader perspective. When beer is ordered to the glory of God and for the good of society, the two goals reinforce one another. The co-founder of the Catholic Worker Movement, Peter Maurin, rightly insisted in one of his Easy Essays that

> As a person
> man cannot serve God
> without serving
> the common good.[1]

Maurin worked for the creation of a society where it would be easier for people to be good, emphasizing becoming better rather than better off. We exist for God and for others and find our happiness in giving ourselves to them. Beer finds its goal or telos only in supporting the overarching goal of human life. As a work of culture, it does not exist for itself, but for the promotion of health and well-being, the social good, and ultimately the glory of God.

## MEANS AND ENDS

A large problem in any consumerist society is the tendency to make a means into an end. The end is that for which you do all else: your goal. Money is a means, as we work to earn money only to purchase further needed goods. Consumerism makes money the major goal of life and success, and continually creates new desires to reinforce an endless, restless search for more means. Just as money is a means, so are all of

---

[1] Peter Maurin, *Easy Essays* (Eugene, OR: Wipf & Stock, 2010), 44.

the consumerist goods and pleasures made accessible by money. And yet, we must ask for what purpose it all exists.

Beer is a commodity and brewing is a traditional method of production. Brewing has been part of the home economy for as long as civilization has existed. It served the good of the family and society by providing a nutritious foodstuff, one capable of fostering some added joy. The monks created the first large-scale breweries in Europe, but small-scale brewing was conducted primarily by women in the early Middle Ages. The medieval English mystic, Margery Kempe (1373–1438), actually set out to get rich by brewing, thereby putting the wrong goal before herself, but the Lord prevented her! She describes the experience in the third person:

> Then out of pure covetousness, and to maintain her pride, she took up brewing, and was one of the greatest brewers in the town of N. for three or four years until she lost a great deal of money, for she had never had any experience in that business. For however good her servants were and however knowledgeable in brewing, things would never go successfully for them. For when the ale had as fine a head of froth on it as anyone might see, suddenly the froth would go flat, and all the ale was lost in one brewing after another, so that her servants were ashamed and would not stay with her. Then this creature thought how God had punished her before—and she could not take heed—and now again by the loss of her goods; and then she left off and did no more brewing.[2]

Contrast Margery's initial motives to Ken and Tom of Blind Faith Brewing, who, as we saw in chapter eleven, began brewing for charitable causes through the Knights of Columbus. They approached brewing from the opposite perspective of Margery: they brewed first to serve the Lord and others, and later entered into it as professional work. A Minnesota brewery, Finnegans, goes even farther by donating 100 percent of its profits to fight hunger, using beer to fulfill a work of mercy.[3]

---

[2]  *The Book of Margery Kempe* (New York: Penguin, 2000), 44.

[3]  Finnegans buys fresh produce from local farmers, thereby supporting the local economy, and donates it to food shelves. See Jessica Trygstad, "Minnesota Beer Company Celebrates 15 Years of Feeding the Hungry," *Catholic News Service*,

Making beer an end leads to the problem of alcoholism, which we addressed in chapter thirteen. In terms of consumerism, we can become too attached to beer and to trying new products and styles. Beer can become a distraction from more important goods, can become our focus and even a minor end in itself. Aquinas treats this overattachment to material goods through the sins of acquisitiveness and covetousness. He argues that we should have the proper measure of external goods, only those we need as means to achieve our necessary ends. "External goods," such as beer, "come under the head of things useful for an end," which must be possessed in a "certain measure" according to the human good.[4] It is a sin to desire the acquisition of external goods immoderately because this does not lead us to our true end, which is happiness in God.

Anders Zorn, *The Little Brewery* (1890). (Wikimedia Commons)

The goal of work is not profit or wealth, but the care of persons and growth in holiness and virtue. The great English distributist, Fr. Vincent McNabb, argued that we have lost sight of just price and just profit.[5] Sometimes prices need to be higher and profits need to be less in order to compensate workers appropriately, make quality products worth

April 11, 2015, https://www.ncronline.org/news/parish/minnesota-beer-company -celebrates-15-years-feeding-hungry.

4   *ST* II-II, q. 118, a. 1, corpus.
5   See Vincent McNabb, OP, *Nazareth or Social Chaos* (Norfolk, VA: IHS, 2009), 41.

purchasing, care for the earth adequately, and attend to the common good. John Senior argued that there are immediate, proximate, and final ends to work. The immediate end is a job well done, the proximate is the love of neighbor, and the final is to know and love God by imitating Christ, especially in the sacrifice of His life.[6] Our work and consumption find their deepest meaning when we order them for the good of others and God.

Therefore, our faith brings us to a deeper reality than profit and acquisition: gift. Our lives are gifts and we find fulfillment only by giving. We are redeemed with grace freely given by God. Drinking responds to the gift of life with joy. Returning to Pieper, he describes how "there can be no festivity when man, imagining himself self-sufficient, refused to recognize the Goodness of things which goes far beyond any conceivable utility. . . . He truly receives it only when he accepts it as pure gift."[7] Drinking in the proper context should not draw us into the consumerist frenzy, but point us beyond it by enabling us to express the deeper movements of the heart in friendship and festivity. It should help us to "waste" our time by seeking things that point beyond utility and profit.

## TIME FOR SMALL BEER?

I was giving a talk at a local brewery last year and during my remarks I raised a glass in honor of locally owned microbrews and named our host brewery as an example. I specifically said that we need local beers to stand against giants like the largest international brewer, InBev. I toasted the brewery, but could see a couple of grimaces in the audience. After I finished my talk, a gentleman came up and said, "I hate to break it to you, but InBev just bought this brewery." The bartender was amused, but said she appreciated her new employee benefits more.

Here in Colorado, we have the largest single-site brewery in the world: the Coors brewery in Golden. It was founded by a German immigrant, Adolph Coors, who arrived in Colorado in 1873 to brew for the mountain miners. For most of the twentieth century, it was a regional brewer with limited distribution. It's now part of an international

---

[6]  Senior, *Restoration of Christian Culture*, 53–54.
[7]  Pieper, *In Tune with World*, 71.

conglomerate: Molson Coors and its subsidiary MillerCoors, the world's third largest brewer.[8] The Miller family left an enormous legacy to the Catholic Church, with Miller's grandson, Harry John, founding the De Rance Foundation in 1946, the world's largest Catholic charity for some time. Although Miller's (and Coors') beers may be a far cry from the Belgians, the foundation was named after Armand Jean le Bouthillier de Rancé, founder of the Trappists. Regardless, the combined company, no longer owned by either family, had 7.72 billion dollars in revenue in 2015, a long way from serving miners.

The Coors Brewery in Golden, CO. (Wikimedia Commons)

Tolkien gives us two views for approaching beer and wealth. First, at the end of *The Hobbit*, the dying dwarf Thorin looks back on his own greed and compares himself to Bilbo: "If more of us valued food and cheer above hoarded gold, it would be a much merrier world." As I discussed in chapter seven, the Shire represents the simple merriment of life in community, which makes its scouring a direct attack on the good life. Contrast Thorin's final reflection with Farmer Cotton's description of what happened while the younger hobbits went on their journey "there and back again":

---

[8]   To give a sense of the dizzying international movement of brewing consolidation, the MillerCoors subsidiarity formed just in 2016, when the joint venture between Molson Coors and SABMiller ended. When AB InBev purchased SAB (South African Brewing Co.), the Department of Justice imposed the sale of Miller as a condition of the merger.

> "It all began with Pimple, as we call him," said Farmer Cotton; "and
> it began as soon as you'd gone off, Mr. Frodo. He'd funny ideas,
> had Pimple. Seems he wanted to own everything himself, and then
> order other folk about. It soon came out that he already did own
> a sight more than was good for him; and he was always grabbing
> more, though where he got the money was a mystery: mills and
> malt-houses and inns, and farms, and leaf-plantations."

Pimple turned from merriment to hoarding wealth, consolidating
malt-houses and inns. Like the hobbits defending the Shire, I witnessed
an enormous amount of pride in local brewing in La Crosse, Wisconsin,
where I finished my last two years of high school in a seminary boarding
school. Part of the city's pride was its Heileman Brewery, founded in 1858.
It produced Old Style, but shut down in 1996 after being acquired by
Stroh's. After years of bemoaning the loss of the brewery, La Crosse got
its brewery back in 2016 when City Brewery reopened the old site and
began brewing Old Style again. The restoration of this defunct brewery
is a small sign that we can restore our losses if we fight back and work
hard for a local economy and culture.

Stephen Mansfield's *The Search for God and Guinness* gives an example
of how beer can serve the community. The Guinness family was part of
the Protestant elite ruling class of Ireland (before independence). The
family ardently supported Unionism with Great Britain and did not
allow Catholics into management until the 1960s. Therefore, it might
be odd to look to them as a model for socially responsible brewing. But
the story of Guinness shows how brewing can serve both employees and
the local community. Mansfield describes how the Guinness family paid
their employees superior wages; invested in training, education, leisure
opportunities, advanced medical care, and adequate housing for them;
and sought to improve the conditions of Dublin's poor. The family also
supported religious initiatives, opening Ireland's first Sunday schools,
with one member of the family, Henry Grattan Guinness, becoming an
internationally renowned preacher. The family's philosophy was "you
cannot make money from people unless you are willing for people to
make money from you."[9] Despite accusing the Guinness family of creating

---

[9] Mansfield, *Search for God and Guinness*, xxx.

"anti-popery porter," Catholics in Dublin nonetheless recognized that the family served the good of the community and its Catholic employees.[10]

Unfortunately, Guinness is no longer family-owned (or even Irish-owned) and is now part of an international conglomerate, Diageo, owned by the Chinese corporation Kweichow Moutai. What's the problem with the enormous beer conglomerates? As Wendell Berry has put it, "bigness is totalitarian."[11] Bill Cavanaugh explains one way in which this bigness impacts business as "it is considered good business practice to maximize the disparity of power between employer and employee to increase the profit margin of the corporation."[12] Consumers take advantage of this disparity by purchasing goods at the lowest possible prices, strengthening their consumerist power. Anonymous stockholders are prioritized by the company over those more present to them, including the employee, family members, and community.[13]

The beer industry has seen an enormous number of consolidations in the last twenty years, as each company seeks to bring down costs and to increase market share. America's great and historic beers are no longer even American! The lesser known breweries, Yuengling (1829) and Schell (1860), are now the two oldest American, family-owned breweries in the country. Brewing consolidation has only picked up in recent years, creating a market dominated by only a handful of companies. *Business Insider* noted in 2016 that

> in 2004, 10 brewers controlled 51% of the global beer market by volume. Ten years later, five beer makers — Anheuser-Busch InBev, SABMiller, Heineken, Carlsberg, and China Resources Enterprise — controlled about the same amount. Anheuser-Busch InBev, which makes Budweiser, merged with SABMiller at the end of last year, giving the new company about 30% of the global market share. Bottom line: Big beer is *big*.[14]

[10] Ibid., 92–93.

[11] Wendell Berry, *The Unsettling of America: Culture & Agriculture* (Berkeley: Counterpoint, 1996), 41.

[12] William Cavanaugh, *Being Consumed: Economics and Christian Desire* (Grand Rapids, MI: Eerdmans, 2008), 21–22.

[13] Ibid., 23.

[14] Dylan Roach, "These 5 Beer Makers Own More than Half of the World's Beer," *Business Insider*, Feb. 9, 2016, http://www.businessinsider.com/biggest-beer-companies

To broaden the scope, another headline noted that "just 11 companies brew 90% of the beers sold in the US."[15] The major brewers consolidated first, but with craft sales rising, many smaller craft breweries have been picked up by the giants as well, with casualties such as Leinenkugel's, Goose Island, and Breckenridge.[16]

Beer may have deep roots in European tradition, but it has become a truly international commodity, with major brewing companies now spanning the globe. The best example of this is the world's largest brewer Anheuser-Busch InBev, which first formed out of a Brazilian takeover of a Belgium company and eventually included America's largest brewer (AB) and its next largest rival SAB (South African Brewing) in 2016 — a Brazilian, Belgian, American, African brewing company spanning four continents! Further, the number one producing country in the world is China, brewing almost twice as much as the number two country, the United States — forty-one million kiloliters to twenty-two million. They are followed in volume of production by Brazil, Mexico, Germany, Russia, Japan, Vietnam, the United Kingdom, Poland, Spain, South Africa, Nigeria, France, Holland, Thailand, India, Belgium, South Korea, the Czech Republic, Columbia, Canada, Argentina, Ukraine, and the Philippines.[17] I list all of these top brewing countries so that you can see every major continent represented.

In spite of this enormous, international consolidation, global beer production has stagnated in recent years. At the same time craft beer sales have been rising, picking up a larger share of the market. The Brewers Association for Small and Independent Craft brewers reported that "overall U.S. beer volume sales were down 1% in 2017, whereas craft brewer sales continued to grow at a rate of 5% by volume, reaching 12.7% of the U.S. beer market by volume.... Retail dollar sales of craft increased 8%, up to $26.0 billion, and now account for more

---

-in-the-world-2016-1.

[15] "Just 11 Companies Brew 90 Percent of Beers Sold in the US," *Fox News*, July 29, 2015, http://www.foxnews.com/food-drink/2015/07/29/just-11-companies-brew-90-percent-beers-sold-in-us.html.

[16] Hence we can see the irony of Anheuser-Busch's 2016 Super Bowl commercial making fun of craft beer drinkers as they continue to purchase craft breweries.

[17] "Kirin Beer University Report Global Beer Production by Country in 2016," Kirin, accessed March 9, 2018, http://www.kirinholdings.co.jp/english/news/2017/0810_01.html.

than 23% of the $111.4 billion U.S. beer market."[18] This phenomenon has been called the "premiumization" of beer, as consumers of craft beer drink less, but are willing to pay more for higher quality.[19] As craft breweries increase their market shares, more brewing jobs have been created. Since 2008, in a "strange and happy" development, in spite of a downturn in production and consolidation, breweries in the US "expanded by a factor of six, and the number of brewery workers grew by 120 percent."[20] This craft brewing revolution has been driven by a development in "taste" as well as by increased innovation and entrepreneurship.

The time has come once again for what Joseph Pearce describes as "small beer." We are no longer talking about the weak medieval beer for children, but an international movement to localize beer production. Pearce notes that "macrophilia—the cult of bigness—has been the prevailing trend in economic thinking for almost two hundred years . . . resulting in huge multinational corporations," as we have seen.[21] A native of England, Pearce traces a similar consolidation of brewing there and the successful emergence of microbreweries, "which went into the competition with the corporate brewers with the bravado and faith of a David facing a Goliath."[22] This miraculous victory meant that "the quality of the product is valued beyond the quantity and economics of its production. That these companies value traditional methods of making beer, and use local skills available to them, is indeed an essential ingredient of their superior quality."[23] Beer provides one amazing example of how *Small Is Still Beautiful*.[24]

[18] "National Beer Sales and Production Data," Brewers Association, accessed March 9, 2018, https://www.brewersassociation.org/statistics/national-beer-sales-production-data/.

[19] Hoalst-Pullen and Patterson, *Atlas of Beer*, 21.

[20] Derek Thompson, "Craft Beer Is the Strangest, Happiest Economic Story in America: Corporate Goliaths Are Taking over the U.S. Economy. Yet Small Breweries Are Thriving. Why?" *The Atlantic*, January 19, 2018, https://www.theatlantic.com/business/archive/2018/01/craft-beer-industry/550850/.

[21] Joseph Pearce, *Small Is Still Beautiful: Economics as if Families Mattered* (Wilmington, DE: ISI Books, 2006), 91.

[22] Ibid., 105.

[23] Ibid., 107.

[24] The title of Pearce's book refers to E. F. Schumacher's enormously important work on economics, *Small Is Beautiful: Economics as if People Mattered*, published in 1973.

Dorothy Day, herself a distributist arguing for more widespread ownership, would have agreed with this vision. Describing her work with Peter Maurin in the Catholic Worker Movement, she reflected: "Ours was a long-range program, looking for ownership by the workers of the means of production, the abolition of the assembly line, decentralized factories, the restoration of crafts and ownership of property. This meant, of course, an accent on the agrarian and rural aspects of our economy and a changing emphasis from the city to the land."[25] She summed up the project with the words, "everything needs to be decentralized," a pressing need for our society.[26] That brewing has shifted in this direction should encourage us to continue to reconsider our consumerist culture more generally.

## CONSUMERISM AND CATHOLIC SOCIAL TEACHING

Consumerism, like drug use, ultimately points to a spiritual problem, an interior restlessness that drives us to cover over deeper needs with the distraction of passing possessions. Christians should evaluate their economic decisions based on virtue, especially charity and justice, which focus on the good of the other. Pope Francis points out how consumerism points us inward and makes us blind to the needs of others:

> The great danger in today's world, pervaded as it is by consumerism, is the desolation and anguish born of a complacent yet covetous heart, the feverish pursuit of frivolous pleasures, and a blunted conscience. Whenever our interior life becomes caught up in its own interests and concerns, there is no longer room for others, no place for the poor. God's voice is no longer heard, the quiet joy of his love is no longer felt, and the desire to do good fades. This is a very real danger for believers too.[27]

Rather than aiming for the common good, "consumerism is, in fact, characterized by detachment from production, producers, and products.

---

[25] Quoted in Mark and Louise Zwick, *The Catholic Worker Movement: Intellectual and Spiritual Origins* (New York: Paulist Press, 2005), 166.

[26] Dorothy Day, *The Long Loneliness: The Autobiography of the Legendary Catholic Social Activist* (New York: Harper Collins, 1952), 190.

[27] Pope Francis, *Evangelii Gaudium* (2013), §2.

Consumerism is a restless spirit that is never content with any particular material thing."[28] It reinforces our culture's attempt to create radical autonomy through detached, individual choice. It also undercuts the sacramentality of Christian culture, which recognizes the material world and cultural goods as signs of deeper realities.

Technology and social media have only furthered our turn away from others. Nicholas Carr has written how automated technologies are "designed to be disinviting. They pull us away from the world. . . . As most people know from experience, the computer screen is intensely compelling, not only for the conveniences it offers but also for the many diversions it provides."[29] Technology gets in the way of reality, leaving only, he says, a shadow of the world. "We render ourselves incapable of perceiving," and "the result is existential impoverishment, as nature and culture withdraw their invitations to act and to perceive."[30] We have forgotten how to see and attend to the realities before us.

We have become even more in need of Belloc's baptism by beer! This metaphorical baptism, renewal by a poetic awakening to the world and others, can combat consumerism by refocusing our attention on our immediate experience and on others. Consumerism affects how we perceive and experience beer as well. It distracts us as "we are too busy getting and spending. . . . Our sensory powers are drained, exhausted, and shriveled by the likes of artificial flavoring, tasteless vegetables grown on Styrofoam and fed artificially — that is, without contact with real soil. Many consumers now prefer the strong and straightforward synthetic flavors to the more subtle and complex ones found in nature."[31] Beer — a product made from basic, natural ingredients — can bring us back to the realities of life, calling us to attend to and appreciate its subtleties. It is to be consumed not in isolation from others, but in community.

Beer rightly made and consumed can point us to what matters most in economics. Rather than profit, Peter Maurin taught that "people are what are important."[32] Brewing, as one form of work, presents us with one

---

[28] Cavanaugh, *Being Consumed*, xi.

[29] Nicholas Carr, *The Glass Cage: Automation and Us* (New York: W. W. Norton, 2014), 219.

[30] Ibid., 220.

[31] Kreglinger, *Spirituality of Wine*, 102.

[32] Dorothy Day, *Loaves and Fishes* (Maryknoll, NY: Orbis, 1997), 11.

particular way of cultivating or building culture. We work for people, to care for people: ourselves, our families, and the common good. Brewing has suffered from our consumerist culture, but has also shown resilience in resisting the global forces that reduce work to corporate profit. As an industry, brewing has shown its ability to promote local, sustainable, and employee-centered economics. Ethical brewing includes quality, fair pricing, wise management of profit, fair and safe labor practices, good stewardship of the environment, proper advertising (which includes the dignified portrayal of women and resistance to consumerist trends), and consumer education.

Pope Leo XIII laid out the manifesto for Catholic social teaching by standing up for workers in his groundbreaking encyclical *Rerum Novarum*: "The following duties bind the wealthy owner and the employer: not to look upon their work people as their bondsmen, but to respect in every man his dignity as a person ennobled by Christian character. They are reminded that, according to natural reason and Christian philosophy, working for gain is creditable, not shameful, to a man, since it enables him to earn an honorable livelihood; but to misuse men as though they were things in the pursuit of gain, or to value them solely for their physical powers — that is truly shameful and inhuman."[33] Leo established principles to govern how we should think about work: work expresses human rationality and creativity; work creates ownership; work must be sufficient to care for one's family; workers must be treated with full human dignity and be compensated adequately; workers should have sufficient leisure, especially on the Lord's Day.

Building on Leo's foundation, two popes explained further the ideal relationship between employers and their employees. First, Pius XI's *Quadragesimo Anno* explains that it is desirable "in the present condition of human society that, so far as is possible, the work-contract be somewhat modified by a partnership-contract, as is already being done in various ways and with no small advantage to workers and owners. Workers and other employees thus become sharers in ownership or management or participate in some fashion in the profits received."[34]

[33]  Leo XIII, *Rerum Novarum*, encyclical letter, Vatican website, (1891), http://w2.vatican.va/content/leo-xiii/en/encyclicals/documents/hf_l-xiii_enc_15051891_rerum-novarum.html, §20.

[34]  Pius XI, *Quadragesimo Anno*, encyclical letter, Vatican website, May 15, 1931,

John XXIII's *Mater et Magistra* describes "the need for giving workers an active part in the business of the company for which they work—be it a private or a public one. Every effort must be made to ensure that the enterprise is indeed a true human community, concerned about the needs, the activities and the standing of each of its members."[35] As Leo had explained, workers impress their very soul on what they produce and thus must reap adequately what they have earned.[36]

Friars farming the Santa Barbara Mission. (Wikimedia Commons)

There is a growing trend toward employee ownership in craft brewing. It presents not only a clear alternative to consolidation by one of the brewing giants, but also a way to improve corporate culture, retain employees, and increase tax benefits. There are three notable examples in Colorado: New Belgium and Odell in Ft. Collins, and Left Hand in Longmont. Other examples include Deschutes in Bend, Oregon; Modern Times in San Diego; and Harpoon in Boston. The founder of Modern Times, Jacob McKean, said he wanted to buck the overarching trend in the brewing industry, where "money is an end unto itself.... Nothing else is more important to them: not beer quality, not business ethics, not their employees' well being." Citing his own concern for business ethics, McKean said embracing employee ownership was the right thing so that employees "share in the company's financial success."[37] In 2012,

http://w2.vatican.va/content/pius-xi/en/encyclicals/documents/hf_p-xi_enc_19310515_quadragesimo-anno.html, §65.

35  John XXIII's *Mater et Magistra*, encyclical letter, Vatican website, May 15, 1961, §91.
36  See Leo XIII, *Rerum Novarum*, 9.
37  Jim Vorel, "Modern Times Beer Is Becoming Employee Owned," *Paste Magazine*,

New Belgium was one of the first major craft brewers to embrace 100 percent employee ownership and it has continued to prosper. As of 2017, it has grown to be America's fourth largest craft brewery and the eighth largest overall, and is also rated one of the best places to work. Deschutes followed with employee ownership in 2013 and is now sitting just behind New Belgium as the fifth largest craft brewer. Employee ownership has worked well for these two pioneers.

Employee ownership is one example of the Church's principle of subsidiarity, enabling decision making to operate at more foundational levels of organization. Local breweries are another example of subsidiarity, as they further the local economy, workforce, and community. One group offers intentional support for local brewing through the website supportyourlocalbrewery.org, which fights local laws that hurt small breweries.

Likewise, the Church's principle of solidarity promotes fraternity and cooperation between brewers and brewery workers. One example is the Brewer's Association, which exists "to promote and protect American craft brewers, their beers and the community of brewing enthusiasts."[38] Its core values and beliefs include principles related to solidarity. Members of the Brewer's Association believe in:

- Promoting unity among craft brewers and recognizing that we are stronger together.
- Working to build a collegial community of craft brewers, homebrewers and beer enthusiasts.
- Supporting and encouraging the responsible enjoyment of beer.
- Promoting and celebrating the small, independent, traditional and innovative culture of American craft brewers.
- Vigorously defending our industry and providing craft brewers with a unified voice.
- Providing stewardship for 10,000 years of brewing history.

The Brewing Association also supports local guilds, harkening back to the primary economic means of solidarity in the Middle Ages. One

---

July 7, 2017, https://www.pastemagazine.com/articles/2017/07/modern-times-beer-is-becoming-employee-owned.html.

[38] See https://www.brewersassociation.org/brewers-association/purpose/.

example can be seen in the Colorado Brewers Guild, which promotes craft brewers in the self-proclaimed "State of Craft Beer": "The Colorado Brewers Guild (CBG) is a non-profit trade association who promotes and protects the Colorado craft brewing industry. With the majority of the 300 licensed Colorado breweries as members, CBG provides information for Colorado beer lovers, and promotes Colorado craft breweries by advocating for Colorado craft beer with policymakers."[39]

Thankfully there are means to stand against the mass centralization of brewing. Craft brewers are embracing the principles of subsidiarity and solidarity to make brewing a more human industry, which can contribute to employee welfare and the common good.

## A NEW WAY TO DRINK RESPONSIBLY

We hear often of responsible drinking, but when the agrarian writer, Wendell Berry, says to "eat responsibly," he means something different. We should not be a passive consumer, but should shape the food and beer industries through our choices. We should ask questions about our food and drink: Where and how was it made? What is the cost and impact of production and transportation? What kinds of chemicals were used? How is it packaged? Berry writes:

> There is, then, a politics of food that, like any politics, involves our freedom. We still (sometimes) remember that we cannot be free if our minds and voices are controlled by someone else. But we have neglected to understand that we cannot be free if our food and its sources are controlled by someone else. The condition of the passive consumer of food is not a democratic condition. One reason to eat responsibly is to live free.[40]

He encourages us to become informed consumers, to get involved in production, to shop local, and to know where the ingredients come from. When it comes to beer, we should learn about the brewing process, visit our favorite breweries, meet people who work there, and listen to their

---

39  See Colorado: The State of Craft Beer, https://coloradobeer.org/.
40  Berry, "The Pleasure of Eating," 323.

passion about their work and their creativity. We can also participate in production by homebrewing.

Our best response to consumerism comes from making good use of our own consumerist power. Our economic choices will drive the industry as we drink locally and sustainably. Berry, not only a writer but also a farmer, proposes a renewed economic sense based on an "old idea": rooting economics in local, immediate, and sustainable realities. This involves confronting the immediacy of one's circumstances, focusing on necessities not fantasies, proposing independence, and engaging in intensive work with "local energies, care, and long-living communities."[41] To address the problem of consumerism, "the responsible consumer must also be in some way a producer."[42] We should take an active part in the economy and not allow ourselves to be pulled blindly by market forces and the latest trends.

We have become detached from the natural world, including how we produce our drinks. Gisela Kreglinger, in pursuit of the spirituality of wine, interviewed a German Catholic vintner, Armin Störrlein. She describes his views on winemaking and the stewardship of creation:

> A good vintner needs sensitivity and a deep sense of responsibility, and Störrlein believes that a great responsibility toward the land and the vineyards has been entrusted to him and his family. He wants to work the land and harvest its fruit, but he must not exploit it. . . . When he thinks about Christian spirituality with respect to his own work, he believes that wine is a gift and product of nature, and nature, in turn, is a gift from God. He feels strongly that his work as vintner includes the conservation and protection of this natural and cultural gift we have received. Today, however, the food-manufacturing industry, with its many technological advances, poses a great threat. The "food" that is produced today with the help of technology and chemicals has little to do with the natural product of the farming world. . . . He believes that "technological" wines lack "soul." There is something indefinably beautiful about crafting a natural wine that reflects place.[43]

---

[41] Berry, *Unsettling of America*, 14.
[42] Ibid., 24.
[43] Kreglinger, *Spirituality of Wine*, 133–34.

The brewing industry should be a good steward of the environment. Water, energy consumption, and transportation are key issues in terms of the environmental impact of brewing. In terms of water alone, it takes about four and a half gallons of water to brew one gallon of beer. Sustainable agriculture can help reduce the impact of pesticides and herbicides in growing barley and hops.

As the brewing industry looks to reduce its environmental impact, it must be careful not to destroy the integrity of its ingredients. Hops consume a good deal of water and so some are looking to genetic engineering to reduce this impact. Yeast has also been genetically engineered. Charles Denby of the University of California led a team of researchers who developed a modified yeast strain, which mimics the taste of hops, splicing genes from mint and basil plants into the yeast's DNA. The mad scientists have claimed success, pointing to results from taste tests reporting that "beers produced using these strains are perceived as hoppier than traditionally hopped beers by a sensory panel in a double-blind tasting."[44] Research has begun on the genetics of barley, laying the groundwork for future modification, but the American Malting Barley Association has noted that "there are no genetically modified (GM) barley varieties for sale or in commercial production in North America."[45]

Genetic modification raises questions about the role of technology in brewing. Obviously, brewing requires tools, but these tools are meant to serve and enhance the natural process of fermentation. At what point do our tools begin to dominate and destroy natural processes, rather than enhance them? Culture expresses human creativity, by which we employ our rationality to shape nature. Culture does not leave the world as it is, but impresses our humanity upon it, to enhance it and even to bring it to perfection. Drinking beer, as a product of culture, is better than munching on barley and hops. Much better. But we have to distinguish between human and non-human uses of technology. The distinction has a lot to do with whether or not the technology embraces natural proportion by harnessing nature, rather than working against it.

[44] Alastair Bland, "GMO Yeast Mimics Flavors of Hops, but Will Craft Brewers Bite?" NPR, April 8, 2018, https://www.npr.org/sections/thesalt/2018/04/04/599147983/gmo-yeast-mimics-flavors-of-hops-but-will-craft-brewers-bite.

[45] "GM Statement," American Malting Barley Association, accessed May 11, 2018, http://ambainc.org/content/58/gm-statements.

Genetic modification is one way that technology threatens the integrity of nature itself, by fundamentally altering the blueprint of an organism. Farmers have always shaped their produce genetically, but until now they did so by selecting desired traits of the organism, not by inserting foreign genetic material into the plant!

We are also placing unsustainable burdens on the earth. Pope Francis's *Laudato Si'* points out the high cost of industrialization on the environment:

> These situations have caused sister earth, along with all the abandoned of our world, to cry out, pleading that we take another course. Never have we so hurt and mistreated our common home as we have in the last two hundred years. Yet we are called to be instruments of God our Father, so that our planet might be what he desired when he created it and correspond with his plan for peace, beauty and fullness. The problem is that we still lack the culture needed to confront this crisis.[46]

Francis is correct that we have a cultural problem in the modern world. We have abandoned the plan of the Father who placed the earth and the poor into our care. A large part of the solution will come from placing God and His plan back in the center, putting more emphasis on people rather than things, and making a better use of technology. Francis rightly points out that we have a naïve view of technology: "We have to accept that technological products are not neutral, for they create a framework which ends up conditioning lifestyles and shaping social possibilities along the lines dictated by the interests of certain powerful groups."[47] We need to form a more human culture, which respects and harnesses the possibilities of nature without destroying them.

Throughout this book, we have looked to monks as the exemplar of Catholic culture and Catholic brewing as one facet of it. When it comes to sustainable brewing, the monks once again provide a model. For example, Br. Pierre of Rochefort reveals an important secret to Trappist brewing:

[46] Francis, *Laudato Si'*, encyclical letter, Vatican website, May 24, 2015, http://w2.vatican.va/content/francesco/en/encyclicals/documents/papa-francesco_20150524_enciclica-laudato-si.html, §53.

[47] Ibid., §107.

You know, if there were a secret, it is to be found in our attitude towards life, in our relation with God and with nature. We believe that everything growing on the field or in nature — and what you brew out of it — is not merchandise but a gift. That is no laughing matter. We make our beers as natural as possible without too much profit seeking. The Trappists are not dealing with compromises regarding price or quality.[48]

A large part of overcoming a consumerist culture, which harms nature, entails reordering our priorities by placing God and others before ourselves and any other utilitarian goals. Thomas Aquinas speaks of the order of charity by which we place God first, our souls next, then our neighbor, and finally our bodies and other earthly goods. If we do not attend to the needs of our soul, we cannot help others and rightly order the goods of the world.

Another example of monks restoring the proper balance in brewing comes again from St. Benedict's hometown, Norcia, with "Monk-to-Table." "In an age of increasing popularity among farm-to-table restaurants and products, where 'food traceability' is a sign of quality and authenticity, buying directly from the monks is a reminder not only of where the beer comes from and how it's made, but of who it goes to support."[49] The Benedictine brewing monasteries of Germany and Austria all express strong concern for sustainable methods and have improved their technology to embrace it. The fullest example, though, comes from the Trappist monastery of Koningshoeven, the brewer of La Trappe, which gives five examples of responsible Catholic brewing on its website:

**Corporate Social Responsibility**. Due to their inner conviction, monks treat what God has given us with great care — people and the environment. For them, this is not a trend. Monks have done this for centuries and we continue their efforts. Corporate social responsibility is inextricably connected with La Trappe. In all the departments of the organisation, employees are aware of the value and power of people and nature. By treating people and nature in a

48 Quoted in Hieronymous, *Brew Like a Monk*, 9.
49 "Monk to Table," Birra Nursia, accessed June 4, 2018, https://birranursia.com/.

Koningshoeven Abbey. (Wikimedia Commons)

respectful and innovative way, they contribute to a more beautiful and healthier world, also for future generations.

**Uganda.** Because La Trappe is an official Trappist beer, part of our profit goes to charity. La Trappe supports a very poor region in Uganda. A Trappist monastery has been established in this region. The brothers of this monastery are mainly specialized in agriculture and cattle breeding. That is how they help the local population build their economy. The money that the brothers currently earn is used to renovate two local schools and provide them with clean and safe drinking water.

**Sheltered workshop.** The Koningshoeven Brewery contributes actively to a sustainable and socially-oriented society. That is why we also work with people from the Prins Heerlijk and the Diamant group: people with learning difficulties and/or mental disabilities. We offer them opportunities by letting them do housekeeping, gardening and packing work, work in the catering establishments or work in the Monastery Shop.

**Barley from the region.** We try as much as possible to purchase raw materials in our own region or at source. Part of our brewing barley is bought in the region. This saves on transportation costs and ensures better control of quality. In addition, our brewery greatly values direct contact with the growers.

**Green products.** La Trappe is genuine and pure beer. We brew our beer only with natural products and reuse our residues and waste. For instance, the monks use our brewery spent grain, a high-fibre residue of beer, for baking bread in their bakery. This explains why our organic Trappist PUUR beer is [organic] certified.[50]

We can also look to craft brewers for examples of sustainability. New Belgium has taken the lead by eliminating wastes (diverting 99.9 percent of its waste from landfills); reducing the amount of water used; supporting sustainable energy; co-founding the Glass Recycling Coalition; and giving financial support for youth environmental education, sustainable agriculture, and water restoration projects—especially for the Colorado River. The Yards and Brooklyn Breweries are run on wind power, while Sierra Nevada, Arcadia, Highland, and Vivant use solar. Full Sail has reduced its water consumption to an impressive two and a half gallons for each gallon of beer. Lakefront turns its spent mash into fertilizer and captures heat energy from the brewing process. Great Lakes runs an organic farm, named Pint Size, and Jester King in Texas began sustainable farming on the fifty-eight acres surrounding the brewery.[51]

Although our consumerist culture has defined beer in the twentieth century by demanding cheap and bland products, the craft brewing industry can now provide a model for how to referment this culture: move back to a local, employee- and community-focused, and sustainable mode of production. These principles provide a model for overcoming our own consumer habits and recentering the economic practices of our society.

[50] "Sustainable and Social," La Trappe, accessed March 27, 2018, https://www.latrappetrappist.com/en/our-story/sustainable-and-social/.

[51] See Mary Mazzoni, "Top 10 Sustainable Breweries," *Triple Pundit*, September 26, 2014, https://www.triplepundit.com/2014/09/3p-weekend-top-10-sustainable-u-s-breweries/; Aaron Sprengeller, "6 Craft Breweries Improving their Sustainability Efforts," *Craftbeer.com*, August 8, 2016, https://www.craftbeer.com/craft-beer-muses/craft-breweries-improving-their-sustainability-efforts.

# CHAPTER 16

# *Concluding with Beer in Perspective*

Eating and drinking are central realities of human life. Leon Kass argues in *The Hungry Soul* that "the meal taken at table is the cultural form that enables us to respond simultaneously to all the dominant features of our world: inner need, natural plentitude, freedom and reason, human community, and the mysterious source of it all. In humanized eating, we can nourish souls even while we feed our bodies."[1] As we have seen, however, our consumption has become cheapened by individualist trends that "diminish opportunities for conversation, communion, and aesthetic discernment; they thus shortchange the other hungers of the soul," especially by creating a "spiritual anorexia."[2] Addressing this spiritual anorexia provides us the right context to end our discussion of beer. Alcohol must ultimately serve and even give way to a life of holiness. This entails approaching beer through virtue while emphasizing the priority of prayer and service. Throughout this book, we have used beer to explore monastic history, to examine local Catholic culture, and to advocate for engagement in a home economy. We have also explored the strong revival in local and monastic brewing—and the advance of more humane brewing practices. This brings us back to the question I asked at the outset: Why a Beer Option?

## RENEWING CHRISTIAN CULTURE

Now that we have come to the end of this book, I have a confession to make. The book is not ultimately about beer. In fact, if you removed beer from it you would still have a coherent narrative: the history of Catholic

---

[1]  Leon Kass, *The Hungry Soul: Eating and the Perfecting of Our Nature* (Chicago: University of Chicago Press, 1999), 228.

[2]  Ibid, 229; 231.

culture, the important elements of culture, the need to engage actively in cultural works, and the need to overcome the cultural problems of our time. My spiritual life has continually brought home to me the limits of beer. In fact, as I began writing this book I was in the midst of a yearlong alcohol fast. Any worldly thing can prove a distraction to our spiritual growth, can divide our heart, and keep us from living an ascetical life. Even the brewing monks themselves must keep beer in perspective. Some Trappist abbeys have preserved the tradition of brewing, but face declining numbers, in part for not preserving their own spiritual charism faithfully and boldly enough.

When it comes to renewing our culture, we must first renew our own lives. This means putting our faith in God first. Having a deep relationship with God in prayer is the one thing necessary, which Jesus explained to Martha (Luke 10:42). The Beer Option must give way to the holiness option: prioritizing God, committing to prayer, and serving others. Once we have our priorities straight, beer can fit within them. If beer distracts us or stands in the way, however, then we need to pluck it out of our lives. We can have Catholic culture without beer, if not without wine! We must consume beer with a perspective on what really matters, as did the martyr St. John Kemble, who on the day he died, August 22, 1679, insisted on finishing his prayers, pipe, and a drink before being led to the scaffold.

When we embrace the one thing necessary in this life, we must also commit to sharing it with others. John Senior pointed out what really matters when it comes to culture: the communal expression of life. "Cult is the basis of culture. An authentic Christian culture, therefore, must be centered on an authentic Christian cult."[3] The Eucharist is the heart of Christian culture, as Christians are drawn together in worship to receive a taste of heaven. We then must bring this taste into the world as leaven, to prepare for the new heaven and new earth. To lay the groundwork for this renewal of creation, we should take the advice of the angel of Fatima: "Make everything you can a sacrifice." Senior laid out the necessary agenda (literally, "what must be done"): "work, pray, sacrifice."[4] We work for the renewal of our world, but this work must join both prayer and sacrifice to be truly efficacious. This includes regularly making a sacrifice

[3]  Senior, *Restoration of Christian Culture*, 132.
[4]  Ibid, 54.

Brewery Wagon at Karlsplatz, Vienna (1825). (Wikimedia Commons)

of our drinking habits, especially during Advent and Lent. Dorothy Day, along with Maurin, gave up alcohol completely in solidarity with the poor and alcoholics, and recommended that we use our beer money to support the poor.[5]

Even as we work for the new heaven and new earth, we live in a time of an impoverished humanity. We have to help people recover a sense of what it means to be human — to be a rational person. The one thing necessary must affect everything we do as we rediscover basic cultural goods: lost traditions, beauty, community, and doing things with our hands. Wendell Berry brings needed sanity by reminding us that "a healthy culture is a communal order of memory, insight, value, work, conviviality, reverence, aspiration. It reveals the human necessities and the human limits."[6] He also reminds us that we cannot give in to a new dualism that separates not only body and soul, but also keeps the body away from its needed contact with the earth and the soul's dependence on others. He notes that we can focus exclusively on the salvation of the soul and miss the complete picture, and asks, "What is the burden of the Bible if not a sense of the mutuality of influence, rising out of an essential unity, among soul and body and community and world? These are all the works of God, and it is therefore the work of virtue to make or restore harmony among them."[7] Holiness embraces the wholeness of human life, our full flourishing, which requires the reintegration of what sin has torn asunder.

5  Day, *The Long Loneliness*, 231.
6  Berry, *The Unsettling of America*, 43.
7  Ibid., 109.

In this vein, beer provides a small but concrete sign of restored Christian culture: it is fashioned from the goods of the earth, it fosters community, and when ordered to God, it can help us catch a glimpse of the joy of heaven. The baptism of beer is a call to return to reality, to rediscover the simple but necessary elements of life. Senior, once again, gives us crucial guidance: "Smash the television set, turn out the lights, build a fire in the fireplace, move the family into the living room, put a pot on to boil some tea and toddy and have an experiment in merriment, a sudden, unexpected hearth, the heart and first step in the restoration of the home . . . and see how love will quicken in a single winter's night!"[8] Renewal will begin by gathering around the hearth and recreating culture with family and friends.

## BACK TO THE BENEDICT OPTION

The Beer Option is an extension of the Benedict Option, looking to the monastic tradition's model for cultural renewal: prayer, work, and brewing united in an organic vision. The Benedict Option has been largely mischaracterized as a withdrawal or retreat from the world. Insofar as it looks to monasticism as a model of culture, there may be some truth in that, but examining monasticism shows that withdrawing to seek God leads to the ability to engage the world in a more profound and impactful way. The Benedictines are credited with rebuilding Western culture in the Dark Ages for a reason. In my opinion, the Benedict Option should be understood as follows: Given the profound crisis of culture (which has affected the Church as well), we cannot look to mainstream institutions for our future. Rather, we need to form intentional communities that more fully embody our Christian faith and in which we are willing to face the consequences of going against the stream. It is from such grassroots communities that real cultural change will occur. Thus, the Benedict Option is about engaging the problems of society. It recognizes, however, that solutions will begin locally, in the relationships that we can influence. Rebuilding will begin there.

The Benedictines are uniquely positioned to provide a model of cultural renewal. They are dedicated to the one thing necessary, which Pope

---

[8] Senior, *Restoration of Christian Culture*, 48.

Benedict described as *quaerere Deum*, but embed that "search for God" within the self-contained culture of the monastery. Putting faith before all else—even to the point of suffering for it—will be necessary to stand against the many obstacles to the Christian life we face. Here are a few reasons why St. Benedict and his monks provide a model suited to our own particular challenges:

Benedict lived in a time of cultural decline and even collapse. This is why Alasdair MacIntyre spoke of the need for "another—doubtless very different—St. Benedict."[9] Benedict did indeed withdraw from society, but in doing so he laid the spiritual conditions for cultural renewal. As MacIntyre elaborated in reference to our time: "What matters at this stage is the construction of local forms of community within which civility and the intellectual and moral life can be sustained through the new dark ages which are already upon us."[10] St. Benedict, more than other spiritual figures, truly provides a model in such a process of rebuilding.

St. Benedict also offers a family-based spiritual vision in a time of great crisis for the family. As a father, I have found inspiration in Benedict's guidelines for the abbot, the spiritual father of the monastery, to whom is entrusted the care of the monks as spiritual children. In *The Benedict Option*, Dreher calls for the family to be a "domestic monastery," where children learn to put prayer and the Church first in their lives. He says, "just as the monastery's life is ordered toward God, so must the family home be."[11] This does not mean living in isolation, but rather calls for deeper community, as "Christian families have to start linking themselves decisively with other families."[12] Dreher also calls families to return to the practice of hospitality and to limit the use of technology in the home. This fits with Dreher's goal of encouraging us to embrace counter-cultural practices and "to focus on prudent, achievable goals."[13] In the end, this means living an intentional and more fully Christian life in our family and in all that we do.

St. Benedict created a culture in miniature within the monastery.

---

9  Alasdair MacIntyre, *After Virtue: A Study in Moral Theory*, 3rd ed. (Notre Dame, IN: University of Notre Dame Press, 2006), 263.

10  Ibid.

11  Dreher, *Benedict Option*, 124.

12  Ibid., 141.

13  Ibid., 87.

Jules Joseph Dauban, *Trappist Monks Welcoming a Stranger* (1864). (Wikimedia Commons)

Although Pope Benedict's Paris Lecture pointed to the search for God as the center of this culture, he also noted how this vision included "a culture of work." St. Benedict taught that "when they live by the labor of their hands, as our fathers and the apostles did, then they are really monks" (*Rule*, ch. 48). And: "The monastery should, if possible, be so constructed that within it all necessities, such as water, mill and garden are contained, and the various crafts are practiced" (ch. 66). Benedictine spirituality can inspire a renewal of more human work, helping us to rediscover skilled labor and the crafts, of which brewing is one. It is particularly important for fathers and sons to work together in rediscovering a home economy.

Aidan Nichols pointed out that in the modern world, we no longer have a culture undergirding and supporting a life of prayer, but rather we live in a spiritual desert. Nichols argued that a distinct form of prayer must arise in response to a secular culture, which, in part, should be characterized by "the complete coincidence of life and prayer."[14] The monks again provide a unique example of this. Comparing monks to angels, Pope Benedict said at Heiligenkreuz: "Their very life is worship." We have to form a daily rhythm of prayer, allowing it to shape how we order our lives,

---

[14] Aidan Nichols, OP, *Christendom Awake: On Re-energizing the Church in Culture* (Edinburgh, T&T Clark, 1999), 208.

rather than squeezing prayer into our distracted lives. Further, we have to make our family life and work forms of prayer, offering everything we do for the glory of God, thereby building up a Christian culture.

Hospitality ensures that intentional communities do not become insular. The focus of the monastery may not be on the outside world, but it is open to the world when it comes to visit: "Let all guests who arrive be received as Christ" (ch. 53). Just as the monastery is open to the outside world, Pope John Paul II in his "Letter to Families" points to the family as a sovereign society that exists not only for its own sake but for the good of others. The family shares in the Church's mission, in part through "the apostolate of families to one another."[15] Building strong families and communities will provide a refuge not only for Christians, but also for those lost at sea, providing a calm harbor in which they can encounter sanity and goodness through hospitality in the home.

The Catholic Worker Movement implements Benedictine spirituality by offering hospitality and drawing people to work and prayer on the land. In addition, the movement seeks to incorporate key ideas of the Church's social teaching such as subsidiarity and distributism. Dorothy Day, under Peter Maurin's influence, became a Benedictine oblate. Peter was an early advocate of the Benedict Option, reflecting on the importance of *Ora et Labora* and the integration of monastic life:

> The motto of St. Benedict was
> Laborare et Orare, Labor and Pray.
> Labor and prayer ought to be combined;
> Labor ought to be a prayer.
> The liturgy of the Church
> is the prayer of the Church.
> The religious life of the people
> and the economic life of the people
> ought to be one.[16]

Day describes how "we need a new economics with a strong emphasis on institutions on the land, decentralization, more study as well as more

---

[15] Pope John Paul II, "Letter to Families" (1994), §16.
[16] Maurin, *Easy Essays*, 29.

laboring at meaningful work. Small industries and hospices on the land mean more employment. There is no unemployment on the land, Peter used to say."[17] The Catholic Worker Movement, despite any flaws and failures, sought to embody something akin to the Benedict Option, uniting work, prayer, farming, community, and hospitality.

Benedictine spirituality has much to teach us about how to draw nearer to Christ through liturgy, prayer, work, and community life.

## CONCLUSION

In Joshua Hren's short story, "The Wrecking Ball," the main character, Blaise, takes an unexpected detour due to his bike's flat tire.

> Pursuing what he first swore was a vaguely-remembered short cut, he soured as the street names lost significance, then slowed in a stop as he found himself small before the ruins of the old Brewer beer grounds, the blocks and blocks of mostly whole but dormant buildings with their dusky yellow windows serving as the stained glass of the industrial age. He set down his bike, almost in awe of these shrines to gods now dead. As he shattered an already neck-less golden-brown bottle against a wall, Blaise was pulled back. . . . Blaise confronted the cream-brick building as though he and it and were caught in an old recurring argument. The cream was mostly charred, but in spots you could see the simple, humble yellow-white of yesterday. The very foundations yearned to be made living, to be clicking, stamping, busy with productivity.[18]

Stumbling upon this brewery graveyard, Blaise recalled his father's and grandfather's work on the site and his own lost prospects of a career there. Like Blaise, we too look upon many ruins and must face our own future. Much has been lost, but can be found again, brought back to life in a slow and faithful movement of renewal.

The Beer Option is one attempt to look at Christian culture anew through one particular, and in the end modest, lens. I have presented a

---

[17] Quoted in Zwick, *Catholic Worker Movement*, 173.
[18] Joshua Hren, *This Our Exile: Short Stories* (Brooklyn, NY: Angelico, 2017), 2.

Pilgrims. Canterbury Cathedral. (Wikimedia Commons)

particular angle on the Benedict Option, entering into the long history of Benedictine life and cultural production through one of its marquee products. Understanding beer within a broader cultural and spiritual narrative helps me to be a better Benedictine oblate and to root my drinking and fellowship within that vision. I hope you come away from this book with a clear sense of how deeply rooted brewing is in the Catholic tradition. I hope even more, though, that you have caught a glimpse of the larger Catholic culture and what we need to rebuild it: community, tradition, and a spiritual vision.

As we go forward, it is certain that we will have to fight intensely to maintain our faith, our humanity, and our sanity in an increasingly senile and violent world. Thankfully, we do not find our hope in ourselves or our own efforts. Christ has already won the victory and has given us a sure hope rooted in him. Pope Benedict beautifully attests how only this hope helps us to move forward in the midst of a broken world:

This great hope can only be God, who encompasses the whole of reality and who can bestow upon us what we, by ourselves, cannot attain. The fact that it comes to us as a gift is actually part of hope. God is the foundation of hope: not any god, but the God who has a human face and who has loved us to the end, each one of us and humanity in its entirety. His Kingdom is not an imaginary hereafter, situated in a future that will never arrive; his Kingdom is present wherever he is loved and wherever his love reaches us. His love alone gives us the possibility of soberly persevering day by day, without ceasing to be spurred on by hope, in a world which by its very nature is imperfect.[19]

Ultimately our hope lies in the Kingdom to come, and yet this hope gives us the courage to face the challenges of our culture to begin rebuilding. Our confidence in God allows us to have true joy not only in the life to come, but in the goodness of this world and the life God has given us within it.

With Belloc, we can look at our once-again pagan world and yet have hope for renewal, rooted in the simple goodness that yet remains:

When they put the food and ale before me, it was of the kind which has been English ever since England began, and which perhaps good fortune will preserve over the breakdown of our generation, until we have England back again. One could see the hops in the tankard, and one could taste the barley until, more and more sunk in to the plenitude of this good house, one could dare to contemplate, as though from a distant standpoint, the corruption and the imminent danger of time through which we must lead our lives. And, as I so considered the ruin of the great cities and their slime, I felt as though I were in a fortress of virtue and of health, which could hold out through the pressure of the war. And I thought to myself: "Perhaps even before our children are men, these parts which survive from a better order will be accepted as models, and England will be built again."[20]

And not England alone, but all of Christendom. May we build it again! I will raise my glass—as well as my work and prayer—to that!

---

[19]  Pope Benedict XVI, *Spe Salvi* (2007), §31.

[20]  Hilaire Belloc, "At the Sign of the Lion," in *Hills and the Sea* (London: Methuen, 1909). I am grateful to Joseph Pearce for pointing me to this passage, over a pint of course.

# RECOMMENDED BOOKS

Alworth, Jeff. *The Beer Bible: The Essential Beer Lover's Guide*. New York: Workman, 2015.

Bamforth, Charles W. *Beer is Proof God Loves Us: Reaching for the Soul of Beer and Brewing*. Upper Saddle River, NJ: Pearson FT Press, 2010.

———. *Beer: Tap into the Art and Science of Brewing*. New York: Oxford University Press, 2009.

Benedict XVI. "Address of His Holiness Benedict XVI." Meeting with Representatives from the World of Culture, College des Bernardins, Paris, September 12, 2008. http://w2.vatican.va/content/benedict-xvi/en/speeches/2008/september/documents/hf_ben-xvi_spe_20080912_parigi-cultura.html

———. *Spe Salvi*. Encyclical Letter. Vatican Website. 2007. http://w2.vatican.va/content/benedict-xvi/en/encyclicals/documents/hf_ben-xvi_enc_20071130_spe-salvi.html.

Berry, Wendell. *The Art of the Common Place: The Agrarian Essays of Wendell Berry*. Berkeley, CA: Counterpoint, 2002.

Carr, Nicholas. *The Glass Cage: How Our Computers Are Changing Us*. New York: W.W. Norton, 2014.

Colicchio, Tom, and Garrett Oliver. *The Oxford Companion to Beer*. New York: Oxford University Press, 2011.

Dawson, Christopher. *Religion and the Rise of Western Culture*. New York: Image, 1991.

Dreher, Rod. *The Benedict Option: A Strategy for Christians in a Post-Christian Nation*. New York: Sentinel, 2017.

Esolen, Anthony. *Out of the Ashes: Rebuilding American Culture*. Washington, DC: Regnery, 2017.

Foley, Michael. *Drinking with the Saints: The Sinner's Guide to a Holy Happy Hour*. Washington, DC: Regnery, 2015.

Francis. *Laudato Si'*. Encyclical Letter. Vatican Website. 2015. http://w2.vatican.va/content/francesco/en/encyclicals/documents/papa-francesco_20150524_enciclica-laudato-si.html.

Hales, Steven. *Beer and Philosophy: The Unexamined Beer Isn't Worth Drinking*. Malden, MA: Blackwell, 2007.

264 *The Beer Option*

Hieronymus, Stan. *Brew Like a Monk: Culture and Craftsmanship in the Belgian Tradition.* Boulder, CO: Brewers Publications, 2005.

Hoast-Pullen, Nancy, and Mark W. Patterson. *Atlas of Beer: A Globe-Trotting Journey through the World of Beer.* Washington, DC: National Geographic, 2017.

Homan, Michael. "Beer, Barley, and שֵׁכָר in the Hebrew Bible." In *Le-David Maskil: A Birthday Tribute for David Noel Freedman,* edited by Richard Elliot Friedman and William H. C. Propp. Winona Lake, IN: Eisenbrauns, 2004, pp. 25–38.

Jackson, Michael. *Great Beer Guide: 500 Classic Brews.* New York: DK, 2000.

Kreglinger, Gisela H. *The Spirituality of Wine.* Grand Rapids, MI: Eerdmans, 2016.

McGovern, Patrick. *Uncorking the Past: The Quest for Wine, Beer, and Other Alcoholic Beverages.* Berkeley: University of California Press, 2009.

Mosher, Randy. *Tasting Beer: An Insider's Guide to the World's Greatest Drink.* 2nd ed. North Adams, MA: Storey, 2017.

Nelson, Max. *The Barbarian's Beverage: A History of Beer in Ancient Europe.* New York: Routledge, 2005.

Palmer, John. *How to Brew: Everything You Need to Know to Brew Great Beer Every Time.* Boulder, CO: Brewers Publications, 2017.

Pearce, Joseph. *Small Is Still Beautiful: Economics as if Families Mattered.* Wilmington, DE: ISI, 2006.

Phillips, Rod, *Alcohol: A History.* Chapel Hill, NC: The University of North Carolina Press, 2014.

Pieper, Josef. *In Tune with the World.* South Bend, IN: St. Augustine Press, 1999.

———. *Leisure the Basis of Culture.* San Francisco: Ignatius, 2009.

Scruton, Roger. *I Drink, Therefore I Am: A Philosopher's Guide to Wine.* New York: Continuum, 2009.

Senior, John. *The Restoration of Christian Culture.* Norfolk, VA: IHS Press, 2008.

St. Benedict. *The Rule.* Translated by Leonard Doyle. http://osb.org/rb/text/toc.html.

Unger, Richard W. *Beer in the Middle Ages and Renaissance.* Philadelphia: University of Pennsylvania Press, 2004.

Vabulas, Sarah. *The Catholic Drinkie's Guide to Home Brewed Evangelism.* Liguori, MO: Liguori Publications, 2015.

Wallace, Caroline, Sarah Wood, and Jessica Deahl. *Trappist Beer Travels: Inside the Breweries of the Monasteries.* Atglen, PA: Schiffer, 2017.

Zmirak, John, and Denise Matychowiak. *The Bad Catholics Guide to Wine, Whiskey, and Song.* New York: Crossroad, 2005.

R. JARED STAUDT is a teacher, writer, and speaker committed to helping others enter into the living and vibrant tradition of Catholic culture. He serves as Director of Formation for the Archdiocese of Denver and teaches at the Augustine Institute. He holds a PhD in systematic theology from Ave Maria University and is a Benedictine oblate. He and his wife Anne have six children.

Made in the USA
Lexington, KY
10 April 2019